JEWS of the RAJ

Mavis Hyman

The front cover photograph is by John Hyman.

It shows Joe Abraham reading from the *Sefer Torah*, Scrolls of the Law. Scribes in Baghdad wrote the scrolls. The *tik*, wooden case would be covered by an outer case of embossed silver or silver and velvet in India. This was typically in the Baghdadi style. The cases were embellished with bells and a pointer. It was customary for families who could afford it, to donate a *Sefer Torah* to the synagogue in the name of a relative who had died.

This book is copyright ©. Apart from any fair dealing for the purposes of study, research, criticism, review, or as otherwise permitted under the Copyright Act, no part may be reproduced by any process without written permission. Inquiries should be made to the publisher.

Design by Mavis Hyman

Hyman Publishers
10 Holyoake Walk
London N2 OJX

Reprographics by Vasim Memon

Printed by The Longdunn Press Ltd
Barton Manor, St Philips
Bristol

ISBN 0 9518150 16

Copyright Mavis Hyman, 1995.

In memory of my grandparents

Meir Ezra and Masooda Musleah

TRANSITION: THE END OF THE RAJ & THE BEGINNING OF INDEPENDENCE.
"THE STATESMAN" CALCUTTA OF AUGUST 19th 1947.

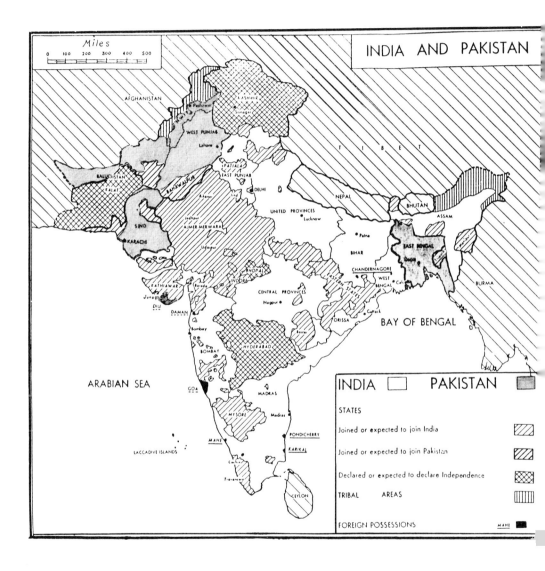

CONTENTS

		Page	
Participants in Discussion			i
Acknowledgements			v
Biographical Note			vii
Glossary			ix
Chapter 1	Historical Background		1
Chapter 2	Approach to the Research		15

PART ONE

Chapter 3	Nahoums		17
Chapter 4	The Servants		27
Chapter 5	Food		41
Chapter 6	Madhupur		55
Chapter 7	Agarpara		67
Chapter 8	An Afternoon at the Races		81
Chapter 9	Sport		89

PART TWO

Chapter 10	Rites of Passage		107
Chapter 11	Faith		131
Chapter 12	Charity		143

PART THREE

Chapter 13	Refugees from Burma		159
Chapter 14	Riots		179
Chapter 15	Zionism		191
Chapter 16	Exodus		209
Sources Cited			229
Notes			233
Index			251

LIST OF ILLUSTRATIONS
Illustrations follow the chapters shown.

	Transition: From the Raj to the independent states of India and Pakistan.
Chapter 1	Hacham Ezra Dangoor and his wife Habiba in Arabic dress, 1895. Manasseh Bassous and his wife Sophie in Arabic dress with their children in European dress. Calcutta. c 1918. The wedding of Rachel and Jack Jacob, Calcutta 1918. Festive *sidarya*, waistcoat, 1920s. Child's *sidarya*, 1930s. Woman's Arabic outfit. Worn in Calcutta until early 20c.
Chapter 3	Part of Price List, Nahoum & Sons, Calcutta. April, 1926. Esther and Jack Silas cut their wedding cake made by Nahoums. One end of Nahoums shop in the New Market, Calcutta. Nahoum in his shop. Calcutta, 1992. Sollo Nahoum with Sally Benaiah aged two.
Chapter 4	Rahim, my grandmother's cook. The tailor, *durzee*. Paroo *ayah* with Leah and Shelley Silas. Shanti prepares food at floor level.
Chapter 5	Preparation of *Matza*, unleavened bread in the compound of *Beth-El*. *Koom-koom*, silver rose water bottle. Silver wine cup made in Shanghai.
Chapter 6	Jews and Indians wait for the train to Calcutta at Madhupur station, c 1928. On the platform of Madhupur station, c. 1928. Paddy fields viewed from the train en route to Madhupur. Ruby Musleah at Madhupur railway station, 1936. Shopping in the *hart* in Madhupur, 1936. "Home" in Madhupur, 1937. Rachel Musleah near the Dak Bungalow, Madhupur, 1937. A picnic in a *tonga*, Madhupur. Boy Scouts from the Elias Meyer Free School hoisting the Union Jack at the start of a day on camp in Madhupur. 1934. Boy Scouts washing by a well in Madhupur, 1934. Boy Scouts on cooking duty in Madhupur, 1934.
Chapter 7	Joe Isaac designed and built the loom in Agarpara. Celebration of *Saraswati Puja*. Enjoying the swimming pool in Riverside, Agarpara. Celebration in the *succa*, Agarpara.

Chapter 8	The Turf Club, Calcutta Race Course. In the paddock.
Chapter 9	Moshe Lanyado at the Wellesley Square Tank, 1933. Joe Solomon, Zionist Institute of Physical Education, 1939. David Einy rides a winner at Tollygunj Race Course, 1945. Rina Einy Margulies at the Los Angeles Olympics, 1984. Members of the Maccabi Basketball team on the Maidan, 1955.
Chapter 10	Chair of Elijah from Bombay, made c. 1790. Naming a baby girl. Silver charms for protection against the evil eye. David Solomon lays *tefellin*. *Sisseth* cases made in Shanghai. Embroidered cap worn by men. Handwritten and painted marriage certificate, Calcutta, 1887. Wedding ceremony in Calcutta, 1953. Marriage certificate of Ruby and Joe Cohen, 1946. *Kettubah* cases in engraved and embossed silver, India.1940s. A Jewish funeral procession. c. 1943.
Chapter 11	Laying the foundation stone of *Maghen David* Synagogue. Display of *sefarim* in *Maghen David* Synagogue, *Simhat Torah*. Iris Moses Ferris with Guides from her Troop. Early 1930s. Interior of *Beth El* Synagogue. *Megilla* in silver and gold scroll holder. Shanghai, c. 1910. Lighting the *Hannukiah*. Made in Calcutta from brass, c. 1910.
Chapter 13	A page from Albert Judah's diary while trekking from Burma, 1942. Permit for Evacuation issued for Albert Judah, Mandalay, 1942. Map showing Albert Judah's evacuation route. Governor of Burma listens to a tale of terror in Rangoon, 1942. Arrival at the Outram Ghats, Calcutta, 1942.
Chapter 14	Communal riots in Calcutta, 1946. Evacuees from East Bengal, 1946.
Chapter 15	Rabbi Seligson addressing a *Habonim* meeting, Calcutta 1943. Gathering at the *Bayit* Calcutta, 1943. *Sha'ar Aliyah*. 1950. New arrivals spent their first five days here.
Chapter 16	Ramah Luddy and Lenny Leight, New Delhi, 1943. Kfar Ofer, 1950. Washing saucepans at a standpipe. Reuben Aaron outside the Sephardi Synagogue, Sydney. Sid Jacob in his store in Sydney. Celebration of *Simhat Torah*, *Maghen David* Synagogue, 1944.

PARTICIPANTS IN DISCUSSION

The countries within brackets indicate places of present residence

Aaron Aaron (Australia)
Reuben Aaron (Australia)
Joe Abraham (UK)
Lillian Abraham (UK)
Marianne Arakie (UK)

Marina Benaiah (UK)
Rahel Benaiah (Canada)
Ruby Benaiah (UK)

Ellis Cohen (UK)
Jackie Cohen (Israel)
Joe Cohen (UK)
Mordecai Cohen (UK)
Mordie Cohen (UK)
Ruby Cohen (UK)
Seemah Cohen (UK)

Danny Daniels (UK)
Noreen David (UK)

Arlene Einy (UK)
David Einy (UK)
David Elias (UK)
Flower Elias (UK)
Sophie Elias (UK)
Aisey Ezekiel (UK)
Maurice Ezekiel (UK)
Norman Ezekiel (UK)
Moses Ezra (UK)

Dan Ferris (UK)

Helen Jacob Himmelschein (UK)
Rose Horovitz (USA)

Diana Isaac (UK)
Joe Isaac (UK)
Benny Isaac (UK

Nissim Jacob (UK)
Sid Jacob (Australia)
Josh Joshua (UK)
Albert Judah (UK)

Michelle Kraft (UK)

Seemah Lanyado (UK)
Sally Lewis (Israel)
Sam Luddy (India)
Ramah Leight (USA)

Mercia Mansfield (UK)
Joe Manasseh (UK)
Rina Margulies (Belgium)
Regina Meir (Israel)
Benny Meyer (UK)
Bertie Meyer (UK)
Ellis Meyer (UK)
Florence Meyer (UK)
Maisie Meyer (UK)
Ruby Mordecai (Australia)
Charlie Morris (UK)
Sally Morris (UK)
Sammy Morris (Australia)
Seemah Morris (Australia)
Sunoo Morris (UK)
Renee Moses (Australia)
Ezekiel Musleah (USA)
Meyer Musleah (Australia)

Ramah Musleah (India)

Hannah Nahoum (UK)
Nahoum Nahoum (India)
Ramah Nahoum (UK)
Ruby Nissim (UK)

Jack Raymond (UK)
Miriam Raymond (UK)

Seemah Sadka (UK)
Elmo Sassoon (Israel)
Anne Shaya (UK)
Rachel Shellim (UK)
Charlie Silas (UK)
Eze Silas (UK)
Simon Silas (UK)
Esther Solomon (Australia)
Joe Solomon (UK)
Eric Sopher (USA)
Helene Sopher (UK)

Mozelle Twena (UK)

Annie Zaccai (UK)
Dick Zaccai (Israel)

ACKNOWLEDGEMENTS

I enjoyed a tremendous amount of cooperation and help from very many people as the project grew and developed.

I would like to thank, above all, those who spent time in discussion. Most people found great pleasure in their recollections but there were occasions when memories were painful, as accounts of daily life are not complete without them.

I would also like to thank the many people who loaned photographs to illustrate the discussion. The older photographs make up in charm what they may lack in quality, and I have been eager to seek these out knowing that photography was a limited part of the lives of the majority of people in the community before the Second World War.

I would like to mention, for special thanks, a number of people who gave additional help.

My aunt, Seemah Cohen, spent many hours in general discussion. She also introduced me to people who were willing to talk about their personal histories.

Naim Dangoor loaned articles and rare books and was informative about the Jewish community in Baghdad.

Flower Elias and Mercia Mansfield read every word as it was written and made very useful suggestions at the early drafting stage. Their friendship and encouragement became a strong source of support.

Rabbi Abraham Gubbay gave permission to photograph the *sefarim*. Norman Ezekiel arranged access, and Joe Abraham kindly gave his time at the synagogue.

I was fortunate to be able to use the library at Jews' College, London, and am grateful to the Librarian, Mr E Kahn for his courtesy and help in directing me to relevant publications.

Sylvia Kedourie, an expert in Middle Eastern affairs, discussed the historical background, particularly those areas which concerned the Baghdadian link. She made useful comments on parts of the manuscript.

Seemah Lanyado's knowledge of the community is as wide as it is deep and I enjoyed many hours in discussion with her. She would say thoughtfully: "Now let's see, what else can I tell you?" It is difficult to do justice to her contribution in giving me advice, introducing me to people who were able to help with photographs, and in discussion, lending me books, pursuing several points herself, and reading and commenting on the completed manuscript.

Benny and Maisie Meyer kindly introduced me to a rabbi who insists on remaining anonymous. He directed me to many sources on the Rites of Passage, which was demanding work. I am grateful for his patience and humour.

My brother, Sammy Morris, gave me the benefit of his views on those chapters where he is familiar with the subject matter.

My cousins, Meyer and Ezekiel Musleah read and commented on the early drafts of most chapters. Meyer never commented without an explanation and Ezekiel added much interesting information and directed me to useful sources.

Esther Silas was helpful in arranging access to some of the photographs.

Helene Sopher gave enthusiastic help, organised access to obscure books and articles, and introduced me to many people who helped in the discussion.

I am very grateful to friends from outside the community - Brian McGinnis, Bernard Marks, and Saty Varma who made detailed comments on the manuscript. They helped me to clarify points which were not as obvious as I had assumed.

It is most difficult to thank my immediate family adequately. My husband, John, has had to live with this project throughout, and he has given me every encouragement, support and a great deal of practical help. Over the years, my daughters, Esther and Miriam, urged me to "write about the community" they found so fascinating. Their help in proof reading has been invaluable.

To each and every one who has contributed to this project, I give my thanks for bringing it to fruition. Any errors are entirely my responsibility.

London, June 1995.   Mavis Hyman

BIOGRAPHICAL NOTE

Mavis Hyman was born in Calcutta of Iraqi-Jewish parents. She is descended, on her mother's side, from one of the earliest Jewish merchants who settled in Calcutta some two hundred years ago. In 1957 she emigrated to the United Kingdom.

She is a graduate from the London School of Economics and has worked in various colleges of London University, where she researched and published work on social care.

After retirement, she published a book on the cuisine of the Jews from India. The continuing depletion of the numbers of Jews in this part of the world since the Second World War has been the spur to preserve the unique experience of this fragment of Jewry while there is still time to do so.

GLOSSARY

Includes foreign words which are repeated. Otherwise translations are in the text.

Abbreviations in text

(A) = Arabic; (H) = Hebrew; (Hi) = Hindi.

Achkan	Hindi	Long fitted jacket with high collar.
Akd-el-yas	Arabic	Celebration on the night before a circumcision.
Aliyah	Hebrew	Immigration to Israel.
Ayah	Hindi	Nursemaid.
Bael	Hindi	Fruit, sometimes used to make sherbets.
Baklawa	Arabic	Sweet made of layers of pastry, sugar and ground almonds.
Bearer	Hindi	Servant - generally a cleaner.
Bene Israel	Hebrew	Children of Israel. Community in Bombay of ancient origin.
Bhaji	Hindi	Vegetables cooked in an onion sauce.
Bhindi	Hindi	Lady's finger, okra.
Cacas	Arabic	Savoury biscuits.
Chappati	Hindi	Flat bread grilled over charcoal.
Chokra	Hindi	Boy or young man.
Choola	Hindi	Brick and clay cooker.
Chumkee	Hindi	Embroidery with sequins.
Chupa	Hebrew	Wedding canopy.
Daroosh	Hebrew	Sermon.
Dhai	Hindi	Yoghurt.
Durwan	Hindi	Security guard.
Estad	Arabic	Hebrew teacher.
Gharry	Anglo Indian	Horse drawn taxi. Probably a corruption of the Hindi word garri, or vehicle.
Ghat	Hindi	River bank.
Ghee	Hindi	Clarified butter.
Gulab pani	Hindi	Rose water.
Gur	Hindi	Jaggery.
Gwala	Hindi	Milkman.
Hakafoth	Hebrew	Circuits.

Hart	Hindi	Open market.
Hartal	Hindi	Strike.
Hazan	Hebrew	Cantor.
Hehalutz	Hebrew	Pioneer.
Hulwaie	Arabic	Sweets, including delicacies made from nuts and candied fruit, coconut, Turkish Delight, etc.
Kabab	Urdu	Grilled fish, poultry or meat.
Kaddish	Hebrew	Prayer of praise read aloud at morning, afternoon and evening services by those who have lost a near relative, for almost a year and which requires a response from a quorum of at least ten men.
Kasher	Hebrew	Permissible foods according to Jewish Law.
Keora water	Hindi	Extract of flowers and young leaves of the Screw Pine.
Kettubah	Hebrew	Marriage certificate.
Khooncha	Hindi	Tray.
Kiddushin	Hebrew	Betrothal.
Koolia	Hindi	Unglazed earthernware cup.
Koom koom	Arabic	Silver perfume bottle used for rose water.
Labree	Hindi	Sweetened clotted cream.
Maftir	Hebrew	Final portion of Torah reading in the synagogue.
Maidan	Hindi	Fields.
Makhbuz	Arabic	Range of baked goodies, both sweet and savoury but without meat.
Mali	Hindi	Gardener.
Ma'on	Hebrew	Meeting place.
Maraba	Hindi	Preserved fruit.
Meela	Hebrew	Circumcision.
Mhendee	Hindi	Henna.
Minhag	Hebrew	Custom or traditional practice.
Misry	Hindi	Crystallised sugar.
Mitzvoth	Hebrew	Good deeds.
Mohel	Hebrew	Man who performs circumcision.
Moshav	Hebrew	A farming collective.
Oseh Haised	Hebrew	Lit. workers of kindness, name of Burial Board, Calcutta.

Parokheth	Hebrew	Curtains or hangings made of rich fabrics, in memory of people. Their families keep them in synagogues.
Pesah	Hebrew	Passover
Pizmoneem	Hebrew	Songs of joy written for festive occasions.
Pugree	Hindi	Turban
Rasagoola	Hindi	Indian sweet.
Rasmallai	Hindi	Indian sweet.
Rosh Hashana	Hebrew	Jewish New Year.
Satyagraha	Hindi	Non-violent civil disobedience.
Sefer Torah	Hebrew	Scroll of the Law.
Seyudah	Hebrew	Meal to honour special occasions, such as the Sabbath or a circumcision.
Shabbath	Hebrew	Sabbath.
Sharbati Dana	Hindi	Sherbet seeds made into a flavoured sweet drink.
Shiva B'rachot	Hebrew	Seven blessings of the wedding ceremony.
Shomrim	Hebrew	Guards or guardians.
Shema Israel	Hebrew	Hear O Israel ... prayer affirming the Oneness of God.
Shohet	Hebrew	Man who slaughters birds and animals according to Jewish Law.
Sissith	Hebrew	Prayer shawl.
Sitti	Arabic	Sixth
Solar topee	Anglo Indian	Sun hat.
Succa	Hebrew	Booth, or temporary structure where Jews eat their meals during the festival of Tabernacles.
Succoth	Hebrew	Festival of Tabernacles.
Surai	Hindi	Earthenware goblet for storing drinking water.
Syce	Hindi	Groom.
Tabees	Arabic	Charms.
Tiffin	Anglo-Indian	Mid-day meal.
Tiryah	Hebrew	Brass holder suspended from the ceiling, to fit seven oil lamps which were lit on the eve of Sabbath and festivals.
Tonga	Hindi	Pony, or sometimes donkey, and trap.
Towlee	Arabic	Backgammon.

Torah	Hebrew	Five Books of Moses.
Ulpan	Hebrew	School for intensive course in modern Hebrew.
Yom Kippur	Hebrew	Day of Atonement.
Zohar	Hebrew	Mystical texts.

Chapter 1

HISTORICAL BACKGROUND

It was not by chance that Jews from Syria and Iraq began to settle in India in the late eighteenth century, for this was the time when earlier European intrusion in the sub-continent paved the way for colonisation by the British. In the previous one hundred years India had enjoyed bouyant economic development, "agriculture was traditional but productive and high-yielding, industry was on an ancient pattern but thriving and efficient, there were many efficient trading circuits and India's commercial and industrial strength was based on a vigorous export trade."[1]

During the period of the Moghul Empire, British territory in India was limited mainly to a few square miles on the island of Bombay and Madras city, and expansion occurred piecemeal in different parts of the country, at different times, by different means. The Emperor Aurangzeb died in 1707 and fifty years later the British established a firm foothold in Bengal. As authority in the great Moghul Empire began to weaken, Indian princes competed with each other in regional battles. This created a vacuum in power, particularly in outlying districts, and the Great Indies Companies of the Dutch, the British and the French, seized the opportunity to get a foothold in the country. Their original purpose was to re-establish stability on terms which they could dictate, in the interests of trade in their favour. "In 1756 Siraj-ud-Daula ... challenged the terms of English trade, to the extent of attacking the English base in Calcutta, (when) Robert Clive captured and sacked Calcutta. Clive's victory at Plassey in 1757 ... established the British as a major political influence on the subcontinent... When Clive returned to India in 1765 to govern Bengal he accepted formal political power at regional level in preference to propping up puppet nawabs. The East India Company slipped into the remnants of the Moghul imperial network ... taking up the revenue administration for Bengal, the richest province in India."[2] This achievement by the British, and the revenues they subsequently enjoyed, enabled them to extend and consolidate their trading posts in the south and west, until political impingement developed into full scale imperial dominion, challenged in 1857-58 by the Indian Mutiny. This was crushed, and soon afterwards the East India Company was liquidated when Queen Victoria became Empress of India, and was represented locally by her viceroy. The era of war and trade which dominated the eighteenth century gave way to peace and settlement in the nineteenth century, ushering in a period of stability, and these changed political circumstances encouraged Jewish merchants from the Middle East to establish communities in Bombay and Calcutta. By the mid-nineteenth century they extended their

HISTORICAL BACKGROUND

settlements all along the trade routes of the Great Indies Companies, mainly in Rangoon, Singapore, Hong Kong and Shanghai.

They were by no means newcomers to the Indian scene, as they had plied the Indian Ocean and the China Sea as traders for centuries. Goitein[3] referred to the India trade, Ghosh observed: "the fortunes of these men (in Aden) were founded on the trade between India and the Middle East ... their part as brokers, financiers ... (and) travelling merchants (dates) to the early twelfth century"[4], and Sassoon wrote: "India was known to the Jews of antiquity as well as to those of the Middle Ages ... reminiscences of India fill the writings of medieval authors."[5] Travellers from the ninth century onwards left accounts of Jewish settlement in the Malabar coast in the vicinity of Cochin, which is confirmed by local evidence from tombstones and copper plates.[6] The Arab conquest of Egypt and Persia in the seventh century closed direct communication between Europe and India. From this time, until the Portuguese incursion which began in the early years of the sixteenth century, the Arabs controlled both land and sea routes to the Far East and held the monopoly of trade in this part of the world. Jewish merchants who lived in Arab lands were able to participate in, and enjoy the profits of, these favourable trading conditions. Indian trading customs were known to be relaxed, and goods on offer from the country varied from the most luxurious to the commonplace. These included the finest silks and coarse cottons, pepper and spices, indigo and saltpetre, precious stones and precious metals, rice and coffee, opium, all of which satisfied demand at most levels of society.

The rise of maritime power in Portugal during the early sixteenth century meant that its merchants set their sights on the rich pickings in India and gradually deprived the Arabs of their dominance over sea routes. In the early seventeenth century Portuguese control was successfully challenged by the Great Indies companies of the Dutch and the English, and the only possession which Portugal retained until 1961 was Goa. However, the main thrust of Dutch interest was in Java, as they had the monopoly of trade in the Spice Islands. This diversion away from the Indian mainland gave the British an advantage which they held firmly in their grasp. The only other contender in the field was France, but "they entered the field too late and failed to show enterprise or to receive backing from their government at home."[7]

The Western merchants established trading posts, sometimes known as factories or settlements, where local markets were connected with trade routes. "Taken as a whole, the system was another form of colonisation - of a purely commercial nature ... Europe sent very small groups of settlers to Asia (who were) in direct contact with the most advanced capitalism in the western world. They were in touch, not with the masses of Asia but with other commercial (groups) who

HISTORICAL BACKGROUND

dominated trade and exchange in the Far East and it was these local groups ... who paved the way for European intrusion, teaching (them) the way through the labyrinth of the 'country trade'. The process had thus begun which was to deliver more than 85 or 90 per cent of India's foreign trade over to the English monopoly by the end of the eighteenth century."[8]

The political climate therefore became favourable for foreign settlement, which included Jewish merchants. They were well placed as they had established connections with powerful commercial groups in the course of trade over a long period of time. In particular, with the Parsis, Zoroastrians who fled Persia after the Muslim conquest and had lived in India since the early eighth century,[9] and the Armenians who are said to have been in India for "at least as long as the Portuguese and possibly before." [10]

From the religious and cultural point of view, India was a haven. Religion was respected *per se*, and people who kept their own traditions could expect approval for this since it was a way of life in the country and almost everyone could identify with it. It was a country where numerous religious groups formed their own tight social and cultural circles, and lived alongside each other in relative harmony. Hindus, Sunni Muslims and Jews were all superstitious and even shared some of these beliefs which were not rooted in religion.

Roland observed[11] - " In the late seventeenth century European Jewish merchants had taken up trade in Surat, ... to be joined in the following century by Arabic-speaking Jews from Aleppo, Baghdad and Basra (and) formed the Arabian Jewish Merchant Colony ... At the end of the eighteenth century, Surat must have included at least ninety-five Jewish merchants and had a synagogue and Jewish cemetery. However, with the growth of ports in Bombay and Calcutta during the period of the British Raj, Surat diminished in importance." One of the first Baghdadi Jewish settlers in Bombay was Joseph Semah, who arrived there from Surat about 1730. In 1828 a traveller, David d'Beth Hillel wrote: "I found there (Bombay) few Jews from Arabia and they are dominated over by Solomon Yakob."[12] But the one man who, together with his sons and grandsons, made the greatest impact of all in India and in China was David Sassoon who left Baghdad as a fugitive and who arrived in Bombay via Bushire in Persia in 1832. The Sassoons were a wealthy and prominent family in Baghdad, having long served the local rulers as chief banker, *sarraf bashi* (A). When the local *walis,* (A) governors, were in financial difficulties for projects which were unlikely to have been met from the capital, Istanbul, they made demands on the wealthy, irrespective of

HISTORICAL BACKGROUND

religion, and even threatened their lives.[13] It is estimated that around the time David Sassoon arrived in Bombay there were approximately twenty to thirty resident Jewish families of Baghdadi origin in the city.

Parfitt[14] observed that "Sassoon's arrival in Bombay coincided with the start of a commercial boom in the city (and)... as the Sassoons and other Baghdadi families, such as the Ezras, Ezekiels and Gubbays prospered, so did the Jewish community which depended upon them. By the end of the nineteenth century two-thirds of the trade out of Bombay was in the hands of the Baghdadi Jews." Roland explains this prosperity by the fact that Bombay's cotton and opium trade was directed to the Far East, and to China in particular, and that this trade was not affected by the British monopoly over trade with the West.

The operations of David Sassoon & Company and of E.D. Sassoon & Company were very successful in Bombay, and the latter firm engaged in business in Calcutta on a smaller scale. By the 1930s "E.D. Sassoon had the largest textile operation in India: eleven mills employed twenty-five thousand workers and produced more cloth than any other group of mills in the country. David Sassoon & Company had three or four mills. The mills provided night schools, libraries, reading rooms, sports clubs and even a babies' creche."[15]

Moorhouse has written:[16] "The start of the eighteenth century sees the middle of the three river villages ... Sutanuti, Kalikata and Govindpur, giving its name, already Anglicized (to Calcutta) to the whole spreading settlement; presumably because the first substantial buildings have been erected at Kalikata", named in honour of *Kali*, a formidable manifestation of the mother goddess. Calcutta is situated on the river Hooghly, a branch of the Ganges, approximately eighty miles from the Bay of Bengal. The delta consists mainly of jungle and marshlands which become flooded during the monsoons. In the hot weather the temperature can soar to well over one hundred degrees for several days at a time, but in the winter months there is respite from the intense heat, humidity, and heavy rains. "On this bog" wrote Moorhouse "the British created their capital in India. Nothing but commercial greed could possibly have led to such an idiotic decision."

There was nothing the British could do about the climate, and very little they could do at the time about the tropical diseases which claimed many lives, but there was a great deal they did to beautify the city. Calcutta was a city built by the British for the British, and Moorhouse wrote[17] "Physically the city was becoming

HISTORICAL BACKGROUND

the first in Asia. When Lord Valentia arrived in 1803 in the course of a world tour he remarked how 'Chowringhee, an entire village of palaces ... altogether forms the finest view I ever beheld in my life'. The patronage of Lord Wellesley was such that he was being hailed as another Medici, and the seat of his government as a second Florence... Europeans at all levels of society lived in Calcutta; administrators, lawyers, merchants, and shopkeepers." "Those of means and sound constitution lived in considerable style and indulged in dancing, parties, gambling and copious drinking."[18] Apart from this group were Parsis, Jews, and certain castes of Hindus, who were bankers and traders, all very involved in the network of local and international trade. The indigenous population provided services in the city, the vast majority being engaged in semi-skilled and unskilled work. This, then, was an overview of Calcutta when the Raj was established in 1857, by which time the founding fathers of the Baghdadi Jews had put down firm roots in the city.

Shalom Cohen from Aleppo was the first Jew from the Middle East to settle in Calcutta. Musleah records[19] "Already a wealthy man ... a jeweller by profession ... he was drawn towards trade in diamonds, silk, indigo and Dacca cloth (and) made three trips to Iraq before finally settling in Calcutta." Like other merchants before him, Shalom Cohen went first to Surat, and then to Bombay and Madras before arriving in Calcutta in 1798. He did not travel alone. Voyages from the Middle East to India and the Far East were times of privation, each traveller taking responsibility for his own provision on board. While they stayed abroad the merchants looked to their Jewish servants for comfort, and they included a *shohet*, (H) who slaughtered birds and animals in keeping with Jewish law, and a cook, at the very least. Business ventures on any scale were kept within the family as far as possible, to try to ensure honesty and loyalty. Shalom Cohen was no exception. Musleah observes: "His relatives aided him in his activities ... his younger brother was his constant commercial envoy to Bombay. His sister's son ... was despatched regularly to Muscat and Basra ... he employed many Aleppo and Cochin Jews" and all these people and their families came to reside in Calcutta, until "the Jewish population in 1822 (reached) over one hundred souls, including children."[20] A single wealthy migrant therefore attracted others from the same family in business, in addition to a number of others who provided personal services for the group. Sassoon observed:[21] "It speaks well for the material well being of the community that in 1831 the entire sum (of Rs. 10,000 out of Rs. 16,000) with the accrued interest of 8 per cent was paid for the site for the synagogue."

Like their European counterparts, the wealthy Jewish merchants also

HISTORICAL BACKGROUND

enjoyed a luxurious lifestyle. Their marriages were arranged, often with kinsfolk from their lands of origin, and their households included Jewish teachers, scribes, and cooks who were often *shohatim*. As news of the emergent communities in India and the Far East reached Baghdad and Aleppo, Basra and the Yemen, those who had skills indispensable to Jewish life, such as Hebrew teachers, cantors, and men who performed circumcision, were attracted abroad. Merchants who operated on a small scale, and hawkers, all hoped for a higher standard of living in the East. By the third quarter of the nineteenth century, David Sassoon's eldest son, Abdulla, "was assigned to re-establish trade contacts with his birthplace. In Baghdad he discovered several promising recruits ... the various overseas branches were almost entirely manned by co-religionists recruited from Baghdad and Persia."[22]

The Ottoman Empire spanned the period 1638 - 1917 and the attitude of the Pashas to the Jews in Iraq varied at different times and in different places in the country. Mahmud II, who reigned between 1808 and 1831, initiated a programme of modernisation and desired "every individual to enjoy the same political rights and my fatherly protection."[23] Policy may have been liberalised but central control was weak, so there were significant differences in local practice. Nevertheless, the "reform movement was to continue after Mahmud's death (and) Abdul Majid (his) successor ... inaugurated the famous programme of reform in 1856 known as *Tanzimat* (A) Regulation"[24] granting, inter alia, equality to all citizens - Muslims, Jews and Christians.

In 1856 the Jews and Christians became exempt from poll tax *jizya*, (A) which gave them protection in Arab lands, but the *badal el-askar,* (A) military exemption fee, had to be paid by those who opted out of service. It was not until 1909 that Christians and Jews were actually required to serve in the army and it was at this time that some looked for other options, like leaving the country. There were a few Jews who, according to their relatives, had settled in Calcutta for this reason specifically.

Rejwan has acknowledged[25] that "the complete equality ... stipulated was not always granted in practice since the situation varied (between) district governor(s) and to the extent of influence Istanbul exerted on them." One example of an oppressive governor, which has been documented by David Sassoon,[26] is Daud Pasha who controlled Baghdad between 1817 - 1831. Sassoon observed: " ... the Baghdad immigration into Calcutta became strong in the twenties of the nineteenth century when the misrule of Daud Pasha compelled many members of the community to seek residence abroad." The wealthiest group were always at the

HISTORICAL BACKGROUND

sharp end of the practice of those *walis* who replenished their treasuries by demanding funds of their officers and bankers, and the latter were usually Jews. Christians and Jews were granted internal autonomy and were self governed by a council of "not less than seven or more than ten, ... certain powers being placed in the hands of the president (such as) supervision of the society for the promotion of religious life in Baghdad *Shomre Miswah* (H) (established in 1868)."[27] One of the duties of the communal leaders was tax collection. When the pasha put them under pressure, the rest of the community was also pressured. Sassoon made the point[28] that "the statutes of the *Shomre Miswa* throw light on the conditions prevailing among the Baghdad Jews (and) that particular care had to be taken by ... trustworthy men for the assessment of taxes ... who should not be paid for their work." A report from one of the *Alliance Israelite Universelle* teachers in 1913, on the progress in the status of the Jewish community, points out that "the management of finances (of the community) has been taken away from the rabbis and placed in the hands of an administrative council named by regular elections."[29] It is possible that before this reform became effective the more affluent Jews of Iraq had reason for migration eastwards.

In 1831 there were devastating floods in Baghdad, accompanied by plague. This was the third plague in ninety years and Rejwan observed that[30] "... those of the Jews who managed to survive, usually the well-to-do, did this through immigration to other places in and outside Iraq." A possible destination could have been India where wealthy merchants would already have established business contacts.

Plagues appear to have been endemic to Iraq. There are several references to this in articles, for example,[31] "Water gathering in great lakes to the westward shows that the Euphrates has again this year burst its banks and is about to inundate the plain and make Baghdad sick with fever in autumn." "The mortality in Baghdad in 1877 was about 5000. The Jews kept an exact register of the deaths in their community which numbers 20,000 and they lost 1200 ... the population of Baghdad (was) 80,000 in ordinary times. The poor principally suffered because they lived surrounded by filth and breathed vitiated air. The overcrowding in the poorer quarters ... is very great ... The Jewish rabbis (on medical) advice got their people to migrate almost en masse into the desert."

In 1869 the Suez Canal was opened and Baghdad became an entrepôt of European products. The new route to India and the Far East via Basra meant that this city became an important business and financial centre and attracted Jews from

HISTORICAL BACKGROUND

Baghdad. There can be no doubt that the boost in trade which extended to countries neighbouring Iraq and extended to India and the Far East, benefitted both large and small scale businessmen who included Jews. Since itinerant merchants were both commuters and migrants, it is fair to assume that some of the latter group chose India, and perhaps Calcutta, as their destination.

As the fortunes of merchants in Baghdad and Basra rose with the opening of the Suez Canal, so the fortunes of those in Aleppo fell. Previously, merchandise shipped from Europe to Iraq and Persia had to pass through Aleppo.[32] As business opportunities shrank, the enterprising would have followed opportunities elsewhere, for the observation of Goitein[33] concerning the Jews of the Mediterranean in the tenth century probably still held good in the nineteenth century, "breadwinners and beggars, the pious and the scholars, all were on the move." They had a saying *"fi'l haraka baraka"*, (A) there is blessing in movement.
He also explained how itinerant merchants were engaged in international commerce, ".. a compelling reason for travel (was) the technique of trade. (It required) personal, intimate knowledge of prospective customers as well as producers and providers of goods to be purchased. (This) was regarded as the foremost prerequisite of successful business." All this is borne out by the fact that emergent Jewish communities in the nineteenth and early twentieth centuries, from India to China, were mainly populated through parent communities in Syria and Iraq.

In the early decades of the nineteenth century political reforms initiated by Mahmud II produced an improvement in the status of Jews and Christians in the Ottoman Empire in spite of opposition from the Muslim religious leaders, the *ulema* (A).[34] These reforms were consolidated in 1856 and created the environment necessary for the significant social and economic changes which were to come. A very important move forward was in education. In 1869 the first elementary school for Muslims was opened and a number of administrative reforms were introduced to control corruption and nepotism.[35] The activities of the *Alliance Israelite Universelle,* founded in 1860 with headquarters in Paris, made an enormous difference to the educational opportunities for Jewish communities. At first the religious leaders opposed the establishment of secular elementary education but in 1872 an *Alliance* school was firmly established in Baghdad, in a new building donated by Abdulla Sassoon of Bombay. In 1890 a school was opened in Basra and early in the twentieth century *Alliance* schools were set up in Mosul, Hilla, Amara and Kirkuk. These schools were attended by Jewish children from all strata in society so that literacy became widespread. Girls were being

HISTORICAL BACKGROUND

educated for the first time and "this opened new paths for women not only in the professional realm but also in contributing to the social advancement of women within the family and within society at large."[36] Boys were being prepared to work in a range of crafts, such as carpentry, typography, tailoring and cobbling, instead of being limited to that of goldsmiths. Elementary schools were therefore being expanded to include vocational and secondary education. Rodrigue quotes reports and letters from *Alliance* teachers in 1913 which state:[37] "The upper class grows every year ... They have almost monopolised the great import trade which once belonged to the Shi'ites ... Emigration has led some of the best of our former students to Europe and the Far East ... in the same manner as the Jew of old (over a forty year period) was humble, servile and accustomed to bowing before the Muslims, today they are conscious and protective of their dignity. The ratification of the constitution has given them hope for a system of justice and freedom which they are anxious to see fulfilled."

At the turn of the nineteenth century the construction of railroads, the expansion of the irrigation system and the increase in administrative and clerical posts meant that economic prospects for the total population were improving markedly in Iraq.[38] As the political, economic and social conditions of the Jews improved and expanded there were fewer incentives for them to set their sights abroad.

The flow of migration from Iraq, Aleppo, Yemen and other Middle East countries to India in general, and to Calcutta and the outlying districts of Bhagalpur, Ghorakpur and Dinapur, in particular, is impossible to chart. We do not know how many from each group came direct to Calcutta and how many moved on permanently or temporarily to other destinations in India and further East. Nor is there documentation concerning the natural increase in the community. In a discussion on the size of the Jewish population in Calcutta, Musleah[39] makes it clear that we are dependent on impressions left by travellers and local Jewish newspapers for estimates in the nineteenth century and he has misgivings about the accuracy of an internal count in 1945.[40] The range of difficulties in the census returns, some of which have been raised by Ezra,[41] shows that they are flawed. Accurate assessments are not required for any practical purposes here, for the main aim is to present an impression of the size of the Jewish population in relation to the general population and the discussion may therefore be limited to the parameters of the populations. If we assume that the Jewish population in Calcutta did not exceed 5000 at its peak in 1942 when the Jews from Burma fled to India during the Second World War, and the total population in Calcutta at about the

HISTORICAL BACKGROUND

same time (1941) was two million,[42] the Jews comprised no more than 0.25 per cent of the general population.

All through their stay in India the Baghdadi Jews did not consider themselves to be "natives" of India, nor did they ever intend to assimilate with the indigenous population. This would have been very difficult, even if they had wished it, because religious groups who were steeped in their own traditions generally formed closed social circles. The Baghdadi Jews were never perceived as being anything other than another religious group. Calcutta has been described by an Englishman in the early twentieth century as:[43] ".. a city of gulfs where nobody knew anybody outside their own particular sphere. The civil servant did not hob-nob with the businessman. The Indian businessman didn't hob-nob with the British businessman. The Bengali businessman didn't mix in with the Marwari businessman." Whenever it was possible, within the terms of their Jewish heritage, the Calcutta Jews modelled themselves on the British overlords. Sassoon,[44] quoting from a traveller's account in 1860 says: "The loyalty of the newcomers in their Indian settlements to England can be seen from many small as well as great deeds." However, as Elias and Elias Cooper observe:[45] "The British kept to themselves and mixed only with other Europeans in their clubs". Arabic was replaced by English as the first language, although the Jews were conversant with at least one Indian tongue. Hebrew, *lashon ha'kodesh,* was reserved for prayer and the study of the Scriptures. When they began to discard Arabic dress, a process which began in the late nineteenth century, they wore European, and not Indian style clothes. First names, and later, family names which were originally Arabic or Hebrew, were Anglicized. The Baghdadis never gave up their struggle to acquire European status[46], but they had little success socially or officially. In general, they were excluded from European clubs, and very few had access to the Indian Civil Service or to directorships of large European commercial houses.

The Baghdadis were not only differentiated from other communities in India, they were also differentiated from other Jews. The time of the arrival of the Bene Israel in the sub-continent is speculative, and historians both from within and outside the community have put forward a series of theories about their presence and development in the country.[47] The reason why they were known as Bene Israel, i.e. Children of Israel rather than as Jews is unclear. They lived mainly in and around Bombay and assimilated in many respects over the centuries. They dressed like local people, and spoke the regional language, Marathi, and Indianised their names. They were engaged in particular economic activities from generation to generation, in agriculture and oil pressing, and were known as *Shanwar Telis,*

HISTORICAL BACKGROUND

(Maharati) Saturday oil pressers, until the end of the eighteenth century. In the absence of documentation, it is difficult to disentangle religious and social traditions, but some of the practices of the Bene Israel which coincided with those of their Hindu and, later, Muslim neighbours, could have made their lives more harmonious with the native population. For example, their widows did not remarry, and they did not eat beef. They ate fish with scales and fins. They retained a few vestiges of Judaic practices when they were "discovered" by a white Jew from Cochin who instructed them in religion and rites. According to their own tradition, this discovery took place by David Rahabi around A.D. 1000. "Rahabi family records show that David Rahabi visited western India and encountered the Bene Israel in the mid-eighteenth century. B.J. Israel, (a Bene Israel historian at the end of the nineteenth century) suggests the Bene Israel might have, in their memory, amalgamated a first discovery by Moses Maimonides (around 1200 A.D.) with the later visit of Rahabi."[48]

When the Baghdadis began to settle in Bombay in the late eighteenth century, the Bene Israel welcomed them to worship in their synagogue and use their burial ground. For their part the Baghdadis instructed the Bene Israel in Judaic law and practice and this reciprocity continued for several decades until a rift began to appear by the mid-nineteenth century, not least over the matter of intermarriage. The Baghdadis opposed this on *halachic* (H) legal grounds in Jewish Law, pointing out that the Bene Israel had remained isolated from Jewish life and learning for hundreds of years and were unfamiliar with the laws of divorce and remarriage, which meant that the legitimacy of their children was in doubt. The position taken by the Baghdadi Jews was that they had a different heritage which gave them the right to be treated differently from "native" Jews. Their aim was to be classified as Europeans, with the same status as white Jews elsewhere in the British Empire. Their arguments, however, fell on infertile ground. [49]

Like the Bene Israel, the origins of the Jewish community in Cochin are also obscure. In 1797 the British replaced the power of the Dutch in Cochin, but Cochin itself remained an autonomous princely state, with guidance from the British resident, *dewan* (Hi). The maharajahs took their role as protectors of the Jews seriously and saw to it that they could keep their customs and practices without hindrance.

The history of the Jews of Cochin has been chequered, and historians have suggested that there were waves of immigration by Jewish merchants over the

HISTORICAL BACKGROUND

centuries from "Yemen, Babylonia, Persia, Spain and even eastern Europe."[50] Originally, their community was located in Craganore, previously called Shingly, twenty miles north of Cochin. The reasons why Jews moved away from this location are not known, but Katz and Goldberg observe, "there must have been traumatic events because to this day (1993) no Jew will spend a night in Craganore." The possibilities they put forward are great floods (1341), internecine fighting, and the terror of the Portuguese who brought the Inquisition to the Malabar Coast. In 1662 the Portuguese burnt the synagogue in Cochin and destroyed their documents. The Jews were forced to flee, but when the Dutch established themselves in place of the Portuguese, they returned and enjoyed a hundred and twenty-five years of monopolistic rights in trade. They were governed by their own elders, the maharaja intervening only in matters where capital punishment may have had to be enforced. The Jews who came from the Middle East and Europe were called *Meyuhasim*, (H) those with attestable descent,[51] and were known as white Jews. From the earliest days of white settlement, a black community also emerged, the *Meshuchrarim* (H) manumited slave.[52] Songs and folk stories suggest that white Jewish traders who settled in Craganore married local girls and their children were educated and brought up as Jews. The white Jews also had slaves from the local population and converted them to Judaism. Their children, whether manumited or not, formed the hard core of black Jews. The black Jews were engaged in agriculture and in poultry and dairy farming, and observed the same laws and customs as the white Jews but there was always social distance between them. For example the black Jews were expected to sit on the floor in the synagogue of the white Jews, and they were not called to read from the Law on Saturdays. The white Jews were predominantly merchants and traders, and when the British succeeded the Dutch, the Jews of Cochin lost their monopolistic trading rights (1795) and their economic situation deteriorated relative to that of the black community. From a position of economic strength, the black community fought for equal rights, but failed until it was almost too late; both communities were on the verge of large-scale emigration to Israel by the 1950s. In 1987/88 Katz & Goldberg wrote:[53] "We are acutely aware that the Jewish community of Cochin is on the verge of extinction. Once there were 2500 Jews in Kerala and 300 in Jew Town (domain of the white Jews). Today the numbers are approximately 60 and 20, respectively."

Although the Jews in India from all communities did not experience anti-semitism (except for the short period of persecution by the Portuguese in the Malabar Coast), they were familiar with discrimination. They experienced discrimination from the British and other Europeans, and the Baghdadi, or white

HISTORICAL BACKGROUND

Jews discriminated against their co-religionists of ancient origin. In the days of the Raj those of Western origin were unquestionably at the pinnacle of the power structure in India, their social status being derived from a political and economic base. An Englishman from the Survey of India Department in 1909 said:[54] "The British reputation in India was extraordinarily high ... we had to rule by prestige ..." At the bottom of the social pyramid were the masses of the indigenous population; particularly the peasants and those in unskilled occupations in the towns. On the whole, individuals from the smaller religious groups, such as Parsis, Armenians, Anglo-Indians and Jews who were educated and had fluent English, did relatively well at the time of the Raj. Many of them were able to enjoy the privileges of a very comfortable life-style. Every sector of the population was pervaded by "a very strong colour bar ... it was accepted by a mutual arrangement and by tacit concensus. It remained one of the least attractive features of British India."[55]

The discussion thus far leads to the question - what was it like, to be a Jew of the Raj ? This project seeks answers from the people who lived there during the latter part of this regime. It is an account of daily life of the Jews of Calcutta as they experienced it, as they knew it, and as they learnt about their history from their parents and grand-parents, many of whom were raconteurs. Their hope is to preserve the memory of the community which was the mainspring of their lives, and which has now all but disappeared. This has been done, not in the spirit of sorrow for something which has been lost, but in the spirit of celebration of a past in which they were free to live without oppression. In this respect it is a past which may be compared with those of other Baghdadis who settled throughout the Far East, from Burma to China from the mid-nineteenth to the early twentieth centuries.[56] It is also a past which may be contrasted with Jewish communities in Europe and other parts of the world where Jews did not live in personal safety and political security. It is a past compounded of the intermingling of a Jewish heritage springing from the traditions of Baghdad, living in the multi-religious society of India where people respected the religious traditions of other groups, and emulating the secular British way of life and aspiring to their culture. It is a past, therefore, for which they must be amply grateful; to providence, to the host communities and to the British Raj.

Hacham Ezra Dangoor and his wife Habiba dressed in typical Baghdadi style with their two sons, Eliyahu (standing) and Moshe in front. Rangoon, 1895.
Courtesy: Naim Dangoor.

Manasseh Bassous is wearing *dagla* (long coat) and *fez* (headgear) and his wife Sophie is in a wrapper and *yazma* (scarf covering her hair). Their children are all in European dress. c. 1918. Back row: L. to R. Hannah Bassous, Joseph Twena, Aaron Bassous, Rachel Bassous. Sitting: L. to R. Mozelle Twena, Sophie Bassous, baby Eze Bassous, Manasseh Bassous. Front: Emma and Flo Bassous. Courtesy: Ruby Cohen.

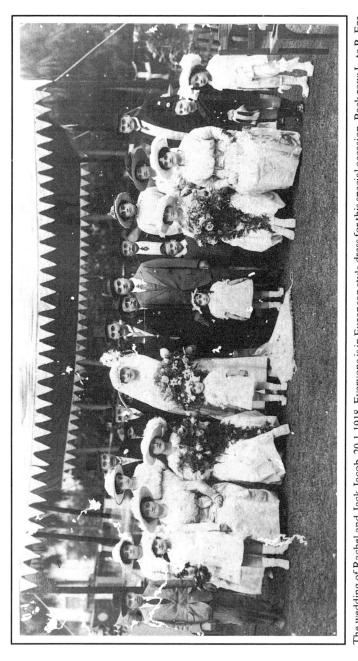

The wedding of Rachel and Jack Jacob. 20.1.1918. Everyone is in European style dress for this special occasion. Back row: L. to R. Eze Jacob, Khatoon Jacob, Hannah Meyer, Yosef Yakob, B. Meyer, the bride and bridegroom. Meroo Meyer, Sir David and Lady Rachel Ezra, Malca Meyer, Ellis Jacob. Front: Seemah Meyer, Diana Meyer, Mozelle Meyer, Margaret Meyer, Sally Meyer, Eric Meyer, Rachel Meyer, Flora Meyer, Nissim Meyer, (Unknown).
Courtesy: Seemah Lanyado.

Festive *sidarya* worn by my grandfather, Meir Ezra Musleah. (1920s). In pink satin damask with gold brocade.
Courtesy: Ruby Mordecai.
Photo: Isaac & Anna Mordecai.

Child's *sidarya*. Pink satin with gold sequins.
Courtesy: Ruby Mordecai.
Photo: Isaac & Anna Mordecai.

Arabic outfit used by women from the Calcutta Jewish community until the turn of the century. *Quassah* (coat dress, trousers), *quamiza* (underdress), *zig* (bodice).
Courtesy: Israel Museum Collection. Gift of Ramah Judah, London.

Chapter 2

APPROACH TO THE RESEARCH

The seeds of this project were sown many years ago but germination and growth took several years. In the tradition of my family I occasionally became an after-dinner story-teller and those that I knew best were about my own experience. In the same way as I had become fascinated by stories of far-off Baghdad in my early years, my family and friends became fascinated by stories of far-off India, and I was persuaded to "write it all down while there is still time". A personal account would have been too limited to portray even a small part of community life, and the idea of a number of personal accounts began to develop, aimed to include experience common to as many people as possible. When I had settled on the topics, advice from friends, and personal knowledge, enabled me to reach those who could assist.

A great deal of time has elapsed between the events and the information collected here, since the main exodus of the community took place in the three decades following the Second World War. It may therefore be argued that memories have faded or have become unreliable. Certain precautions were taken to minimise these effects. For example, evidence on the same topic was sometimes collected from more than one source, documents, both published and unpublished, were checked whenever possible, and a careful watch was kept on the consistency of information as it was collected.

Without exception, all the people quoted here agreed to their names being used as they were my primary sources of information. It was only when the material became sensitive that I suggested anonymity. Married women from the community invariably use their husband's family name, but for ease of identification here I have generally used maiden and married names.

The questions asked were unstructured as each dialogue was unique. I had to do no more than introduce a topic, suggest where it might be focussed, and assist with a little prompting and probing. The discussions took place between March 1994 and February 1995, and were generally face to face, but there were a few telephone conversations, particularly with those who live overseas. More often than not, the meetings were with one person, at other times two or three people got together, as this stimulated discussion.

APPROACH TO THE RESEARCH

A tape recorder was not appropriate for this purpose as there was naturally some overlap between personal conversation and information for the record, and in the latter case it was written verbatim in shorthand. As each discussion was transcribed it was sent to the the contributor to be checked for accuracy.

I have played a dual role in this work, which is unusual. On the one hand I have been coordinator and commentator, and as such I have stood outside the community. On the other hand, sections of this work are autobiographical, as I too have been witness to aspects of life within the community and I have clearly identified with it.

While we still lived as a single community in one place, bound by religion and tradition, information about our past was transmitted orally. Now that we are dispersed and open to influences of a wide spectrum of Jewish thought and practice within a Gentile world, what is still left to be preserved must be done in writing. The general acceptance of this is reflected in the very high response rate and in the great enthusiasm with which people co-operated. Three out of the eighty-three people approached did not respond positively, one because of ill-health, another because of fading memory and the third person gave no reason. On the whole there was a feeling that something worthwhile was being achieved in a joint enterprise, and after a career in social research, this project has been most rewarding.

In recent years historians have become increasingly aware of the valuable place of personal histories in improving our understanding of social and economic events, by exploring values, feelings, and attitudes. In the same vein, sociologists appreciate the use of case studies to complement statistical surveys. If the history of the Jews in India has stimulated interest among Jewish and non-Jewish communities both within and outside India, this additional piece in the jigsaw may take its place in the greater picture and complement the work which has been done.

The topics selected fall within three groups. Part I concerns the domestic situation, such as family, servants, food, holidays and leisure. Part II concentrates on values and practice derived from our religious background, covers rites of passage and an attempt to trace the sources of the rites and customs which surround them. Part III covers events in the period when the community emerged from its cocoon-like existence, spurred by the pace of the nationalist movement which led to India's independence, the Second World War, and Zionism, all of which contributed, directly or indirectly, to the exodus of the community from Calcutta.

PART ONE

Chapter 3

NAHOUMS

I was about seven years old when my mother first read the story of Aladdin with me. We came to the end and she asked: "If you had just one wish from the genie, what would you ask for?" Without a moment's hesitation, I replied: "I would ask to be locked up by myself for one whole night in Nahoum's shop!"

Nahoum & Sons, Confectioners, or Nahoums, as everyone calls the shop, is one of the largest in the Sir Stewart Hogg Market, commonly known as the New Market, in Calcutta. This is probably the biggest covered market in India, the shops and stalls being roughly grouped together by produce. You can buy almost everything there, from expensive jewellery to a pin. Nahoums dominates the confectionery shops towards the middle of the New Market. The shops radiate from a central point in broad, neat rows outwards towards the streets and there are several exits and entrances. Some shopkeepers perch on stools at the doorways of their shops and urge passers-by to come in and look at their stock. "Table cloths, napkins, pillow cases, anything you want" one cries, while another outcries him with "ribbon, tape, elastic, buttons". Once inside, no trouble is too much to display their goods. Bolts of cloth are unrolled one after another, box after box of shoes is opened and closed, every variety of nut and dried fruit is on offer. Competition is keen, forceful and vociferous; and this can be overwhelming for the uninitiated. In the middle of all this bustle, coolies with large baskets on their heads follow customers for hours, piling purchases higher and higher in their baskets. Then there are the young messenger boys, *chokras,* (Hi) either relatives or employees of the shop-keepers, rushing to buy hot tea, cold drinks, or coconut water for customers who seem to be worth entertaining while they decide which curios to short-list, or which carpet they might be able to afford. The story of how the Nahoums came to have a shop in the New Market goes back to 1868 when Nahoum *Ibn* Israel arrived in Calcutta with his two cousins from Baghdad. It was the custom, in some Baghdadi families, to be known by their own name or names, followed by the form *Ibn* or 'son of" (A), and then the father's name. Family names were used sometimes, and according to Rejwan,[1] "In the beginning of the seventeenth century the custom spread among the Jews of Baghdad to adopt family names and was a means of identifying place of origin, profession, or lineage such as Cohen, Levi, Nasi." When a man is called to read a portion of the Law in the synagogue, he is addressed by his own name, followed by those of his father, and sometimes the paternal grandfather. When Baghdadis came to India they were required to fall in with the British way of using family names. When Nahoum *Ibn* Israel's son, Elias Barook, enrolled his children in school, and was asked the child's name and the family name, at the spur of the moment he gave his father's first name 'Nahoum' for the family name, and as Nahoum they came to be known ever since.

Nahoum *Ibn* Israel and his cousins lived in one joint family home in Baghdad, as he used to tell his grandchildren. The reasons why they left Baghdad are not clear and may have been personal. From the middle of the nineteenth century, Jewish communities were becoming established even further east than in India, extending to Burma,[2] Singapore,[3] Java and China.[4] The settlers came mainly from Baghdad, but also from different regions of Iraq, such as Basra and Mosul, and from other areas in the Middle East, such as Palestine, Syria and the Yemen. As news of the promise of business opportunities in India and the Far East reached Baghdad and the Middle East through relatives and friends,[5] it is possible that a spirit of adventure and hope for riches, could have attracted many a young man to these exotic lands. It is said[6] that as long ago as the tenth century, Saadia Gaon wrote about a myth that every man who went to India became rich!

When he arrived in Calcutta via Bombay, Nahoum *Ibn* Israel was twenty-one years old. He was a baker by trade and knew the recipes for *makhbuz, hulwaie* and cheese, that the Baghdadi Jews loved so much. *Makhbuz* (A) covered a wide range of baked goodies[7] - both sweet and savoury, but without meat. *Hulwaie,* (A) sweets included delicacies made from nuts and candied fruit, coconut, Turkish Delight, sesame sticks, and many more. Two types of cheese were common - plain and plaited, preserved in salt water.[8]

There was a gap in the market for Nahoum's skills, and as oven cooking was difficult in the brick and clay fires, *choolas* (Hi) in most homes, he saw reasonably good business prospects in a community which was growing steadily, both from natural increase and from new arrivals from Baghdad and the Middle East. Nahoum started his business by making everything himself and then going round to sell from house to house in the Jewish community. A coolie, carrying a large box on his head, filled with delicacies baked by Nahoum, would follow him. Within a couple of years it became clear that the business could flourish and Nahoum decided to settle in Calcutta. According to the family, his two cousins

NAHOUMS

travelled on, looking for possibilities elsewhere. Eventually one of them is said to have settled in Shanghai and the other made his home as far away as New York.

When Nahoum's business in Calcutta grew to the point where he could support a family, he married and had several children. As they grew up, his daughters began to help with the preparation of confectionery and his sons assisted with sales. Coolies going around to houses with boxes of goodies on their heads were no longer able to fill the growing demand, and a cart was used instead. When cartloads became insufficient, a small shop was rented in the New Market in 1912 to sell goods which were now being prepared in a small factory next door to their home; a distance of no more than a few hundred yards from the shop. It was at this time that they started to expand their repertoire from solely Baghdadi to Western type patisserie. Nahoum & Sons began to open windows on the wider world and their customers, both Jews and others, were able to enjoy a range of new products.

The landlord of the factory in Tottee Lane watched the expansion of the business with a keen eye to profit himself, and made incessant demands for a rise in rent. This was during the First World War and the sales for Nahoum's products had grown to the extent that it became worthwhile to take over a large shop in 1916.[9] This is the shop which they still occupy and very few of the furnishings have been changed. They still use the original till, the original desk, and the original display cases. "We could have lived in Alipore, or any other choice suburb of the city, for the rent we were paying for our house and factory" a granddaughter said. "So we got fed up and the family decided to buy two cottages in Hartford Lane, which is convenient as it is so near the New Market." The cottages were pulled down and replaced by a new development. A purpose-built factory, which is still being used for the same business, was built on the ground floor, and flats for residential use by the family and tenants, were built on the floors above.

By the mid 1920s the Nahoum family were employing several workers in their factory and sales assistants in their shop. All Nahoum's sons were actively involved in various aspects of the business, from supervising production at the factory, ordering and maintaining appropriate machinery from abroad, exploring sources of supplies in the U.K. and Europe, to keeping the books and assisting with sales in the shop. His daughters did a great deal of work behind the scenes. Helen Jacob Himmelschein describes a typical sight from those days. "My granny took me to music lessons twice a week, and my teacher lived only two streets away from

NAHOUMS

the Nahoum's home in Hartford Lane. While I was at music, my granny went to the Nahoums' house and I would join her there after my lessons. I can still picture it. The Nahoum ladies and a few of their friends would be sitting around a round table, chatting in Arabic, and wrapping chocolates and sweets which they made in the factory. I would always get a paper bag with unwrapped chocolates in it." The daughters also made jam and pickles - which took the form of local vegetables cooked in spices, usually in an oil base, which was sold in the shop and by mail order as shown in a price-list of the time. (See illustration).

Their advertising in the mid-1920s shows that Nahoum's products became known at home and abroad. They had several sole agencies in India, Burma and Ceylon, and their supplies extended to both large and small centres in India, which is clear from their reference to *Mofussil* areas. This is an Anglo-Indian word meaning small settlements in outlying provincial districts. "For *Mofussil* orders a remittance of 25 per cent should be accompanied with the order ... post ... your valued orders some days in advance to enable us to have the goods properly packed and sent out for despatch." Since many of their goods had a reasonably long shelf life, and movement by rail was swift and efficient, they were able to extend their business interests. Space was set aside in Hartford Lane to deal specifically with this side of the business. Nahoum's granddaughters remember that whenever wedding cakes were ordered from outside Calcutta, one of their assistants would travel with the cake to make good any slight damage to the decoration that may have been caused in transit. Their wedding cakes were supplied with a silver stand and a silver knife which were brought back by the assistant.

They employed one man whose only task was to pack cheese. Once he was told the weight of cheese to be packed he made up a container of suitable size to take the cheese, with salt water to preserve it. He would then seal it himself. The Nahoums had orders for cheese from communities throughout the Far East. Rose Horovitz, who was brought up in Shanghai explained: "Each family had their own contacts abroad, in the Middle East and India from whom they would order delicacies."

This was the time of the British Raj, when manufacture in India was not encouraged and when imported products, mainly from Britain, but also from other parts of Europe, filled the markets. Nahoums imported a very wide range of confectionery, biscuits, fruits in syrup, and assorted jam, as shown in their advertisements in the 1920s. They also imported *kasher* cheese from Holland. One of Nahoum's granddaughters, Ramah, remembers her father showing her

NAHOUMS

catalogues with information on these cheeses and how one could distinguish between what was, and what was not, *kasher.*

By the 1920s the family were installed in Hartford Lane, and Nahoum's grandchildren were growing up under his loving eye. They described the days on which consignments would arrive from abroad. "Everything was delivered in enormous containers, which came by the lorry-load. All of us kids became terribly excited and shouted to one another 'the lorries are here, the lorries are here!' This was the signal to come and get it. Every large pack had a sample and we knew we could have these. Chocolates from Cadbury, Caley's, Fry's and Rowntree, biscuits from Jacobs and Peek Frean. Sugar sweets filled with syrup from Perugina in Italy, and from Clarnico's in France. Cake decorations of the finest quality came from Germany. Cupids and angels, silver bells, horse shoes, wishbones and tiny bunches of artificial flowers wrapped with ribbon, Father Christmas and babies in cribs. There were Christmas stockings and Christmas crackers. We waded through everything until we were sure not a single sample had been overlooked. Our aunts and uncles would call out to us 'look out; come away from there; mind your head; clear out of here!' but we were all too busy to hear, or too involved to care if we were in the way. And that's not all. The manufacturers didn't only send samples, there were gifts too which we knew we could have, such as mantlepiece clocks, powder bowls, combs, hair brushes and perfume sprays. These were unforgettable, red-letter days in our calendar."

The extent of Nahoum's business dealings with Rowntree alone were so sizeable that in the early 1930s they invited Raymond Nahoum, a son of the founder, to their factory in the U.K. with all expenses paid. Unfortunately, because of pressure of business in Calcutta, he could not take up the offer which would have meant an absence of a few months.

When I was a child and my mother took me to the New Market, we usually headed straight for our cakes and goodies so that there would be no danger of my nagging "when are we going to Nahoums?" The shop was always full of customers and the atmosphere was full of *bonhomie.* People seemed to have all the time in the world to talk about themselves, their families and their friends. Members of the Nahoum family never seemed to mind that their shop was being used as a meeting place. In fact they themselves jokingly referred to the shop as the 'Judean Club'. Sometimes they joined in the conversation, sometimes they were too busy to stop. But everyone; adult, child, and the elderly, felt welcome. I grew into adulthood when some of the young grandsons of the founder were working in the shop and I have fond memories of talking and laughing with them while my mother did the buying. I don't remember what we talked about, or what we laughed about, but I do remember having a great deal of fun and I knew I wasn't the only one.

The Nahoums had a reputation for hospitality. Helen Himmelschein recalls: "My father was a special friend of Israel Nahoum (a son of the founder). Almost every Sunday he went to the cinema, and from there he would go to the shop where he sat down for a couple of hours, meeting friends, watching people come and go and enjoying a cup of tea and pastries. This was way back in the late 1920s, early 1930s, but even in the next generation, particularly on a Sunday, there was always a knot of people around the cash desk, close friends of the family, who spent many a pleasant social hour as a guest in the shop.

"They were so thoughtful, every year after the services were over on *Yom Kippur,* (H) Day of Atonement, one of their servants would come to the synagogue in a rickshaw with two large containers of cold drinks. One had fresh lemonade and the other had *Sharbati Dana* (Hi), sherbet seeds made into a sweet drink flavoured with rose water. The idea was that the *hazan,* (H) cantor and the *tokay'ya,* (H) man who blew the ram's horn at the service, should be able to break their fast and refresh themselves immediately afterwards, but these drinks were there for anybody who wanted them. Of course this was a great *mitzwa"* (H) good deed.

Charlie and Simon Silas, who attended the *Sha'aray Rason* Synagogue, where their father was the *hazan* (H) cantor, recall that every morning after *Selihoth* (H) penetential prayers read before sunrise for forty days before *Yom Kippur,* Nahoums would provide tea and *cacas* (A), savoury biscuits for the whole congregation, without charge.

A few Jewish children went to boarding schools in the hills, some distance from Calcutta. This meant being away for nine months in the year, between March and December. Nahoums often arranged for food parcels to be sent to them as their parents requested, but when they returned to Calcutta they were able to choose for themselves. Maisie Sadka Meyer recalls: "when we started our holidays in Calcutta my sisters and I went to Nahoums as soon as possible. It was like going to wonderland. It wasn't just the cakes which were the attraction, although they were superb, of course. It was also the people. First there was the family, who were such fun, and then there were friends. Everyone who

NAHOUMS

went to the New Market was sure to drop in to Nahoums somewhere along the line while they were shopping, so you never knew who you were going to meet."

Christmas day was a holiday but many food shops were open, including Nahoums. It was the most rushed time in the year, when they would take on additional sales staff, when the factory workers stepped up their earnings with overtime, and when close friends volunteered help. Helen Himmelschein recalls further, "My father used to sit at the cash desk. It used to be a struggle for him to push his way through from the entrance in the middle, to the cash desk at the end of the shop." (A distance of some ten to fifteen feet).

At every party in the community, at every festival except for Passover, Nahoum's goodies would be on the table, particularly after the fast on the Day of Atonement. I can remember the scene in my grandmother's home when we returned from the synagogue, which was probably typical of many homes. She had a large dining-table which the servants had covered from end to end with every variety of sweet and savoury products from Nahoums.

There were certain days following the death of a person, when a table was laid with food so that blessings could be said in their memory either just before or after evening prayers, and when Nahoum's produce was in demand. Since it was always open house for prayers it was a good opportunity for poor people to enjoy these delicacies. This was on the seventh day, the twenty-first day, the month, eleventh month and full year after death. One way or another, the Jews kept Nahoums busy. But it was by no means only the Jewish community who kept Nahoum's business brisk. Once they opened a shop they attracted the attention of many other communities, particularly as so many of their goodies were unique and not known to Europeans, Anglo-Indians, Armenians, Chinese, Hindus and Muslims. Their 1926 price-list (see illustration) shows that they were producing Armenian specialities at that time, catering beyond their own community.

The outbreak of the Second World War meant an immediate halt of all imports to India. Fortunately for the Nahoums, they had bought machinery from abroad for making bread and confectionery before 1939, and were therefore in a position to expand production locally. Sweets were made in their factory, chocolate were manufactured and sold under their own brand name, Ralfe's, and a variety of biscuits such as ginger, butter, and raisin, were on the market. As manufacturers of confectionery they were given a special quota of sugar during the war. Their products were popular and apart from confectionery, included foodstuffs such as oil and fruit drinks, which they sold to the armed forces in bulk. It was not easy to win such contracts, as competition was keen, but their success here helped to offset the difficulties involved in the cessation of imports.

Nahoum's grandchildren recall that while they were growing up they were never surprised to find strangers at their table on a Sabbath night, or on a festival night. Jews from abroad, arriving at railway stations, would ask coolies there if they knew of Jewish families and would be directed to Nahoum's shop. Jewish soldiers based in Fort William in Calcutta would find their way to the New Market and coolies would escort them to Nahoum *Sahib's* shop. Jewish sailors coming ashore at the Outram Ghat would find a similar route to the shop, and on festivals and Sabbath evenings they were invited to a meal at their home.

Anyone who has owned a shop over many decades will have a stockpile of stories and incidents to recount, and the Nahoums have their own fair share. There are numerous funny incidents of people only vaguely aware of what they were after - such as cream rollers or lump cake. The lump cake inquiry was not so easy to answer. "I want one of those cakes where you mix everything up in one big lump" said the customer. "Every cake, even the plainest one, means that various ingredients have to be mixed together. Can you give us clues about what might be mixed in the lump cake?" Gradually it became clear that the man wanted a mixed fruit cake! The joke has passed into the family and anyone asking for lump cake now will be understood immediately.

With the joy there has also been sadness. Sadness in seeing the community dwindle from day to day since the end of the Second World War and hearing that one family after another was emigrating. There were many who left while the Nahoums stayed on, and this must have brought about a certain sense of loss. This is not to say that they lacked friends from other communities. There were many friends who rallied round the family when one of their younger brothers, Solomon, died at a young age in 1987.

Sollo, as everyone knew him, was a great favourite. A broad smile was never far from his lips and his easy-going manner endeared him to all those who knew him. Sollo made a very substantial contribution to the business throughout his working life, both in the factory and in the shop. He was an innovator, constantly looking for new ideas and new lines, not only for the promotion of business but also for the enjoyment of customers. In the tradition of his family he was kind-hearted and charitable, and this is illustrated by his friend, Benny Meyer,

NAHOUMS

who remembers Sollo's twelfth birthday party. "When the party was over there was still plenty of food left over, which Sollo collected. He then got on his bike to deliver it himself to the poor." He knew, at a very early age, about caring for others and this is how he was throughout his life.

My aunt, Ramah Musleah, was at his funeral, and told me afterwards, "people from many communities were there, all in tears, saying that they would miss him sorely. Many more talked of the goodies which he gave to people who would not otherwise have had the chance of eating cake." One of their friends who runs a school bus for children arranged transport for all the factory workers to go to the cemetery, for Hindus and Muslims alike wished to pay their last respects. The Little Sisters of the Poor, and Anglo-Indians, held church services for him. It was a tribute of love for one who had given so much while he lived.

Since Sollo's death Nahoum has had the main responsibility for the business. His grandfather dearly wished to have a grandson named after him, but when sons were born before Nahoum, there always seemed to be a good reason to name them after someone else. When he finally got his wish, the old man was delighted. He would have been proud if he could have seen the efforts of his namesake.

Nahoums is still *the* hub of the community although there are hardly more than seventy Jews living in Calcutta now. For at least five decades their shop was a place where the community sought and found the familiar. Familiar confectionery, familiar friends and a familiar family. It was a way of reaffirming our Baghdadi roots. As Nahoum's products expanded to include those of other countries and communities, particularly those of the United Kingdom and Europe, we were able to extend our eating experience beyond the orbit of Baghdad.

For those who return on holiday there is a certain sense of security in the knowledge that they are still there, carrying on the same business in a city which has changed so much and in which the points of contact for the Jewish community have all but disappeared. They are now the hub of a much wider network of communities. Flower Elias illustrated this when she told me she went to Calcutta recently and hoped to visit a Muslim friend of one of her daughters. She had been in the city for no more than a day when the same lady called upon her. "Darling!" exclaimed Flower "How lovely to see you! How did you know I was here, and how did you know where I was living?" "From Nahoums" came the simple reply.

NAHOUMS

When I was in Calcutta in 1992 I arrived on Christmas eve and was eager to go to the shop. Unfortunately there had been a robbery there a couple of days after Christmas and the news spread quickly all over town. It was sad that I had reason to commiserate when I visited with my family. But neither the shock, nor the loss, stood in the way of the warm reception and hospitality we enjoyed. We drank *dhab,* (Hi) fresh coconut water, tasted as many goodies as our stomachs could endure, but not as many as Nahoum would have liked us to try. There were superb new varieties of fudge, an expansion in the range of savoury delicacies, and every kind of old favourite of the very best quality.

We were not the only visitors singled out for hospitality as all old friends are made equally welcome. I had a letter from Renee Moses[10] now living in Australia, after a recent visit to Calcutta. "The first place we visited was Nahoums in the New Market. There we ate the authentic cheese sumoosucks and everything else he wanted us to taste!! Of course we were immediately invited to Friday dinner which we accepted with great pleasure. That night was an eye opener for Heather (her daughter) as everything was done in the traditional way of years gone by. The *tirya,* (H) sabbath lights, (seven oil lamps set in a flat brass chandelier) was hanging from the ceiling, which looked so beautiful that she thought it was a pity not to continue it. The usual Friday night dishes kept coming in, and we really had a feast to remember."

I made my home in London and for many years had treated my family to stories of Calcutta, not least about the Nahoums. They had heard about the family, the shop, the goodies and could hardly believe that they were seeing everything with their own eyes. During the few days I was in Calcutta I often visited the shop. I always saw people there, both Jews and non-Jews, visiting as I did, and taking *makhbuz, halwie,* and cheese back to their homes in the United States, Canada, England, Israel and Australia. While we were in the shop we allowed ourselves, for a few brief moments, to imagine that time had stood still.

Nahoum & Sons,

MANUFACTURING CONFECTIONERS
AND
STORES, PROVISIONS & GENERAL MERCHANTS.

F. 20, Sir Stuart Hogg Market, CALCUTTA.

CONFECTIONERY

CAKES.

	Rs	As	
Almond Paste with Cream Sandwich	1	8	per lb.
,, Cacroons	1	8	,,
,, Icing Rich Plum Cake	1	8	,,
Cream Roll only	1	8	,,
Cocoa-nut Drops Cake	1	8	,,
Petit Fours (assorted design)	1	8	,,
Fresh Fruits Cakes such as Grapes, Peaches Apricot, Pears, etc	1	8	,,
Chocolate Cake with Grapes	1	8	,,
Ecclair Cake	1	8	,,
Baby Cake	1	4	,,
Madeira Cake	1	4	,,
Genoa ,, (on cut or in whole)	1	4	,,
Cherry ,, ,,	1	4	,,
Heart ,,	1	4	,,
Pastries (assorted) including Cream Rolls—Almond Macroons—Almond Paste Cakes	1	4	,,
Rich Plum Cake	1	4	,,
Sponge Lemon Cream	1	4	,,
,, Finger	1	4	,,

CAKES (Contd.)

	Rs	As	
Seed Cake	1	4	per lb.
Cheese Cake	1	2	per doz.
Sponge ,,	1	2	,,
Hot Cross Buns	1	0	,,
Venetian Loaves	0	8	per loaf
Current ,,	0	8	,,
Fancy cake in shapes of apple orange pears, peaches, carrets, bananas, etc. (between 8 to 16 cakes to a lb.)	1	8	per lb.

FANCY CAKES.

	Rs	As	
Fancy Cakes in shape of—Apple, Pineapple, Orange, Cabbage, Trunk of a Trees, etc.	1	8	per lb.
Lemon, Raspberry, Apple, Apricot & Chocolate Cakes in different flavour	1	8	,,
Walnut Cake	1	8	,,

Your enquiries for any other goods not mentioned in this Catalogue will receive our prompt and careful attention.

NAHOUM & SONS, F. 20, Sir Stuart Hogg Market, Calcutta.

FOR AFTERNOON TEA.

	Rs.	As.	
Cheese Patties	1	8	per doz.
,, Puffs (large size) ...	1	8	,,
,, ,, (round) ...	1	8	per lb.
... ...	1	4	per doz.
,, ...	1	4	,,

DELICIOUS TOFFEE.

FOR DESERT.

	Rs.	As.	
Pistachio Cream Toffee ...	2	0	per lb.
Cocoanut Iced Toffee ...	1	8	,,
Rich Cream Toffee ...	1	8	,,

BOILED SWEETS.

Assorted Drops such as Acid, Lemon, Rose, Rasberry, Orange, Lime Juice Drops, etc., etc. ... ... 0 12 per lb.

ARMENIAN SWEETS.

	Rs.	As.	
Goozumgami (or Gaz) ...	2	0	per lb.
Pistachio Nut Louse ...	2	0	,,
Almond Louse (Rose flavour) ...	1	8	,,
Nazook (Biscuits) ...	1	4	,,
Halwa Ardah (available in cold season) ...	1	0	,,

EXTRA SPECIALITIES.

	Rs.	As.	
Assorted Chocolate, "Nahoums" ...	1	12	per lb.
Nougat Stick Chocolate ...	1	12	,,
Walnut Chocolate (without Tinfoil)	1	12	,,

EXTRA SPECIALITIES (Contd.)

	Rs.	As.	
Dates Marzapan	1	8	,,
French Sweets in Fruit shape such as Peach, Apricot, Pears Cherry, etc., etc.	1	8	per lb.
Italian Sweets	1	8	,,
Turkish Delight 1 lb. Packet ...	1	0	packet
,, ,, ½ lb. ,, ...	0	8	packet
Vanilla Chocolate, "Nahoums" ½ lb.	1	0	per slab
,, ,, ,, ¼ lb.	0	8	,,
,, ,, ,, 2 oz.	0	4	,,

PASCALL'S FRENCH SWEETS WRAPPED

	Rs.	As.	
Butter Brazils	2	8	per lb.
,, Almonds	2	4	,,
,, Walnuts	2	4	,,
,, Hazelnuts	2	4	,,
,, Lemons	2	4	,,
,, Nougat	2	4	,,
,, Ginger	2	4	,,
,, Bon Bons	2	4	,,
,, Apricot	2	4	,,
,, Pineapple	2	4	,,
,, Murshmallows ...	2	4	,,
,, Creme de-menthe ...	2	4	,,
Barley Almonds	2	4	,,
,, Cocoanut	2	4	,,
,, Walnut	2	4	,,
Cherry Almonds	2	4	,,
Paradise Fruit (Pascall's Speciality)	2	4	,,
Cabinet Bon Bons	2	4	,,

Your enquiries for any other goods not mentioned in this Catalogue will receive our prompt and careful attention.

PASCALL'S FRENCH SWEETS WRAPPED.
(Contd.)

		Rs.	As.	
Jordon Toffe ...	... ...	2	4	„
Fruit Bon Bons	... ...	2	0	„
Mint Bulls eye	... ..	1	8	„
Silver Mints ...	... ...	1	8	„

PASCALL'S HERMETICALLY TOFFEE.

Lilly Butter Scotch	... ...	0	14	„
Chocolate Butter Scotch	...	0	14	„
Valencia Nougat	... ...	1	0	..
Almond Rock	... ...	0	12	„

SWEETS.

View Tins Butter Scotch	...	1	0	per tin.
Creme-de-Menthe	... ...	1	0	„

Pascall's Specialities—(Bottle Sweets.)

Mixed Fruits, Lemon Drops, Acid Drops. Raspberry Drops, Butter-Scotch Drops. Fruit, Nuggets, Glace Pralines, Barley Sugar (Assorted flavours) etc.		0	12	per lb.
Pascall's Rose Gums ...	...	2	8	„

PASCALL'S CHOCOLATES.

Ambrosia	½ lb.	1	8	per slab
.. ..	¼ lb.	0	12	..
Nut Milk	½ lb.	1	4	..
.. ..	¼ lb.	0	10	..
Milk	½ lb.	1	4	..
.. ..	¼ lb.	0	10	..

PASCALL'S CHOCOLATES *(Contd.)*

		Rs.	As.	
Furzedown (plain eating)	1 lb.	2	0	..
.. „ ...	½ lb.	1	4	„
.. ..	¼ lb.	0	10	„

Rowntree's—

Mixed Pastilled	... ...	2	8	per lb.
Dessert Fruit	.. ...	2	8	„
Clear Mixed ...	... ...	2	8	„

CADBURY'S CHOCOLATES.

King George ...	1 lb.	3	4	per tin.
.. ..	½ „	1	12	„
Imperial	1 ..	3	4	„
.. ..	½ „	1	2	„
Bournville Nut ...	1 „	3	4	„
.. ..	½ ..	1	12	„
Tropical	1 ..	2	12	„
.. ..	½ ..	1	10	..
Almond	1 ..	3	4	„
.. ..	½ .	1	12	„
Selected	1 ..	2	8	..
.. ..	½ ..	1	8	„
Bournville Chocolate Biscuits	...	2	14	„
King George (in fancy boxes)	...	4	0	per box.
Ruby Assorted ..	...	3	10	„
Milk Chocolate ...	...	0	8	per slab
Mexican	...	0	8	„
Chocolate Biscuits ...	...	3	0	per tin.
„	...	1	8	per box
Nut-Milk (large) ...	...	1	0	per slab
Bournville Neapolitans	...	1	4	..
.. Chocolate ...	½ lb.	1	2	..

Your enquiries for any other goods not mentioned in this Catalogue will receive our prompt and careful attention.

Esther and Jack Silas cut their wedding cake made by Nahoum & Sons, Calcutta.
Photo: David Mordecai.

One end of Nahoum's shop, Calcutta. 1987. Nahoum and Sollo with Danny and Rachel Isaac.
Photo: Cheryl Isaac.

Nahoum in the shop.
1992.
Photo: Miriam Hyman.

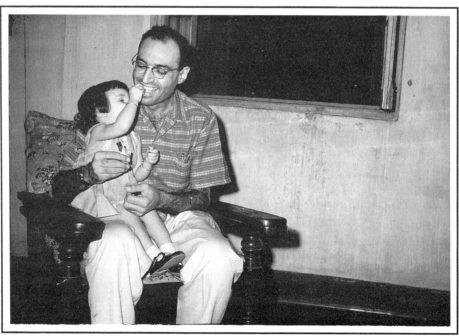

Sally Benaiah, aged two, offers Solo Nahoum one of the sweets she found in his pocket.
Photo: Florence Benaiah.

Chapter 4

THE SERVANTS

Most domestic servants in Calcutta were from farming communities in the neighbouring provinces of Bihar and Orissa, where the system of land inheritance was such that holdings became increasingly smaller over generations, and the land increasingly over-farmed until produce and income gradually diminished. Many farmers therefore needed to look for another source of income and this usually meant finding work in the cities. It was the only way to pay for the repair of their modest houses, to renew their livestock, and to replace their meagre farming equipment.

The two main options in the city were domestic work or work in small factories, and the former had certain advantages. The work was less monotonous, but more important was the freedom to return to the village whenever necessary and sometimes at very short notice when there was an emergency, such as attention to a sick child or a natural disaster, like the flooding of fields. Those in domestic work were able to spend at least four to six weeks in their village every year to help with the harvest and attend to their families and homes. It was not unusual for them to play a set game, known widely in the country, to ease such departures. An article in the local newspaper[1] describes this play-acting perfectly. "I once had a mali who liked to go home every year for the month of March. Every year, at the end of February, he would approach with a solemn face and hand me a telegram. 'Mother hopeless come quick'. Eventually his mother really did fall ill and die. I thought 'this will be the end of the telegrams'. But I was wrong. The following year he waylaid me again with the familiar pink form 'Haridas assaulted your wife come quick'."

The servants could usually borrow from the family whenever they were in urgent need of a little capital without worrying about interest, and every month a small amount would be deducted from their wages until the loan was paid off.

The older servants would try to arrange for a *budli* (Hi) substitute, or someone else to stand in for them while they were away in their villages, but this was not always possible, nor was it considered to be essential to employment.

THE SERVANTS

An important part of domestic work for some was the close relationship they built with the families who employed them. They paid a high price for working in the city which meant separation for ten or eleven months in the year from spouses, children, relatives and all that was familiar from childhood. Conseqently they depended for care, at least partly on their employers, who they would look upon as *ma-bap* (Hi) mother and father, or the ones to whom they could turn in times of trouble. In return, the family usually enjoyed a high degree of loyalty and affection from their servants which was most apparent when the families themselves were going through a crisis or preparing for a celebration which meant a great deal of extra work for the servants. A system therefore developed which was based on reciprocity. It was customary, for example, to entertain large numbers of people to dinner for seven nights after a wedding, and although this was exceptional, there was an occasion in our family when brother and sister were married a week after each other and there were no less than fourteen consecutive nights of feasting. Money was not enough to compensate the servants for their extra time and effort, and it was only their commitment which made the celebrations possible in the first place. The kitchen in my grandmother's house was totally unequal to the task and a temporary kitchen was set up in the compound, so that the cooks of all my grandmothers' married daughters could work together without treading on each others' toes.

In Jewish households, only Muslims were taken on as cooks and trained in the culinary arts of Baghdad. High caste Hindus would not cook in non-vegetarian households and lower caste Hindus usually did less exalted work, like cleaning floors and toilets. It was not at all uncommon for families in the city to employ father and son, from one generation to the next, or two people from the same extended family. A father taught his son, not merely how to cook, but all the Jewish dietary laws, his position vis-a-vis the family, his rights and general responsibilities. Families were always open to scrutiny, and to know the strengths and weaknesses of each member, their status within the community, their values, beliefs and superstitions, could all be enormously useful to those servants who wished to play their cards well.

In an average middle income home, the cook shopped and prepared meals for the family, himself and his son. In the early 1940s, he would have earned between thirty and fifty rupees a month, depending on the size of the household, which is approximately £2 , plus *nachta,* (Hi) breakfast, which would consist of a mug of tea and a sizeable portion of bread. He would probably have sent at least half his earnings to his village. Another servant, again a Muslim, would serve

THE SERVANTS

meals, then clear and wash up afterwards. Sometimes he would also do the daily dusting and cleaning but in larger households these jobs were divided between two men. His wages would have been about twenty to thirty rupees a month. Calcutta was a dusty city, in spite of the fact that the streets were washed down twice a day during the Raj. Windows and doors were generally left open, and dust settled quickly on the large, heavy Victorian pieces of furniture, cleaned once and sometimes twice a day.

If a family owned a car, a chauffeur was employed full time. He was the highest paid of all the servants, usually earning double the wages of the cook. Drivers always wore uniform, white trousers and a white jacket in the summer and dark blue serge in winter. After the days of the Raj they wore khaki all the year round. Uniforms were provided and laundered and were worn proudly, like a badge of skill, and skill was certainly necessary to steer through a maze of streets over-crowded with private cars, taxis, buses, tramcars, *gharries*, handcarts, bullock carts, rickshaws and cyclists, to say nothing of jay-walkers and animals.

In general, household servants in Jewish homes dressed as they pleased. Men wore long or short sleeved shirts over pyjamas, trousers or *dhotis* (Hi) cotton fabric draped over each leg. In the homes of the wealthy, however, they wore uniforms which was the way in the houses of Europeans. *Ayahs* wore saris in the style of their local district. Full-time servants worked a minimum of twelve hours a day, but they generally had a long break in the afternoon.

A house which stood within its own grounds, required a full time security man, *durwan* (Hi). He was provided with a stout stick which he used on his rounds of the house during the day and night. His earnings were in the region of ten to twelve rupees a month plus accommodation within the grounds, which was a bare lock-up room, without electricity or furniture. Apart from being responsibile for security, he was required to do odd jobs during the day, such as running errands, washing the car, or doubling up for servants who were away or under pressure.

Children in a household needed an *ayah,* (Hi) nursemaid, but occasionally a bearer looked after small boys. Those who could afford it had an *ayah* for each child. In the early 1940s, an *ayah* with responsibility for one child only would get thirty rupees a month plus breakfast and a room on the premises if one was available. Wages varied greatly, depending on the number of their charges and the

THE SERVANTS

extent of their responsibilities. They did absolutely everything a child required, from personal care to chief entertainer. Relationships between *ayahs* and children were generally close, resembling that of grandparents, because the matter of discipline was usually left to parents.

There were also part-time servants. Sweepers and gardeners came in once or twice a day, for a couple of hours each time. They earned about two rupees and four rupees a month, respectively. *Dhobis,* washermen came in once a week but less often during the monsoon months when it was difficult to dry clothes. They were paid up to twenty-five rupees a month, but some washermen preferred to be paid by the piece. It was quite an entertainment for a child to watch the *dhobi* place all the clean clothes in neat piles on a bed, and then count each piece aloud to see if it tallied with the account book. The dirty clothes would be collected from the *patara* (Hi) soiled linen box, sorted, counted, entered in the book by the *memsahib,* then wrapped in a large bed-sheet which the *dhobi* would place on his head, ready to be taken to the washing *ghats* (Hi) river bank.

The *durzee* (Hi) tailor, called as frequently as a family might require, to take in all the sewing, from curtains to caps, and from cotton pyjamas to fine silk dresses. He charged three rupees for sewing pyjamas and five to eight rupees for a dress. A simple alteration or an urgent job could be done in the house. The tailor would spread a mat on the verandah floor, prop the sewing machine in the middle of the mat, and work with a will. Our tailor had enough work from the extended family to keep him busy all his working life. He spent hours discussing patterns and fitting each and every one in the family. He knew all our temperaments, our foibles, our demands. He himself had a calm, soothing manner and never lost his patience or his temper, which we must have tested almost to breaking point at times.

Quite apart from the services of those we employed, were those who were self-employed and who eased our lives considerably. They were mainly hawkers, who carried their wares in baskets, boxes or cloth bundles, perched on a roll of cloth on their heads, such as *maywah wallas,* (Hi) fruit vendors, *mettai wallas* (Hi), sweet vendors, *box wallahs* (Hi) haberdashery men. Chinese men sold silk suit fabric such as tussore, finely embroidered handkerchiefs, table and bed linen, and silk lingerie from the Far East, and called "Silk!" in a soft, melodious voice, as they passed through the streets. As a child I knew exactly what each hawker had to sell,

THE SERVANTS

and even the order in which the goods would be arranged, as it never varied between one time and another. But the magic of the gradual unpacking process was never lost.

When the water supply failed, or was cut off for periods during the day, the *bisti* (Hi) water carrier was called in. For a few annas he supplied water drawn from a tube well in the street, for use other than in the kitchen. He carried several litres at a time in an enormous dark coloured goat skin bag.

The *Gwala,* (H) milkman called before breakfast and tea-time with his aluminium container in his hand. Quantities were ordered a day in advance. He was often warned not to mix water with the milk and he always gave assurances, but guarantees were another matter!

The *buruf walla* (Hi) ice man, brought to order, large blocks of ice, covered with saw dust, no less than eighteen inches square and six inches deep, and each block was tremendously heavy. Ice was very cheap and the man who delivered the ice was given a small tip for his trouble. In the days before refrigeration, most people had ice boxes to keep dairy products cool. They varied in size from that of a trunk to a large cupboard with a number of shelves, the whole interior being lined with zinc for insulation. There was an ice compartment at the bottom, with a tray underneath to collect the water as it melted. One of the servants emptied the tray every few hours.

The *bikri walla*, (Hi) salesman, was called in from time to time to clear out our stocks of old newspapers, empty bottles, tins and clothes which were of no use to anybody. For this we asked a price - not a high one - but still going through the motions of the bargaining process. In many households the servants dealt with this and it was understood that they kept the income for themselves.

People in the Jewish community were mainly flat dwellers, who rented their property at very reasonable rates. The front of the buildings, with open or closed verandahs, generally overlooked the street. This was convenient for both hawkers and residents. The main entrances were also directly on the street and hawkers who had regular customers would not wait to be called in. All these hawkers and salesmen would go through the streets, advertising their presence with their own particular cry, hoping that someone in the flats would call them in and even buy what was on offer. Their expectations were not generally high and the

THE SERVANTS

patience and fortitude with which they showed their wares and the dignity they displayed on rejection, were studies in the art of accepting what providence had in store. An Englishman, writing about the Raj admitted[2] - "Some disliked the Raj (because) cheap labour was another jewel in the crown ... at the back of the jewel was the squalor, hunger, disease and beggary ... such criticisms come with hindsight."

Rahim was my grandmother's cook. His father, Karim, had worked in the family when he was a young lad, and his son Ishmael came after him. Rahim was very tall and thin, with a goatee beard. He was a man of few words, and when I was a child he was never particularly pleased to see me in the kitchen, so it suited him well to use my grandmother's instructions to oust her children and grandchildren from the kitchen, politely but firmly. The kitchen was not considered to be "our place" - it was acceptable for us to go in there for a specific reason, but we were not to meddle with the servants. One corner of the kitchen was separated for washing-up by a one or two brick "wall." This was necessary to contain the flow of water from the tap to the draining hole. All the preparation of food was done at floor level. Spices were ground between heavy grinding stones, fresh for every meal, and the cook would squat on the floor to do this job. Vegetables, peeled and cleaned by my grandmother or her daughters, would soak in pans on the kitchen floor until ready for use. It was customary, in most homes, for the women of the house to take responsibility for this job, and for picking over rice, lentils and other grain, to remove parasites, grit, and husks, and ensure that the dietary laws in this respect were observed. Chickens and fish, apportioned for various dishes, would be spread out on *tukhtas,* (Hi) chopping boards with stubby legs, until ready for the saucepans.

Having small children in this setting was a recipe for disaster. The time I most liked sneaking into the kitchen was when the servants were cooking their own food and when I could beg for wholemeal *chappatis* (Hi) flat bread grilled over charcoal, which they ate every lunch time. The family ate *chappatis* made of highly refined white flour, not nearly so aromatic or tasty. My mother and grandmother would scold if the children of the house asked the servants for their food as they knew we would never be refused. Another good time to be in the kitchen was when preparations for a tea party were under way and finger-foods such as *nimkis, filowreees,* (Hi) and the like, were being deep-fried. "Look! that one's ready now, can I have it?" would be met at first with indulgence. Indulgence slipped into tolerance, and tolerance into impatience, as the demands grew and the

THE SERVANTS

food visibly vanished. "There will be nothing left to put on the table at this rate, and I'll be blamed. If you don't clear off at once I'll call your mother and then you'll be sorry." Servants who were old timers felt free to tell us how to spend our money, live our lives, and even to scold us.

When I started work, Rahim managed to find me by myself one day. He inquired with concern about my job and working conditions. "Are they respectable people who run the show there? Do they understand about speaking to a woman with respect? Do they lower their eyes in the presence of women?" When he was satisfied that the important matters were going well, he turned his attention to the mundane. "Paying you well, are they? I should hope so! They would have to go around searching with a candle to find the likes of you!" Having boosted my ego, he then went on to reflect "you know *Baba*" (Hi) child "I've been thinking that as things have turned out so well for you, you will easily be able to afford so many rupees a month to cover the cost of my smokes. Now that is not too much to ask of someone whom I watched growing up from the day she was born?" How could I refuse? If ever I missed the handout by so much as a single day I would be gently reminded by the raising of an eyebrow or a tilt of the head. Many, many years later, long after Rahim had died, two cousins and I met in London. Inevitably, we talked of the old days and the conversation turned to the servants. One cousin leaned back in his chair and said "I wonder how poor old Rahim managed for his smokes once I left?" "What do you mean, when *you* left? When *I* left, more likely!" said the other cousin. "No" I chimed in, "when *I* left!" Clearly, all three of us were paying for Rahim's smokes and what is also probable is that five other cousins, absent on that occasion, were also paying for the same thing. There must be a down side to not letting your left hand know what your right hand is doing.

The servants who worked in our kitchens knew the Jewish dietary laws as well as any observant Jew. In fact they knew all our customs and practices, for example the required interval between eating meat or poultry and dairy products. I remember on one occasion when I was a child, cheating on the interval and being caught out by a servant.
"What are you eating?" he demanded.
"Milk chocolate" I replied brazenly.
"You know very well you shouldn't be eating it for another half hour."
" It's O.K." I insisted. "I had lunch at 12.30 and now it's 3.30, so why the fuss?"
"The fuss, as you know, is that you finished lunch at 1 o'clock and that's when the counting starts. The next time you want to fool somebody try it out where you

THE SERVANTS

might get away with it. This time I'm going to let it pass but I'm warning you, if this happens again I shall have to tell your mother."

A somewhat more serious matter arose when a visiting rabbi from England was living at the home of one of my relatives. Seemah Lanyado explains: "His wife had been ill and he was waiting for news from her. It was a Friday and there was nothing in the post. The next day when he returned from service in the synagogue he found there was a letter from his wife and asked that the servant be informed. The servant was told and responded - 'I'm happy to hear it'. This was repeated four times that day, at which point the servant exploded 'How many more times will you tell me? Doesn't the rabbi know that we cannot open letters on the Sabbath and that we have to wait until *havdala*?'" - (H) short ceremony to mark the going out of Sabbath. The rabbi could not ask the servant directly to open the letter, as this would have meant violating the Sabbath but hoped that he would oblige with a nudge in the right direction. He was wrong.

On the Sabbath we relied on our servants to switch lights and fans on and off when we went from one room to another, without having to ask them to do so. In some families they paid our fares to rickshaw men and tramcar conductors for which they were given an advance. Somewhere along the line they must have been asked to do these favours for us, but as they got to know our ways, they didn't have to be asked and we were content in the belief that we were not desecrating the Sabbath.

On the eve of Sabbath it was customary for our servants to cut sprigs of *yas* (A) myrtle, which was generally grown in our gardens or in large pots on our verandahs. This was placed on the table in readiness for *havdala*, to make a blessing on the fragrance. Kadir, the table servant in Seemah's household, had forgotten to cut the sprigs one Friday evening. He realised this after Sabbath had come in and said to the same servant who had chastised the rabbi, "I had better slip out and cut the myrtle, or the *Memsahib* will be angry." "You will do no such thing" came the curt response "Sabbath has come in and I will explain to the *Memsahib* myself that you simply forgot." That week the family made the blessing on rose water and nothing more was said about the myrtle.

Flower Elias remembers an *ayah* she employed who made sure the younger children in the family said a prayer at bedtime. "Come on" she would say *"Shema Israel ... "* and read the whole prayer, Hear O Israel ... in Hebrew. She had

THE SERVANTS

learnt it from the older children and passed it on to the younger ones with great devotion, and the fact that she herself was a Christian did not matter at all.

I don't know how school children would have managed for hot mid-day meals if it wasn't for the servants. Our cooks would have lunch, or *tiffin*, as we called it, ready by late morning, and three or four dishes would be stored in tiffin-carriers. Each container, made from aluminium and about five inches in diameter, would be stacked and connected by aluminium rods on each side, with a handle on the top. One container was usually filled with rice, and the other dishes could have been *murug,* (A) chicken stew, a curry, or a *bhaji*, (Hi) vegetables in an onion sauce, and probably an entrée dish, or dry food. This was a fairly typical menu for a child from a middle income family. The 'boy' who served at table, or a *chokra*, would take the food to school, with a tiffin-carrier in one hand, and the crockery and cutlery in the other, wrapped in a *jharan*, (Hi) dishcloth. We were usually allocated our own seats at long dining tables in school, and by the time we took our places, the servants would have laid the table, fetched water, and unstacked the tiffin-carriers. They gossiped as we ate, pausing occasionally to eulogise over dishes we were reluctant to eat, or to goad us into getting on with our meal instead of chattering. When we finished eating we went off to play, leaving it entirely to the servants to rinse our dishes, restack the tiffin-carriers and make their way home on foot, by bus or by bicycle. I can't remember that anyone of us ever felt a sense of gratitude for this service. We simply took it for granted as part and parcel of our everyday life.

It was not only at lunch time that servants converged on schools. They often accompanied youngsters there and back, meekly carrying school bags. My cousin Ruby Musleah Mordecai remembers the time when she was about sixteen years old, going to school with the servant walking a few paces behind her, carrying her books. A Hebrew teacher from Palestine, who had recently joined the teaching staff happened to have seen her and was most concerned. "What is wrong with you, Ruby?" she asked. Ruby was puzzled. "Why is the servant carrying your books, are you ill?" That evening Ruby made it clear to the family that she intended to go to school without an escort and that she was perfectly capable of carrying her own books. No one said anything, but everyone probably thought they could have managed without the interference of a foreign school teacher!

Rachel Shellim reminded me of the days when there were no telephones, and the servants made up for this by passing messages around. As they met nearly

THE SERVANTS

every morning in the bazaar, they heard a great deal and talked a great deal. Every night they made an account of their purchases to the member of the family who held the purse strings, and would casually remark: "the so-and-so family have returned from Darjeeling and their youngest daughter fell from her horse and broke her leg." Or, "so-and-so *sahib* lost a lot of money at the races last week and now there's ructions in their house." Although people lived near each other there were times when arrangements had to be made at short notice, urgent information had to be passed on, or there were pressing inquiries to be made, and this was all done by sending a *chitty* (Hi) note, back and forth through the servants. "Take this to so-and-so but you don't have to wait for a reply." Or, "tell so-and-so to let you know whether her answer is 'yes' or 'no'."

We cultivated the custom of exchanging delicacies which was only possible because we had servants. If a family was preparing something special they knew to be a favourite of a friend or neighbour, they would ask a servant to take a portion round with compliments. *Dodail*, (Hi) a coconut sweet would be sent round to Sarah *Memsahib*, or a servant would arrive with a plate covered with a spotless white napkin saying "filowrees from Leah *Memsahib* with *salaams*" (U) greetings. Another custom was for the family of a prospective bridegroom to send his fiancée a dish of sweets with a gift of jewellery on the eve of a festival, or on the Sabbath before the wedding. The mother of a bride would send her and her husband a tray of *baklawa* (A) on the morning after the wedding. Gifts of delicacies would be exchanged between families and friends on the festival of Purim, and all this coming and going would be entrusted to the servants, who were rewarded with a tip for their trouble.

It would be quite wrong to give the impression that everything always went smoothly and happily between ourselves and our servants. Weren't all women scourged by the aggravation of having to put up with them? Didn't they have to get rid of their anger by making them their favourite topic of conversation? They outdid each other, hour by hour, with their sad experiences of disloyalty, disobedience and deceit. Servants, especially the newly employed, could be blamed for everything; anything that was missing or mislaid; for bringing bad luck, for causing misunderstandings. There were times, happily before my day, when families carried out weird and wonderful tests of guilt among their servants whenever money was missing. For example, they demanded that all the servants chew a mouthful of uncooked rice and then spit it out on a banana leaf. The one whose rice was driest was said to be the thief because it was argued that their saliva

THE SERVANTS

would have dried up from guilt and fear. This evidence was enough for punishment which was usually instant dismissal.

I have been told about women in our community who head-hunted cooks who worked for particular families. Visiting the homes of friends and relatives was a very casual matter and it was the custom for people to drop in whenever they pleased without warning, in the mornings, afternoons or evenings. If visitors happened to be around at meal times they were invited to join the family, and in this way women got to know the quality of the cooking in each other's homes. There were some cooks who had learnt all they could from women who had come straight from Baghdad; there were those who had picked up many culinary skills from women who had come from other Jewish centres in India, Cochin in particular, where there were dishes unique to that part of the world. There were cooks who worked in households where the range of cooking included everything from pickles to preserves, and there were some women who entertained in European style by reading magazines, travelling, and widening their social circles, who taught their cooks to prepare many 'fancy' dishes. Cooks with such special skills could sometimes be lured away, with the promise of better wages, to households where they could use their training to their own advantage. This was a cause of feuds and bitterness between families, and even after decades I was told of these incidents with great emotion.

The lives of servants and families, families and servants, were all bound together in a tight mesh of mutual dependence and it was in this relationship that the Jewish community came into closest contact with the native population. They depended on us for an income to supplement their meagre produce from the land, for their medical needs, and for a certain amount of emotional support. Servants in Jewish households were more fortunate than most because they had the best part of every Saturday off, while others generally worked a seven day week. They had their own feast days off, when they gathered together to pray and to eat. At the end of their festival they brought us Indian sweets and in exchange we gave them a gift in cash, making sure it was well in excess of the cost of the sweets.

For our part, we became thoroughly dependent on the servants to do all our chores. The conditions under which they were done were not easy. We cooked on brick and clay fires which meant that wood and coal had to be brought in every day, chopped, laid and lit. It took so much time and energy that a whole hour could pass before a kettle would come to the boil. Water was not always available

THE SERVANTS

at the turn of a tap. Quite often it had to be fetched from a main pipe during certain hours of the day and carried up at least one flight of stairs. Drinking water had to be boiled, strained, and stored in *surais* (Hi) earthenware goblets, to keep cool. It seemed everything had to be done the hard way, made harder still by the heat and humidity. We were lucky to be able to afford to pay for the labour but I'm not sure that we knew this at the time. An Englishman wrote in a similar vein in the local newspaper:[3] "No one retiring from India can fail to miss his servants. Indian servants, especially those of long standing, grow roots in a household that it is painful to have to break. Their housepride is equal or greater than your own."

Perhaps it was not until we had left India that we understood fully how fortunate we were to have had servants and appreciated how spoiled and helpless we had become. Most of the women who emigrated to the West did not know how to cook. I remember one of my mother's friends complaining, "by the time my daughter comes home from work and relaxes over a cup of tea and a cigarette, it is already 7.30. Only then does she start preparing dinner and by the time we've eaten and cleared up it is past 10 o'clock, which used to be our bed time in Calcutta. All day I wait for a hot meal and look back with longing for a hot lunch at 12.30, a hot dinner at 7.30, all ready and served up." It gradually became clear to the older women that they could not depend on their children in the West as they had depended on their servants in the East. With mod-cons to assist them and many friends and relatives to consult, they learnt the basics of cooking. Then they became ambitious and turned their hand to baking and preparing the goodies which used to come out of Nahoum's shop. Competition became intense, their standards soared, and they sat in judgement on each together. The race to become prize cooks was on! In the early days following migration, the greatest domestic handicap was not being able to cook, but there were innumerable other difficulties to overcome. It was a shock, coming home from work, to find that clothes dropped on the floor in the morning were still there in the evening. It was humiliating to see how easy it was to iron more creases into a shirt than out of it.

We have come to understand more about our relationships with our servants now that distance enables us to see it all more objectively. Marina Benaiah said "it is disgraceful that they worked for us all their lives and we didn't provide them with a pension for their old age." Lillian Abraham added "we ought to have been more concerned about them than we were; we weren't concerned enough" and Rachel Shellim said "I can't believe we were so helpless it never occurred to us to cross the floor to fetch a glass of water. It was really too bad that

THE SERVANTS

we thought nothing of our little children making such demands of grown men." The gentleness of the servants, their patience, their fortitude in the face of adversity, and their unquestioning acceptance of their lot could not have left us entirely unaffected. The British admit " ... there was ... nostalgia for Indian qualities that were not always appreciated in their time; the gentleness of the Indian, his courtesy and heightened sense of hospitality that so rarely allowed an Englishman to feel that he was not welcome in another man's land."[4]

Shortly before leaving India I went into the kitchen and upset a pot of potatoes. The servants were delighted. "Can you see yourself in England?" they cried. "We give you a month at the outside and you're bound to be back because you can never manage without us." It is true we couldn't manage without them in India, but how could they know that in the West there were ways and means of being weaned off constant domestic service? I didn't return after a month, or even after a year. Like so many others from the small Calcutta Jewish community, when we did return it was not to live permanently, but to visit elderly relatives and friends briefly, to wind up business affairs, and to tour the country. In the meantime the old guard servants had passed on; in some families their sons carried on for a while, but it was to be the last page in this particular history.

Rahim, my grandmother's cook.

The tailor, *durzee*, carries his work, neatly wrapped in a cloth.

Paroo *ayah* with Leah & Shelly Silas, aged four and two years, respectively. The Maidan, Calcutta. 1961.
Courtesy: Esther & Jack Silas.

All food preparation was done at floor level. Shanti rolls out dough for chappatis & nimkis.
Photo: Miriam Hyman.

Chapter 5

FOOD

Claudia Roden, an authority on both Middle Eastern and Jewish cooking[1] once asked me - "How would you categorise Indian Jewish cooking?" There could have been only one answer. "In a class by itself!" This was to be taken literally and metaphorically. Metaphorically, because those reared on Jewish cooking in India would probably agree this cuisine is second to none. Literally, because in its two hundred year history, the roots of Indian Jewish food were in Baghdad and Syria and its branches in the main areas of Jewish settlement in India - Bombay, Calcutta and Cochin. In the course of expansion, certain elements of the Middle East remained, such as the method of food preparation, while the influences of the new environment became increasingly important. Gradually, something new developed, something unique, which did not quite fit in comfortably into one type of regional cooking or the other.

Those who have travelled through the rows of spice shops in the bazaars of India, particularly along the Malabar Coast and South India, will not fail to know the excitement of the Arab and Jewish merchants, going back at least to the ninth century.[2] The sheer range of *masalas* (Hi) spices, in the form of roots, seeds, bark, powder, heaped high in conical mounds are contained in round-bottomed vessels of all sizes. The colours are a feast for the eye; vermillion chilli powder, pale gold and green cardamom pods, brilliant yellow turmeric powder, cloves, carraway, and cinnamon, in a variety of earth colours. The textures are fascinating. Rough gnarled roots of ginger and turmeric, smooth round seeds of coriander, smooth irregular seeds of fenugreek, rough round peppercorns, and flaky irregular pieces of cinnamon bark. The air hangs heavy with the aroma of ginger, pepper, cumin, and many other spices which merge into one another, so that it becomes impossible to distinguish them, one from another.

Spices are used to flavour everything; meat and poultry, fish, vegetables, pulses, and even rice and flour. They are also known to have medicinal properties. Jewish women who settled in India from the Middle East were no strangers to these spices, because of centuries of trade in these commodities,[3] but there was still

FOOD

much for them to learn. For example, the delights of the taste of ginger, garlic and chilli, indispensable in the kitchens of India, were not as widely explored in Baghdad. Neither was the pleasure derived from mixing onions, garlic and ginger as the basis of substantial dishes. Most Jewish settlers employed Muslim cooks in their households, and it is mainly from them that they learnt how to combine indigenous spices with each other, and with a variety of ingredients, to bring gradual changes to their cooking.

Spices go hand in hand with herbs. *Dhunnia putta* (Hi) coriander leaves, glistening with water to keep them fresh, *pudeena* (Hi) mint, with a strong, fresh aroma, *madanoos* (Hi) Greek parsley, *soowa sag* (Hi) fennel leaves, and *karfas* (Hi) celery leaves, were used in the Middle East. However, these herbs did not play as important a part in cooking as they did in India where they were used to flavour pounded meat, poultry, fish, and pulses, and thus brought variety to single dishes.

Flavouring of sweet food is just as distinctive. Rose water is perhaps the greatest favourite for sweets and confectionery in India, whereas orange blossom water was used more widely in the Middle East. We called the orange blossom extract *farsh*, (Hi) which some people distilled in their own homes, and used for medicinal purposes, such as mild heart problems, rather than for flavouring food. *Keora* (Hi)[4] water, extract of a species of screw pine and imported by Indian grocers in the West, was another means of making sweets and sherbets more appetising. The Jewish community often combined sweets, particularly those made with nuts for example, with the flavour of both rose water and ground cardamom seeds, bringing a superb taste to well known Middle Eastern delicacies such as *baklawa, mulfoof,* and *loozenas* (A).

Since some of the dishes using vegetables available in the Middle East are also grown in India, such as aubergine and okra, we were able to continue cooking them in a similar way. Sometimes we modified the old recipes and at other times we produced completely new ones. But there are many vegetables and fruit in India which were scarcely known, or not known at all in the Middle East and which the Jews used imaginatively. Coconut is a good example. Dessicated coconut gave a distinctive flavour to fish pickle, and cream of coconut formed the base of a delicious fish soup and a range of curries. It is in the preparation of sweets and puddings that coconut has been used most flexibly, combined for example, with agar agar, cornflour, ground rice and jaggery. Sour green mangoes is another example of an Indian product which was sometimes adapted to cooking

FOOD

methods of the Middle East. The mangoes were combined with chillies and spices to make chutney and were pickled in brine, the old way, and in oil, the new way. They were cooked with onions, spices, and chicken to make a main meal eaten with rice. They were also preserved in syrup to make a unique, sharp *maraba*, (Hi) fruit preserve, extending the range beyond that known in the Middle East, of orange, lemon, dates, sour cherries and quince.[5]

In a discussion of food eaten by the Jews of Spanish origin in Jerusalem at the turn of the century, John Cooper writes - "Turkish coffee was brewed in an urn and offered to visitors at all times of the day and night. The guests were always offered coffee with a *dulce*, or preserve... these *dulces* of preserved fruit were of Middle East origin." This was also a custom among the Jews of the Raj, particularly in the homes of those who were comfortably off. If a guest called in between meal times they were offered unsweetened black coffee, into which a pod of cardamum was occasionally added, with a side plate of *maraba*. This was also served at the end of dinner parties and was a signal to guests that they should bring the evening to a close. Preserves were usually made at home with peaches, pumpkin, guavas, gooseberries and mangoes.

When the Moghul rulers established themselves in India, they brought with them many culinary traditions of the Middle East and Persia. Elaborate rice dishes, such as vegetable *pilaw* (Turk), *pilaw* with chicken and meat, and *kababs*, (Hi) grilled poultry, fish and meat were well known in North India and called Moghli dishes. These foods were reflected in the cuisine of the Baghdadi Jews in India. We cooked a wide range of food on skewers over charcoal; mainly chicken dishes in Calcutta, and those who were in Bombay and Cochin were able, in addition, to indulge in mutton and beef. These dishes were spiced in many different ways and were occasionally combined with herbs to produce variety in a single range of food.

Our cooking was influenced by the Muslims in India principally because we had Muslim cooks who were familiar with local produce and with local dishes which could be adapted to the *kasher* kitchen. As we do not mix dairy products with meat or poultry,[6] where the Muslims thickened their meat and poultry curry sauces with yoghurt, we thickened ours with potatoes. If they used milk in meat dishes, we substituted with coconut milk. If *ghee*,(Hi) clarified butter, was their favourite cooking medium we used ground-nut oil.

The Hindu influence was also significant. The use of spices and local herbs predated the Moghul conquest, and so did the range of bread adopted by the

FOOD

Muslims themselves. Indian bread, such as *chappati, parata,* and *puri* all became part of our own diet. Eaten with vegetables sauteed in an onion sauce, or with spiced potatoes they made a welcome change in our food. As there are certain castes among the Hindus who are strict vegetarians, we bought cooked food from their shops with impunity. *Singaras,* (Hi) spiced potato and peas pasties, *dal puri,* (Hi) small round flat bread filled with spiced lentils, *pakowras,* (Hi) boiled potatoes, cauliflower, and onions, fried in a batter of spiced powdered lentils, were among the savoury favourites. Sweets, made basically from milk products, such as curds, were treats, and included *rasgoola,* (Bengali) steeped in syrup flavoured with rose water, *rasmallai,* (Bengali) soaked in cream and filled with pistachio and other nuts, and *sandesh,* (Hi) a creamy sweet made from curds and sugar, flavoured with rose water and ground cardamum seeds.

Although Jewish cuisine was influenced by both Muslims and Hindus, there is no evidence that it was affected by other communities, except by the British in small ways. Leavened bread from the West was common in many bakeries, and recipes for gateaux, cakes and other baked goodies found their way to India through imported magazines and cookery books. The multi-tiered, rich fruit cake coated with marzipan and royal icing which became the centre-piece of wedding receptions was a way of imitating a British custom, and so too was the introduction of ice-cream, made at home and in factories, from the 1920s onwards.

Clearly, our food was subject to local influence but we do not appear to have influenced any of the communities among whom we lived for about two hundred years. Armenians, Parsis and Anglo-Indians ate at our homes from time to time, and although they had their own culinary traditions[7] there appears to have been no interchange of cooking methods and food between us.

The cooks in most Jewish households went to the bazaar six mornings a week but there were those who preferred to do their own food shopping. Either they enjoyed it, or didn't trust their servants to get the best produce. Some thought that servants used the opportunity to subsidise their own food purchases. [8]

When the cook returned from the market he discussed the menus for the day with the *memsahib*. Like many housewives, my grandmother and her daughters prepared all the vegetables themselves to be sure they were perfect and that everything was thoroughly washed, sometimes using condies fluid (potassium permanganate) to take special care. They also picked over rice, lentils and pulses to satisfy themselves that all the husks and grit were removed. They apportioned

FOOD

fish and poultry for various dishes, salting the chicken themselves for an hour, and discarding those parts of the bird which had to be removed. This degree of supervision to observe dietary laws to the full did not necessarily exist in all homes, particularly where women were content to leave these things to their servants, or where they had no inclination to involve themselves in matters concerning food preparation. As more women began to go out to work they had less time for domestic detail.

Ingredients which went into food also went into home cures; it was simply a matter of getting the right combinations and roughly the right quantities. "My mother never took us to the doctor when we were growing up, she just knew what to do for us when we were ill because of what she learnt from her mother" Diana Isaac remarked. She would not have been alone in this experience because we were raised on many home remedies based on products which were used in everyday cooking, and spices in particular. Here are some examples. Crushed ginger and garlic, seasoned with salt, and applied to the temples was said to work wonders for dispelling migraine. Powdered turmeric mixed with alum and made into a paste with water was effective for injuries. Finely powdered nutmegs, mixed with water and just a little brandy, applied as a fine paste, relieved body pain. Clove oil brought comfort for toothache and drops of mustard oil with crushed cloves relieved ear-ache. The yolk of a duck's egg mixed with *hing* (Hi) asafoetida, made an ointment to take all the distress out of an abscess. I don't know many children who escaped *moghlee* (Hi) tea when they had a cold on the chest. According to Ruby Nissim, two cups of water should be brought to the boil and infused with a few cloves, cardamom pods, a stick of cinnamon, a bay leaf, two slices of fresh ginger, two sticks of aniseed and a lump of *misry*, (Hi) crystallised sugar. All this is simmered until reduced to half a cup of liquid. A little honey may be added, according to taste, although how this can be judged in a pungent brew, it is difficult to tell! This remedy was supplemented by rubbing warm mustard oil over the chest, sometimes with a little crushed garlic or crushed cumin seeds.

It is perhaps just as well that some remedies were easily accessible at a low cost because doctors' fees and medication were not always within the means of poorer families who had to eat street foods from time to time. *Khoi* (Hi) puffed rice and a small packet of roasted chick peas, could be bought for a few pice, and as they contained carbohydrates and protein they were both sustaining and had nutritional value. The hazards of street foods came mainly from cut vegetables such as cucumber, or cut fruit such as papaya and pineapple, which attracted

FOOD

hordes of flies, and produced disastrous results from time to time, particularly in the hot weather. Home remedies such as camphor water and essence of peppermint were powerless antidotes in these circumstances.

Most children were tempted by snacks sold by hawkers or in tiny corner shops, some of which were conveniently positioned near schools. Although we were not let out at breaks at the Jewish Girls' School in Pollock Street, a brisk trade was carried out through the bars of the locked iron gates, where children flocked on one side and hawkers took up their stand on the other. There was our favourite "ting-ting" man, who tinkled on a little bell to attract attention in the melee of trade, with a tray full of *koor choor* (Hi) small dried plums in chilli powder, and the gram man, selling *chunna jor*, (Hi) gram crushed in chilli powder and salt, and *seow*, (Hi) roasted strands of lentil paste, spiced and seasoned. Those with a sweet tooth had a choice of *simsimee,* (Hi) sesame sticks, pink and white coconut balls, and caramelised *cheena badam* (Hi) peanuts. For the benefit of the entire school, the *punkha buruf* man (Hi), who sold crushed ice on a stick, was actually let into the school grounds during the lunch break. He came with large blocks of ice packed with sawdust, which he would hack off into manageable bits and dip them into a not too clean bucket, in not too clean water, as the sawdust accumulated. He would crush the ice on a thick blade supported by wooden blocks, into a cup. When the cup was full he packed the ice down with his hands, pushed a stick into it, released the crushed ice from the cup, and sprinkled it with thick raspberry syrup. In the hot weather he brought a great deal of joy to countless small children who would crowd round him, hands extended with small change.

Some children were not allowed to eat street foods, but I know of those who saved money given to them for fares, and who walked long distances to be able to pay for *chutputey,* (Hi) and *aloo dum,* (Hi) varieties of spiced potatoes, *poochkas*, (Hi) puffed, crisp wheat cakes, punctured to order and filled with spiced tamarind water, best eaten in a single gulp. These snacks were mouth-watering.

Just as "the Sephardic women were accustomed to lighting wicks of oil lamps ... instead of kindling Sabbath candles"[9] among the Spanish Jewish households in Jerusalem at the turn of the century, so too did the married women among the Jews of the Raj. By late afternoon on a Friday the table was laid with the best linen and tableware, and adorned with flowers and a bowl of *yas* to be used at the close of the Sabbath. Covered glass bowls, placed down the centre of the table, contained a variety of relishes; *halba,* (A) a sauce made from the soaked

FOOD

seeds of fenugreek, pounded fresh coriander leaves and crushed ginger, *zalatta*, (A) finely sliced cucumber, chopped fresh ginger, and Greek parsley, and tomato *chutney*, (Hi) chopped fresh tomatoes, spring onion, coriander leaves and fresh green chillies. Freshly baked loaves, covered with an embroidered satin cloth, were placed at the head of the table, with a large silver wine cup which would be filled to the brim later, with wine made by Jews in the synagogues, extracted from *zibeeb*, (Hi) large black raisins.

After the benedictions over wine and bread the servants brought in the food and placed the dishes on the table, when each member of the family would choose what they liked in whichever order they wished. We helped ourselves to the food, although in some households a table servant served each member of the family individually, which was the way of the British. The servants hovered about, as they did when every meal was served, absorbing the dinner table chatter as many of them understood Eglish, but did not admit to it. They filled glasses with water as soon as they were drained, cleared away dishes which were not required, brought in bowls of fruit, and passed messages to and from the cook in the kitchen. A typical Friday night dinner in a middle to higher income family, would consist of *aloo makalla*, parboiled potatoes deep fried very slowly until a golden brown crust formed on the outside, while the inside remained soft and succulent; chicken pieces simmered in onion, garlic and ginger, spiced with turmeric, cloves and cardamom; *hushwa*, (A) chicken skin stuffed with rice and chopped chicken gizzards, seasoned with cloves and cardamom; *mahashas*, (A) aubergines, tomatoes, cucumbers, and onions stuffed with rice, pounded chicken, lemon juice, sugar, and flavoured with chopped fresh mint leaves; *pilaw*, rice flavoured with turmeric, cardamom, cloves and cinnamon. In some households there were additional dishes such as boiled *buckulee*, (Hi) dried red beans, or another chicken dish.

When the men in the family returned home from synagogue service on Saturday morning, *humeen* (A) was served, a typical Sabbath dish cooked slowly overnight. Cooper[10] observes that "different kinds of *hamin* were consumed depending on whether it was winter or summer ... in the autumn ... a special *hamin* was prepared ..." *Hamin, humeen, humeem*, appears to be a generic name given to the hot meal served on the Sabbath, without violating the Sabbath laws. The ingredients used by the Jews of the Raj were basically rice and chicken cooked with onions, garlic, ginger, and spiced with cloves, cardamom, turmeric and black pepper, but even in one small community there were many variants. This was achieved by adding other ingredients, such as tomatoes, carrots or fresh fruit, such

FOOD

as quince when it was in season. On *Shabbath Bayshallah,* (H) which is in mid-winter, around the time of the New Year of Trees, *Tov Shebath,* (H) *humeen* was made from barley instead of rice, with quince.

The lid of the saucepan in which the *humeen* was cooked was usually inverted, and eggs and green bananas steamed gently on the top. The bananas were sweet and would turn into a deep maroon colour while the skin turned a very dark brown. Other dishes served at lunch time on Saturdays would include a salad made out of the leftovers of the chicken and *aloo makalla* on Friday night, which tasted very different when cold. Mixed with chopped mint leaves, chopped green chillies and dressed with lemon juice, it looked and tasted good. Potatoes boiled the previous day would be chopped and mixed with ground cumin and coriander seeds, seasoned with salt and tamarind water. This would give a sharp edge to the dish of *chutpatay.*

It seems unbelievable, but in well-to-do families four substantial meals were eaten every day. Each family had its own preferences for food and there were as many differences in eating habits between the homes of the Jews of the Raj as in most communities. Nevertheless, a very general pattern is sketched here to give an indication of the food we ate, when we ate it, and how it was eaten.

Those who did not have a preference for a light breakfast had porridge in winter, or porridge substitutes such as *semai,* (Hi) fine vermicelli roasted until brown, then covered with sugar and milk, or *kheer,* (Hi) made with boiled rice, milk and sugar. These were Indian foods. This was followed by an egg dish, very much in the British style. Scrambled, fried or soft-boiled with toast, and for more excitement there was *ujja* (A) a flat cheese omelette, or a rolled omelette flavoured with chopped coriander leaves and green chillies or French fried toast. Occasionally there was *mahmoosa,* (Indian Jewish) chopped onions and potatoes, scrambled with eggs. This was a hybrid dish which we seem to have invented from our knowledge of Middle Eastern methods of cooking. To add to the variety of breakfast foods there was a range of dairy products; plaited and plain cheese made by suppliers in the community, cream and fruit preserves, *labree,* (Hi) sweet thickened cream made at home, and *dhai* (Hi) yoghurt, both sweet and sour. This was washed down with tea. *Murug,* (A) chicken stew with rice was a staple for lunch. It was a fall-back for children who might have balked at the other dishes which were often vegetable *bhajis,* (Hi) in their basic form, vegetables in an onion sauce, or a fish dish. Non-poultry food was popular in the middle of the day, especially for those who were orthodox and looked forward to tea with dairy

FOOD

products but waited for an interval of six hours after they had eaten poultry. Four o'clock in the afternoon was tea time and was a British custom. Tea was often accompanied by a treat, such as pastry, or gateaux, baked goodies of Baghdadi origin, such as spiced or savoury biscuits, *cacas,* (A) or Indian sweets and savouries. At dinner there was usually an entrée dish which meant something fried, *koorket,* (A) like rissoles, *pantras* (A) pancakes filled with pounded chicken and onion, or a chicken salad. The main dish was often chicken cooked with vegetables in a great variety of ways which depended on the size and the tastes of the household. Fresh fruit was served both after dinner and after lunch. When all the dishes had been cleared, a servant brought in a brass basin and ewer of water for the elderly in the family to wash their hands.

This was not the manner in which the poorer people in the community were raised. I was told: "We did drink tea, but not made with tea leaves, it was actually tea dust. Coffee was expensive and therefore out of the question. For breakfast there was a bite of bread and butter. Butter was sold in tiny portions for one pice a portion in the shape of a pyramid put on a banana leaf, secured with a clove. Eggs were quite cheap and it was possible to eat them about three times a week. Cheese was a great luxury and not for us, as was *ghee,* clarified butter. Sometimes we went out and bought a load of *dal purees.* They cost no more than a couple of pice a piece, but this would be instead of, and not as well as, bread and butter. For the main meal of the day we ate boiled rice every day, except on the Sabbath. This was eaten with *dal,* (Hi) lentils, three times a week at least, and on other days we ate *bhajis*, vegetables cooked in oil and sauted onions if we were lucky. Sometimes there was just boiled rice helped down with a little pickle, or a piece of cucumber, or *aloo bharta*, (Hi) boiled potatoes mashed with chopped onions and flavoured with lemon juice. Fish was expensive and so were tinned provisions, such as tinned fruit and fish, so we couldn't afford these things. We never had cakes or confectionery and sugar was expensive. So was fruit, but when the fruits became soft they were sold cheap, and that is where we got in. No matter how poor the family, there was chicken and *aloo makalla* with *halba* somehow or another on Friday nights. Boiled eggs and potatoes, cooked on Friday, was the main meal for lunch on Saturday and on *Motsae Shabbath* (H) after Sabbath, we had boiled rice with a piece of cucumber." Rahel Silas Beniah said: "When the Jews from Burma started arriving we had to help them on the spur of the moment and one day a boat arrived on a Saturday. My mother went round to all the neighbours to ask for any food they could spare for the refugees. We didn't live in a rich neighbourhood and at every house she was given boiled eggs. In no time at all she had countless eggs - nothing else."

FOOD

The community did help the poorest families with rice and oil for example, for the festivals of Passover and the New Year as it was hoped that no one went without a small taste of luxury. In addition, there were many people who made provision for the poor privately. Bread was distributed to many families on a Friday by individuals but not by the community.

The food eaten during the festivals by families who were in comfortable circumstances was very much the same as for Friday nights, although a lunch time favourite was a sweet-sour ragout, *khutta,* (Indian Jewish) a typically Middle Eastern method of cooking. Neither the Hindus nor Muslims make sweet-sour dishes. These ragouts were made with chicken, *koobas,* or *kooftas,* minced chicken balls combined with onions and a herb, together with any one of a range of vegetables, such as tomatoes, beetroot, lady's fingers, and pumpkin. Sometimes a ragout was made exclusively with these vegetables. Another variety of ragout was *mahmoora,* (A) a very festive dish because almond slivers and raisins were added. On festival days we sprinkled the top of *pilaw* with fried raisins and almonds.

On *Rosh Hashana,* (H) the Jewish New Year, bread was dipped in sugar and not in salt for the usual benediction which preceded a meal. We did not eat anything sour on that day, so that the popular sweet-sour ragout was replaced by *murug,* chicken stew. And like Jews the world over, on the eve of *Rosh Hashana,* we ate apple dipped in honey, only our way of doing this was by preparing apple preserve, spiced either with cloves or cardamom, or with both. We prayed for a year "from the first day to the last, as goodly as the apple and as sweet as honey." In the tradition of other Sephardi communities we ate other symbolic foods in a specific order. Before the apple came dates as a beginning of happiness, blessing and peace for all men, and pomegranate full of seeds, eaten in the hope that their numbers would be matched by a similar number of *mitzvoth,* (H) good deeds. After the apple came boiled *lubia* (H) black-eyed beans, preceded by the prayer that we would be full of merit and taken to God's heart. Boiled pumpkin came next, with the supplication that we be guarded against our enemies, boiled spinach for protection from those who had harmed us in the past, fresh garlic sprouts in the hope of being lucky. The brain of chicken or lamb symbolised going ahead and not backwards in the coming year, and was intended to remind us of "Isaac our Patriarch, son of Abraham our Patriarch, who went ahead in peace." This refers to the sacrifice of Isaac, which is included in the synagogue service on the second day of New Year.

FOOD

After lunch on *Rosh Hashana*, my grandparents hosted a large gathering of men who took it in turns to read from the Book of Psalms. Meanwhile, the women in the family peeled, cut and displayed fresh fruit in season and set out almonds and dried fruits, *loozenas* (A) diamond shaped sweets made from nuts, guava and quince and pumpkin. When the reading was complete the table was laden with food so that the men could recite the appropriate benedictions.

Most families fasted on a rich meal of *aloo makalla, pilaw, khutta,* and chicken, before *Yom Kippur,* (H) the Day of Atonement, but there were those who preferred a light meal of their own choosing. Some people broke their fast on *sherbet* (Turk) in the synagogue after *Yom Kippur* and recall that the whole synagogue would smell of *Kaiora* and *Gulab Pani*, (Hi), rose water which was used to flavour a local drink made by soaking seeds called *Shurbati Dana* (Hi). Many looked forward to a hot cup of tea with a variety of sweet and savoury baked goodies. In some homes grilled chicken, *kabab* was served a few hours later.

The festival of Tabernacles, *Succoth,* (H) was a time when those people who had the space and the inclination, built a beautiful *succa,* (H) booth with a temporary bamboo structure covered with palm leaves. It was customary for those who built a *succa* to invite guests for lunch and dinner throughout the eight days of the festival. The *succa* was decorated, among other things, by hanging every type of fruit in season. As the fruit ripened we would take it down to eat during the festival in my grandmother's house. Each member of the family was given at least one opportunity to invite their closest friends and the richest and most complicated dishes were prepared in this week. This was a festival of great socialising and those who called in between meal times were traditionally served toasted and salted almonds, pistachio nuts, and pine nuts.

On the seventh night of *Succoth, Hoshanna Rabba,*(H) many friends, mostly men, would gather at my grandparents' house after dinner. The men sat in the *Succa*, and took turns to read the Book of Deuteronomy, which was completed before midnight. Afterwards they made blessings over a range of fruit and sweets, which was then passed round among the women, in much the same way as on *Rosh Hashana.* Prayers continued until dawn, when the men went to synagogue to read the morning prayer, *Sha' areet* (H). Some of the women brought dough, from which they pinched a tiny piece at a time, rolled it between their forefinger and thumb and dropped the pieces to dry out on a tray. It was a Baghdadian custom. On the festival of *Simhat Torah* this pasta, called *Sha'aree*, was deep fried and mixed with rice in the preparation of pilaw. The end result was a colourful mixture of yellow rice with golden brown *Sha'aree*.

FOOD

Passover was a festival associated with relative deprivation of many foods. We did not buy oil or sugar, for example, because there was no certainty that these products were free from *hametz* (H) leaven, in the course of production. Instead we had to rely on chicken fat as a cooking medium and *halek,* (A) date juice to sweeten many foods. People usually prepared *halek* in their own homes by picking over dates, removing the stones, soaking them, and extracting the juice, which would be cooked for several hours until it thickened. It was mixed with walnuts for *haroseth,(H)* at the *Seder* service to symbolise mortar used by the Hebrews in ancient Egypt to build cities.

Spices were not used during this festival because the seeds and powder might have mingled with leaven products. However, there appeared to be no objection to dried roots such as turmeric and ginger which were ground at home. We bought rock salt which was also ground at home. Coffee beans, roasted and ground by the servants, replaced tea, as the tea leaves were loose and might have been in contact with leaven. Cows were brought round to our homes and milked into our own utensils. The milkmen took this in their stride, never questioning, never objecting. Those who lived in houses and kept their own cow gave the spare milk to their friends during Passover. Rice was a staple in India as it was in Baghdad, and we brought the *minhag,* (H) custom, from there of eating rice during Passover. There were no cakes, confectionery or sweets, but as on the Festival of Tabernacles we offered guests roasted almonds and nuts. *Matza,* (H), unleavened bread, was baked in the compound of the synagogue to meet the demands of the entire community and soon after Purim the preparations would start in make-shift kitchens. Many Jews were able to get casual work, assisting with the preparation of dough, rolling out the *matza* in large rounds and baking the bread. A family's supply of *matza* was wrapped in enormous white sheets fitted into large baskets which would be suspended from the ceiling to provide protection from mice, household lizards, spiders and insects. The servants would climb on a stool to bring down the *matza* as it was needed.

When Passover was ended, the servants of most Jewish households would converge on the Hindu sweetmeat shops to buy *hametz,*(H) leaven products. Bengali confectioners of quality, such as Bhim Nag and K.C. Das would make sure there was a choice range of sweets for this night. My grandmother would order a large pistachio *sondesh,* a green sweet which took on the colour of the pistachios, in the shape of a fish. Bengalis are very fond of fish and often use the shape in sweet production. It was called *Santak Khadra* (A) night[11] - literally, let your year be green, symbolising fertility or fruitfulness. When the table was laid it would be

FOOD

strewn with soft willow branches and we would tap each and every member of the family on the shoulder with a branch saying "*Santak Khadra, Santak Khadra*, may you ... pass your exams ... succeed in your business ... marry a good man", etc. etc. whatever seemed appropriate to the particular circumstances of the person being blessed.

Shavuoth, (H) the festival of Pentecost is celebrated for agricultural and historical reasons. It is the time of the grain harvest and to commemorate this we ate meal from roasted corn, mixed with water and sugar, *suttoo* (Hi). Pentecost is the time when the Hebrews were given the Law on Mount Sinai. The Law is likened to honey and the Jewish people to milk, so we ate dairy products such as cheese *sumoosucks* (A) cheese pasties. We also ate *kahi*, (A), which was a tradition from Baghdad. This is puff pastry and was eaten with something sweet, such as *halek* left over from Passover, or fruit preserve. Some people preferred a generous sprinkling of sugar.

The eve of *Shavuoth* was also spent in studying from religious texts all night, and as on *Rosh Hashana* and *Hoshanna Rabba*, a meal of baked goodies, sweets, dried and fresh fruit, was served in between the reading for the appropriate blessings to be recited.

Few preparations were made at home for the minor festivals of *Hannukah*, rededication of the Temple, and for *Purim*. At *Hannukah* some families ate *halwa,* (Hi) made from semolina, sugar, and oil, flavoured with rose water and garnished with slivered almonds. For *Purim* we bought in *makhbuz* and *halwie*, to exchange with friends and relatives. The goodies were taken to and fro by servants in covered *khoonchas* (Hi) trays, and, as they were given a small cash reward for every trip, they were quite happy to help out.

In the week from *Rosh Hodesh Ab,* the first day of the last but one month in the Jewish calendar, until the eighth of the month, we prepared for the day of mourning on the ninth, to remember the destruction of the Temple, marked by a twenty-five hour fast. In that week the intention was to avoid fine food, so we did not eat poultry or meat, and some people would not even eat fish.

On the whole, the Jews of the Raj prided themselves on eating well. Those who could afford it bought the best quality of fresh and dry food, on which they were quite prepared to spend a sizeable proportion of their earnings. Eating was a very pleasurable activity, usually in the company of family and friends. It

FOOD

was not unusual for an entire family to get together for at least two meals a day, breakfast and dinner.

In what way can it be claimed that the food of the Jews of the Raj was basically Jewish cooking? Primarily because the Jews from Iraq or the Middle East carried to India a cuisine distinctive of their countries of origin. In its original form, the foods might not have been exclusively Jewish, but when modified and eaten in India, they formed part and parcel of a repertoire exclusive to the Jews, and distinct from other communities. Our cooking shows clear signs of influence from India, and for this we must be grateful to our Muslim cooks and to the produce of the land. The fact that many Hindus are vegetarian enabled us to enjoy their sweet and savoury products on the market, both in and outside our homes. In this respect too, we were able to "experience" India and enjoy what it had to offer. However, we usually retained the basic cooking methods of Baghdad and the end product is a hybrid cuisine derived from two traditions and which in all fairness could be labelled Indian-Jewish cooking.

PREPARATION OF *MATZA* UNLEAVENED BREAD IN THE COMPOUND, *BETH EL* SYNAGOGUE, CALCUTTA.

Unleavened dough is rolled out by local women for Passover. The casual work was done by Jews during the Raj.
Photo: Cheryl Isaac.

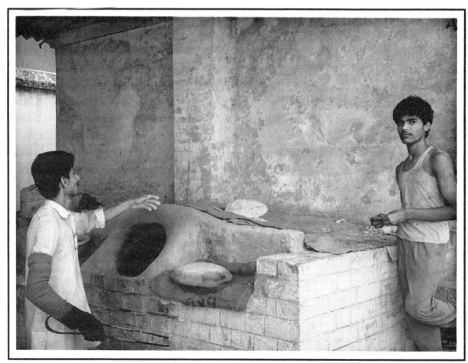

Brick and clay oven to bake the *matza*. This was always done by local bakers.
Photo: Cheryl Isaac.

PREPARATION OF *MATZA* UNLEAVENED BREAD IN THE COMPOUND, *BETH EL* SYNAGOGUE, CALCUTTA.

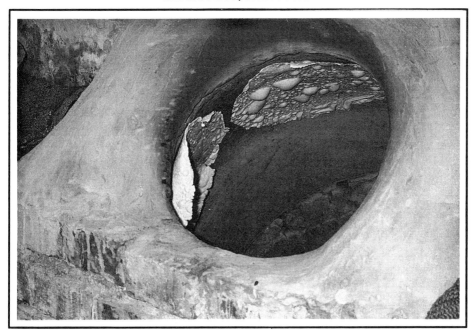

The *matza* being baked on the walls of the oven.
Photo: Cheryl Isaac.

The *matza* is stored in baskets, ready to be weighed and sold.
Photo: Cheryl Isaac.

Koom-koom, silver rose water bottle with sprinkler on the top. Traditional pattern from Shanghai.
Courtesy: Ruby & Elias Mordecai.
Photo: Isaac & Anna Mordecai.

Silver wine cup, traditional pattern from Shanghai.
Courtesy: Ruby & Elias Mordecai.
Photo: Isaac & Anna Mordecai.

Chapter 6

MADHUPUR

When the Calcutta Jews took their vacations they often chose to congregate in the same place. It is possible that the tight social circles which coexisted in the wider society compelled members of various communities to turn in on themselves. Two influences, working in the same direction, could have been important. On the one hand the Baghdadi Jews may have had a preference for socialising between themselves, but on the other hand the norms which existed right across the board, may have left them with little alternative. This could have come into sharp focus when they took vacations and when parting from the main group left them in social limbo, so they could have decided to create a home-from-home.

Darjeeling was the favourite mountain resort in the hot season, and Madhupur during the winter months. Madhupur was particularly popular from the mid 1920s until the mid 1950s, when the exodus from Calcutta began in earnest. Situated in the neighbouring state of Bihar, Madhupur is a mere one hundred and eighty mile train journey from Calcutta which could take anything from six to eight hours. It was quite usual to travel overnight, when bedding, carried in a neat holdall, would be rolled out on bench seats. The movement of the train would soon lull the traveller to sleep but as the engine came to a halt at each of the several stations en route, the passengers would be rudely awakened by the cries of hawkers on the platforms, even in the dead of night. Each cry had its own musical character and accent, and it is a pity it can't be reproduced here. *"Cha garam, garam chai!"* (Hi) Hot tea, hot tea! *"Meetha Lameboo, Meetha Lameboo!"* (Hi) "Oranges, oranges!" *"Pan, berrie, cigarettes" Pan* (Hi) betel-nut and other spices encased in an edible leaf which is chewed very slowly, and leaves a red stain in the mouth. *Berrie* (Hi) is a cheap form of smoke.

Arlene Einy recalled: "For those who travelled by day, the view was not spectacular, just mile after mile of paddy fields, separated by low mud ridges, or meadows with a few goats or cows grazing. There was the occasional cluster of trees, mostly palm, with a few mud huts sheltering in their shade. Mongrels wandered through villages and men and women worked in the fields nearby. The women were in brightly coloured saris - red, blue, green and yellow but the men wore pale colours; blue or grey.. From time to time you could pass a village pond

MADHUPUR

and see the women washing clothes, beating them on a stone. Or a group of youngsters would be fishing in pools. At level crossings, men were waiting with their bicycles, with loads of maize in tin containers. Most eye-catching of all were the lorries and other vehicles, painted in the brightest colours imaginable and decorated with floral designs from end to end. The lorries were laden with farm produce. After the journey it was a relief to get a hot cup of tea at Kellners in Madhupur station. I drank it from a *koolia*, (Hi) unglazed earthenware cup, which was always broken after use. It was possible to get a full breakfast at Kellners; eggs, toast, butter, jam, the lot, and this was welcome for overnight travellers. The bookshop in the station had a wide choice of paperbacks displayed on wheeled stands. I usually bought a few to keep me going as there was never much to do. But this didn't stop us from returning to Madhupur again and again."

Madhupur was a village in Bihar, small enough to be able to cross from one end to the other in no more than half an hour on foot. It has changed almost beyond recognition now, as it has grown into a town in an industrial area. In the days when it was a popular holiday centre for Jews it was not particularly well known, not singularly beautiful, neither were there local amenities to attract visitors. There were no made-up roads, there was no electricity, tap water, or sanitation. During the winter it was even cooler than in Calcutta. Yet year after year, a large number of Jews and their cooks would pack their bags, their bedding, their separate kitchen and tableware for milk and poultry products, and take the train to Madhupur. They stayed there for at least a month over the school holidays, and even longer - up to three months - whenever this was possible. "In the early years, Rev. E.M.D. Cohen, senior minister of Calcutta's Maghen David Synagogue, would take along a *Sefer Torah*, (H) scroll of the Law, (to Madhupur) so that he could conduct Sabbath services at his home while he was away from synagogue. He was joined by large congregations of vacationers".[1] This meant that men who were reading *Kaddish*, (H) could go on holiday with impunity. *Kaddish* is a prayer of praise read aloud at morning, afternoon and evening services, for almost a year, by those who have lost a near relative, and which requires a response from a quorum of at least ten men.

The *Dak* Bungalow, which literally means Post House in Hindi, is a fine building and imposing by Madhupur standards, just outside the station, and was used for many purposes. For example, it was the location of the district small causes court, with long lines of litigants awaiting their turn outside the magistrate's office. There was short-stay accommodation for government officials while on circuit in the province, or for travellers, as there was nothing approaching a hotel

MADHUPUR

or a guest house in those days. There was also space for their servants. *Dak Bungalows* were used in this way throughout the provinces in India. It was a meeting place in Madhupur, with vast tracts of land all round, which meant that a child kicking a ball was like a light to moths. Soon there would be enough children to make up a football team, with plenty of reserves on the sidelines. The sounds of children at play would carry across the fields. "Pass the ball here!" - "It's my turn!" "Go home, you're useless!" and triumphant yells of "goal! goal!" "I scored!" There were different sounds in the night; the howling of jackals, the barking of dogs, and the tap, tap of the night watchman's stout wooden stick as he walked through the streets, calling to people fast asleep in their beds *"Samalow, samalow!"* (Hi) Take care!

Madhupur is a railway junction, and all connecting goods trains to Bengal have to stop there for refuelling, taking on water, and cleaning. There was always a sense of hustle and bustle at the station, with people coming and going, greeting each other and saying their good-byes for everyone to hear. There were people shouting orders to coolies, hawkers and *tonga wallas* (Hi) men with pony and trap. Trains would be moving slowly on to sidings and moving off them, with a heavy puff, a hiss of steam and a crunch of wheels on the lines. The Jews would be bringing and taking news and messages, bringing gifts of baked goodies from Nahoums and taking back sweetmeats and mint. Some are convinced that one of the attractions of Madhupur was the ease with which Nahoums could send large basket-loads of goodies, and families were known to order a basket every week. There were friends and relatives to be seen off and family to welcome, particularly just before the weekend, when those men who were working in Calcutta would join their families in Madhupur.

It was also a convenient point for changing railway personnel, such as engine drivers and guards who were mainly Anglo-Indians and who settled there with their families, so that it came to be a railway colony. The Anglo-Indians lived in railway quarters around the station and many stayed on in Madhupur after they retired, when they bought their own houses. Some of them rented part of their homes to Jews who would return unfailingly every winter. "The Anglo-Indians coexisted in their own railway communities beside the local British (and other) communities with a deep gulf in between ... it was a sort of social taboo."[2]

The railway employees had an Institute or club house in the *Dak Bungalow* and were quite relaxed about young Jewish men using their billiard room, joining their carrums matches (a board game) and attending their weekly

MADHUPUR

dances to a small band. On New Year's eve they would have a gala dance and young Jews were always welcome, as they were on New Year's Day when they played bingo, or housey, as it was called. The Anglo-Indians organised sports activities in which Jewish children sometimes participated, and their annual sports day during the winter holidays was a special event which attracted Jewish boys and girls, who were generally outstripped. A few Jewish boys did excel and when they carried off prizes and trophies the whole resident community cheered. While it seemed perfectly natural for teenage and younger boys and girls to mix freely with Anglo-Indians, it was uncommon for the older people of the two communities to socialise, and this separateness was the choice of the Jews. The Anglo-Indians had few taboos, if any, and this made it easier for them to cross cultural barriers.

There was no shortage of accommodation as several houses were owned by Jews, some specifically for renting, and many had English name such as Home, Hermitage, Anchorage, and Rose Bank. The houses and bungalows were usually spacious, surrounded by gardens, some the size of a playing field, with beautiful trees. There were cashew nut trees and *pad badam* trees with purple pods, each pod containing a single large nut which was deliciously juicy when it was fresh. There were a variety of fruit trees and in winter there was a riot of colour when the flowers were in bloom, looking rather similar to English country gardens. The soil was fertile and commercial growers, as far away as Bengal, had their gardens in Madhupur and the surrounding area. Sometimes the Jewish children strayed into the large gardens of absentee landlords and persuaded the gardeners to give them flowers. But far more exciting for the children were the fruit trees, to climb and to plunder. "I'm not getting out of this tree until I find a guava with a pink centre." "Neither am I, even if I have to eat them all before I find one!" and this would have been the case in a tree which didn't produce this particular variety. My mother once found one of my brothers eating papaya straight off a tree just before lunch. "You'll ruin your meal" she remonstrated. "Not a chance, this is only my third one!" Considering that each papaya weighed at least three pounds, my mother's amazement was understandable.

"What I enjoyed most about being in Madhupur" my brother, Sammy Morris, recalls "is that when we were kids we had complete freedom from responsibility while we were there. We took no school books and we were not followed around by adults or servants wherever we went. We had a free rein and we made the most of it. When we were tired of playing cricket, hockey and badminton with cousins, we went off to the *Dak* Bungalow to look for new company. We knew there would always be other kids there, kicking a ball in the

MADHUPUR

fields, or playing soccer, and we could join them. We went for walks through the village, through fields, and to the ravine. We climbed fruit trees and ate to our hearts' content, we went to the *hart*, (Hi) open market, and gorged ourselves on Indian sweetmeats and filled our *solar topees,* (Anglo Indian) sun hats, with *khoi*, (Hi) puffed rice, for one pice, and then we would go home complaining that we were starving!"

Since Madhupur was a train junction, train spotting was great fun. Some of the children were able to identify each steam train by name and they were always encouraged to visit by Mr Cohen, the assistant station master, who was a direct descendent of Shalom Cohen, the first Jew to settle in Calcutta.

The large gardens and vast areas of open space made a wonderful change for the Calcutta Jews who were essentially flat-dwellers. Young and old; men, women and children, went for walks in the mornings and evenings. Photographs taken in the late 1920s and early 1930s show ladies in fashionable hats, coats and high-heeled shoes. They carried parasols to protect their complexion from the sun as a high value was placed on fair skin. These outings meant there were ample opportunities for meeting friends, making new friendships, and developing romances which would otherwise have been difficult in Calcutta. Right up until the war, and perhaps some time after in certain families, chaperones were necessary. Cousins had easy access to each other's homes which probably explains why there were so many marriages between them. In Madhupur, on the other hand, opportunity could combine with luck to open up the way for romance and even marriage, in a wider group. This is how it was with one of my aunts. It was 1929 and her family were living three doors away from the family of her future husband. As they were not related, it was difficult to become acquainted under the watchful eye of over-protective parents, so luck had to step in. My grandmother returned to Calcutta for a few days to see a dentist and left the household in Madhupur, which included several daughters of marriageable age, in the charge of her eldest daughter who had not been married very long herself, and who was sympathetic to young people and their problems in becoming better acquainted. Therefore, when the enterprising young man from three doors away called with a portable gramophone under one arm and an album of records under the other, saying "would you like to hear songs from the latest picture shows?" he was not given marching orders but was allowed, and even secretly welcomed, to entertain with his gramophone, but only in the garden. Having set his foot in the door, he became a regular visitor by the time my grandmother returned. She was not at all pleased, either with the audacious young man or with her remiss eldest daughter.

MADHUPUR

"Is this the way you've looked after your sisters while I was away? Is this your idea of taking responsibility? The whole community must be talking about this by now!" But a portable gramophone in Madhupur in 1929 could not fail to break the social ice, and eventually even my grandmother relented. Perhaps she was old enough and wise enough to see that this young man had a serious interest in one of her daughters. The friendship started in Madhupur and gradually grew into a full-blown romance within bounds set by my grandmother. They returned to Calcutta and the young man asked my grandparents for permission to marry their daughter but he was reminded that protocol demanded his father should be the one to make the proposal. Late that same night he returned with his father, my aunt was officially consulted, and her parents accepted on her behalf. Sweets were passed all round and the engagement took place four weeks later.

Winter was the only time of year when picnics were possible because of the weather, and those who spent that time of year in Madhupur had no shortage of pleasant and private spots to spend the day. David Einy recalls: "We usually headed towards the ravine but sometimes we got on a train and went to Giridih, an hour's distance away. There are waterfalls there and it is much more beautiful than in Madhupur, besides the thought of getting *poochkas*, (Hi) was always something to look forward to. Still, you couldn't go to Giridih in quite the same style as going to the ravine, which stretched out a good two miles. As soon as the food was cooked the servants would load the *tongas* with *deckchie* after *deckchie*, (Hi) aluminium saucepan, of cooked food. There was chicken, *pilaw*, chutney, the lot. And all the fruit in season. Then we piled in ourselves and drove off in a convoy of *tongas*. Those who wanted to walk took a short cut through the paddy fields and got there in no more than half an hour. Those who drove had to plod over rough roads and this took a bit longer. We unloaded the food and scrambled on the rocks or dipped our feet in the spring water, playing games, teasing each other and enjoying the sheer space. If there were no other picknickers or walkers we'd have the whole place to ourselves, stretching as far as we could see. But more often than not, many families would arrange to gather together and we would have a great time and swap our food. We'd tuck into lunch, eating with our fingers, in the good old Indian style, using banana leaves as plates. After we'd eaten and rested, told a few stories and exchanged jokes, we would walk right along the ravine and back. As it gets dark early in winter, before we knew it, it was time to repack the *tongas* and make our way back, singing all the way home."

No one missed the *hart*, if they could help it, although I'm told some people would only rent a house en route to the *hart,* so that they could stop the fruit

MADHUPUR

and vegetable sellers on their way to market, to get first choice. Marina Benaiah remembers that when she was a child, she would sit by the garden gate, alongside her sisters and brothers, each with a bowl of water. As the men would pass by on their way to market, crying *"Dheem! Dheem!"* (Bengali) eggs, they would stop them and test the eggs for freshness by dunking them in their bowls of water to see if they floated, which meant they were bad, or sank to the bottom.

The *hart* was held twice a week, on Mondays and Fridays. Arlene Einy said "The area covered by the *hart* was even smaller than half a football pitch, although it seemed enormous to the children. It was always crowded with people of all ages, buying, selling, or just looking on. At one end were the permanent, brick built shops which opened every day and from where we would buy dry goods such as lentils and rice, for instance. The open space in front was for the *chassawallas,* (Hi) people with home grown produce, who would arrive as early as eight o'clock. Those who had plenty to sell carried their produce in two baskets, balanced at each end of a pole slung across one shoulder. Some came to market with very little to offer, perhaps no more than a dozen eggs and a couple of chickens. They were often approached by a middleman who bought what they had, added it to that of other villagers, and made a small profit on the whole lot. The fruit and vegetables would be put down on the ground in baskets, or displayed on pieces of cloth. They grouped together, product by product, the fruit and vegetables on one side, the fish, chickens and ducks, and eggs on the other. Everything was weighed on home-made, make-shift scales, made from wickerwork and sticks, with stones for weights, representing and not pretending to be correct measures, but everything was so cheap, no one was too bothered. There were women who ground grain and mustard seeds by hand and people took home freshly ground flour and oil. In another section there were baskets, goblets and clay toys made in the small potteries in the area. The toys were made from terracotta and black clay, shaped into tea sets and kitchenware, which the children loved. Basket after basket of these toys would be packed for children in Calcutta. There were glass bangles in all colours and sizes, and decorations made from coloured paper. The three sweetmeat shops were always encircled by eager customers. The stuff they sold was so superb that I have not tasted better anywhere else. As it happened, the long wait of the trains at Madhupur station was a good opportunity to milk the cattle being transported into Bengal and the milk was therefore sold off cheap locally. *Gur,* (Hi) jaggery, was also plentiful which meant that the main ingredients for Indian sweetmeats could be combined to make fine *gurpayrah,*(Hi) a dry sweet, *labree,* (Hi) sweetened clotted cream, and *rasmallai,* to mention only a few of the mouth-watering things they sold. The quality of

MADHUPUR

everything was superb, even the fruit and vegetables, although the variety was not fantastic. Papayas, plums, pineapples and tomatoes had much more flavour than in Calcutta. As for herbs, such as mint and coriander, they were more aromatic than you could possibly find anywhere else. We took back as much as we could for friends and family in Calcutta as they would look forward to it. On the days when there was no *hart* there were always a few men with fruit and vegetables who could be relied on to fill the mid-week demand. One thing is sure, no one ever went short."

"Going to Madhupur was like being let out of a coop" Seemah Musleah Cohen said. "Even the very old, and those who were feeble on their feet, had only to walk as far as the garden gate where they were bound to see people out on their walks and as time was of no particular consequence, it was possible to socialise on the spot. The less mobile could spend many a pleasant hour in the garden, sitting on a chair and dealing with hawkers who were constantly on the round, from house to house, selling chickens, *ghee*, (Hi) clarified butter, sweet and sour *dhai*, (Hi) yoghurt, buns, and many other products." Arlene Einy added: "Buying and selling was never a straightforward business. The origins of the product would be discussed, slightly disparaging remarks would be made by the buyer, hot defences would be put up by the seller, and all this before they even got to haggling over price. This was the ritual, no matter how mundane the product or how ridiculously low the price." Marina Sopher Beniah said: "There was the daily round of the milkman, *gwala,* to supervise. Each milkman would go from house to house with his cow, the bell around the animal's neck announcing their arrival. The cow would be milked in a pail right in front of the family so that there could be no question of diluting the milk. Even so it goes without saying that the cows would be given plenty of water to drink beforehand!"

No one moved from Calcutta on holiday without their *towlee*, (A) backgammon board and it was no exception in Madhupur. Players could be seen on the verandahs of many houses at all hours. This was a favourite game of both young and old in almost every family. On the whole there were friendly matches, but those with a strong gambling streak played for money. Whether for money or for matchsticks, the excitement, the emotion, the enthusiasm for the game came through with every call of the dice in a variety of languages. "*Shesh-besh!*" (A) six and five. "*Koobus*" (H) three diagonal dots, "double sixes" the highest number, would be given the warmest welcome "*Gan Eden!*" (H) Garden of Eden. The black and white men would be moved noisily on the board, punctuating every single move with a loud tap, tap, tap. I've seen many a friendly game lead to a

MADHUPUR

heated argument, with pleas for arbitration to all those present, for sleight of hand was not above the tactics of some players.

Although there was no electricity, oil lamps were adequate for ordinary household needs. Lack of street lighting didn't seem to matter. On moonlit nights it was clear enough to go out for short walks, and the village looked enchanted in a soft glow. When there was no moon, people went out with torches which flickered like fireflies in the dark. So much time was spent out walking, each pothole and puddle must have been firmly imprinted on everyone's minds.

To this day people still talk about the purity of the water in Madhupur and some claim it has medicinal value. My grandmother would say with utter conviction "it was good for everything, no matter what was wrong with you, whether it was indigestion or rheumatism" and her sister would have only one request if she was unable to go to Madhupur herself - "don't bring anything back for me except a goblet of water." Most of the houses had wells but sometimes a well was located between two houses. This was the only source of water and it was plentiful. The servants would draw it by pulley and fill large earthenware goblets, buckets and zinc bathtubs.

On the whole one didn't expect to find sanitation when travelling outside the major cities during the days of the Raj, so this was no particular hardship in Madhupur. As long as servants could be hired locally, and they always could be, everything was made bearable for us.

Madhupur was a very popular venue for camps - particularly for the Boy Scouts of the Elias Meyer Free School. Norman Ezekiel recalled the days of his early teens. "The whole year we looked forward to only one thing - going to Madhupur. Our fear was that we would either become ill or be punished and not be able to go. Our lives were very tough as school children because of the strict discipline of the principal. He may have been a very good man but he believed in 'spare the rod and spoil the child'. I liked being a scout but hated the idea of being forced into it. The best part of being in Madhupur was being completely released from school discipline. It was a different world.

"Our Scout Master, Mordy Cohen never pushed anyone around. He shouted and threatened but there was a special pleasure in knowing that his threats were empty and we would get away with being slack. For example, the bugle call was at 6 a.m. but we seldom got on parade before 6.15 or 6.30 and for Boy Scouts

MADHUPUR

that's pretty bad going! Our physical training and our morning walks were supervised and we would always end up in the *hart* to buy sweets with the little pocket money our parents gave us once a year by making a special effort. Luckily, money went a long way in Madhupur.

"We had a camp fire most nights. Everyone joined in the sing-song and we would compete with each other to sing the loudest." Mordy Cohen confirmed this. "We had boys who could play the flute, mouth organ and the banjo and we would make up our own songs. We had dancing, concerts, comedies, plays, and the boys would get into bed exhausted but happy. The Station Master would let us have disused sleepers from the railway lines for our camp fires. People from the community joined us practically every night and some of the local Anglo-Indians would come too."

Norman continued: "Sleeping under canvas was lovely. We were never cold in our tents as we slept on gunny bags filled with fresh hay and this kept us warm. Can you imagine what it meant, coming from a crowded city, and a crowded flat, where we were lucky to sleep only six to one room, to be out in the fresh, open air, with all the space our hearts could desire?

"We drew water from the well for all our needs and washed ourselves as quickly as we could, around the well. The water was tepid but the air temperature was so cold we wanted to get this part of the day over as soon as we could."

Moses Ezra said: "When I left school I would still go to camp to help. I would be in the advance party, to book the land twenty-four hours beforehand. About fifty boys between the ages of thirteen and fifteen would be on the camp site for about two weeks each year. We would also go to the *hart* and buy hay to stuff the gunny bags which were used as mattresses. Mordy Cohen was an A1 Scout Master. He saw to it that everyone ate well, played well and had a great time."

Mordy Cohen said: "Aaron Aaron took the first camp, as Scout Master of about half a dozen scouts of the Elias Meyer Free School in 1934 and again he took the whole Troop in 1935. I attended both the camps as Troop Leader. I took over as Scout Master from 1936 and continued till the late fifties, ending up as Group Scout Master, having started the Wolf Cub pack in the School in 1937 which my wife took over in the same year as Cub Mistress after a training course. I took the scouts to camp from 1936 until 1941 every year and then again I took the scouts, wolf cubs, other boys and girls from both the Jewish schools to camp at

MADHUPUR

Madhupur from 1946 until 1951. There were no camps betweem 1942 and 1945 because of the war."

Aaron Aaron said: "I remember going from house to house to collect the boys and their luggage. The luggage would be loaded on to bullock carts en route to the station. The mothers would follow me to the front door, shouting their instructions - 'its not necessary for my son to bathe in the cold everyday, so don't force him', 'don't forget to rub my son's chest every night with the ointment I gave you', 'make sure my son wears his winter vest every day, I'm relying on you!' They drove me mad, and I wondered why I ever got involved. If anything had gone wrong the first person I would have had to answer to would have been the principal, Ezra Arakie. That in itself should have been enough of a deterrent, but I would also have had to face the parents of the boys, and finally my own parents. I was crazy! Then I remembered the faces of the boys, their joy and excitement and knew that it was well worth it."

Mordy Cohen recalled: "We would reserve three bogeys and travel on assisted fares. We travelled overnight and none of us would have a wink of sleep. We would sing all the way to Madhupur and keep ourselves going on nuts, fruit, and tea from the hawkers in the stations.

"My mother-in-law came with us from 1946 until 1951. She would do the shopping and supervise the cooking. My cook also accompanied us although the boys did have their daily tasks which included help with the preparation of meals. In the weeks before we went to Madhupur my mother-in-law's house would be bursting from one end to the other with stores for our holiday. We took tea, cocoa, sugar, butter, oil, rice, salt and Jewish cheese which we bought out of the Scout fund. We would take our own *shohet* so that the boys could eat chicken most days. Members of the community who were on holiday sometimes invited us for tea or for a meal and this made a pleasant change.

"We started the day with prayers and the hoisting of the Union Jack. There was a general inspection and physical training. Every day we had a programme for each patrol, such as route marches to the ravines, where we would stop and relax, but the leadership was very informal. The patrols would take it in turn to keep guard at night in case there were animals on the prowl, and sometimes we had trouble with a group of local people - the Santals.

"In the course of the year we would have two dances, a concert and other

MADHUPUR

entertainments to raise money for Madhupur. The boys would feel that it was through their efforts that they were able to enjoy those unforgettably happy camps."

Madhupur may have been no more than a little-known village, the amenities may have left much to be desired, and the landscape may not have been awe-inspiring, but the vast majority of those who went there were agreed they had wonderful holidays and returned to Calcutta thoroughly refreshed. "All of us kids came back with rosy cheeks with all the tearing around in the outdoors", Marina Beniah recalled. Sammy Morris said: "One of our old friends, Ben Jacob, used to make a pun on the word Madhupur and called it, instead, *Modhupur*, (Hi), place of honey." Aaron Aaron and his family would call it "Little Jerusalem, not only because the Jews congregated there, but also because of the toast - 'next year in Jerusalem!' at Passover". The regular holiday-makers kept cheerful on the thought that from one year to the next they could enjoy the anticipation of the simple but good times in Madhupur.

A group of Jews wearing European clothes with solar topees and another group of high caste Indians, wait for the train to Calcutta at Madhupur station. Coolies wait in the background. c. 1928. The group of Jewish men in the foreground include, L. to R. Dick Cohen, Isaac Musleah, Abraham Shalom Cohen, Unknown, and Isaac Cohen.
Photo: Elias Musleah.

Waiting on the platform of Madhupur station for the train to Calcutta. Group in foreground, L. to R. Isaac Musleah, Dinah Cohen, Flora Musleah, Rachel Cohen, Dick Cohen. c. 1928. Photo: Elias Musleah.

Paddy fields en route to Madhupur. View from the train.

Ruby Musleah in Madhupur railway station, 1936.
Courtesy: Ruby Musleah Mordecai.

Madhupur, 1936. My grandmother, Masooda Musleah in the 'hart' local open market, with her daughter Rachel. The coolie follows behind, carrying all their shopping in the basket on his head.

"Home" in Madhupur. In the 1930s it was owned by an Anglo-Indian lady who lived on the top floor and rented the bottom floor to Jewish families for winter vacations.

My aunt, Rachel Musleah, in front of part of the Dak Bungalow, Madhupur. 1929. Courtesy: Ezekiel Musleah.

A Jewish family enjoying a snack in Madhupur while the tonga driver and his donkey wait patiently.
Courtesy: Noreen David.

The day starts in Madhupur for the boy scouts of the Elias Meyer Free School by hoisting the Union Jack. 1934.
Courtesy: Aaron Aaron.

Boy Scouts from the Elias Meyer Free School at their early morning wash by the well on the Camp Site, Madhupur, 1934. Sitting: L. to R. Aaron Sultoon, Mordy Cohen, Aaron Aaron, Isaac Isaac and Ezra Elias. Standing: Menahem Menahem.
Courtesy: Mordy Cohen.

Boy Scouts from the Elias Meyer Free School on cooking duty at the Camp Site, Madhupur. December 1934. Sitting L. to R. Isaac Isaac, Aaron Sultoon. Standing: Mordy Cohen, Menahem Menahem, Aaron Aaron, Ezra Elias.
Courtesy: Mordy Cohen.

Chapter 7

AGARPARA

Agarpara, and the areas around it, form an industrial complex on the River Hooghly, about nine miles north of the centre of Calcutta. For those of us who now live in large cities in the West, this distance would be thought of as a mere suburb away. In Calcutta it was a world away, a world which could only be reached, in the early 1940s, by taking three buses, or a bus and train. It was either a walk to the railway station which was about a mile away from the houses, or a ride on a trolley during the day. The trolley was a platform on wheels which ran on narrow gauge railway lines and was pushed by a couple of coolies. A bench on the platform could take six people, three sitting back to back on each side. There was none of the hurly burly of the city, dotted with shops and imposing commercial buildings. There were no blocks of flats standing cheek by jowl, each one completely different in style and size. There were no taxis and rickshaws competing for customers and road space. There were no buses and tramcars filled to overflowing, with passengers travelling on every inch of footboards and bumpers.

B.N. Elias & Company, with its head office in Calcutta, employed the majority of Jews of working age in the community by the end of the Second World War. The Agarpara Jute Mill which they owned, "went into production in 1928 with a comparatively small number of looms ... the profits it generated provided the base on which the industrial empire of the B.N. Elias family was built ... the capital was provided almost exclusively by the family". [1]

When Joe Isaac, who was to become engineer of the jute mill and then Assistant Manager, joined the company in 1942, "the mill had 900 looms for hessian and sacking and 1000 looms for webbing tapes 2" x 5", used for upholstery. This was a medium sized mill." He explains that jute was the cheapest fibre on the world market at the time, used in the manufacture of hessian and sacking. "Hessian is not waterproof and has a fine weave which is suitable for domestic use. Sacking has a coarse weave, has no synthetic fibres, and is very useful as a packing material. There was no lack of demand for these products. When I started work there were no more than thirty-five Jewish families living in

AGARPARA

Agarpara. The Manager, Assistant Manager and supervisors were all Jews, while the mechanics, machine operators and clerical staff were Hindus and Muslims."

"... in 1932 the B.N.Es set up a small (cigarette) factory in Beliaghatta ... the National Tobacco Company of India Limited." [2] In 1936 the factory was moved to premises in Agarpara, within a short walking distance of the jute mill. There were twenty to thirty Jewish and non-Jewish supervisors, including Sunnoo Morris, who transferred from Beliaghatta to Agarpara and were living near the factory.

"In those early days" Joe recalls, "Agarpara was a jungle, where wild monkeys lived in the thick growth of trees, where spiders, the size of quarter plates, could be seen both out and indoors, where foxes roamed freely and where the call of jackals was heard every night. Snakes were common and often found their way into our homes. In fact the very first night I spent there, there was a cry from the *durwan*, 'Don't move, there's a snake under your bed, wait till I deal with it.' Worst of all, the land was swampy and this attracted mosquitoes. It was impossible to sleep without a net."

Sunnoo Morris, who was to become General Manager of the cigarette factory and its subsidiaries, says that "there were no shops, even for basic food." One night he and his flatmate ran out of bread and they had to cycle two miles before they found a small tea shop which was open. The *chaiwallah*, (Hi) tea shop owner, refused to sell them bread as he was holding on to his stock for his breakfast trade next morning. They were crestfallen, when Sunnoo's gaze fell on a most improbable sight. A violin was hanging up in the shop. "What's that doing here?" he asked. The man said he had the instrument on approval for a few days, but had no idea how to use it. "I'll show you" Sunnoo volunteered, his eye on the bread. He gave as convincing a rendering as he could of "Daisy, Daisy", the only piece he could play at the time. The *chaiwallah* was delighted and the four mile cycle ride, after a twelve hour shift, paid off.

"In the mid-1930s" Sunnoo remembers, "the land just two to three miles away from Agarpara was covered by jungle and I used to hunt wild boar there. This was done late at night. I went out with one of the factory hands by truck for about a mile and a half. There the road stopped and we had to go on foot. It was dangerous as the grass was tall and there were tunnels of water deep enough to drown a man. The object was to reach a mound of slightly high ground and wait for the movement of what appeared to be shadows in the dark, and then switch on

AGARPARA

our torches, aim, and fire at the boar. I had done quite a bit of hunting in Burma, before I came to Calcutta, so I knew the routine. Boar hunting was a matter of sport but as the jungles around Agarpara were cut down to make way for housing, these wild animals disappeared. Sometimes we got up early in the morning for duck shooting. We ate the birds, even though they were not *kasher*, as they were killed in this way. My Muslim companions would simply say *'Bismillah rahman rahim'* (A) in the name of the most merciful God, and eat the duck, as they said this satisfied their religious requirements."

Sunnoo and Sally Morris recall the time when their chickens were dying and they were advised to turn over the soil in case it had become contaminated. What they found instead was a nest of baby cobras, one of which was double-headed!

Joe's wife Diana, and Sunnoo's wife Sally, said that everyone did their main shopping in Calcutta once a week, although it was possible to travel half a mile away by cycle rickshaw to get a limited variety of fruit and vegetables from the village shops in Kamarhati. Most people visited their families in town at weekends and this was the time to shop for groceries and greengroceries, which would have to be carried through tedious journeys. It was also the time to visit friends, attend weddings, go to the cinema, eat ice cream, and catch up with all the news.

There was a doctor employed in the mill and the factory, and a compounder to make up simple prescriptions, but most people went to town for medical care. However, there were challenges to be met in Agarpara on a daily basis. Sunnoo Morris said: "we turned our hand to everything in those early days, family counselling, getting each other out of all sorts of personal scrapes, first aid and even giving injections. I've given tetanus injections in my time." Mozelle Twena, whose husband worked in the cigarette factory backed this up. She could have been described as a voluntary health visitor. "I used to mother the young mothers. I taught them to bath their babies and gave encouragement to those who were not confident about their little ones."

The early "settlers" in Agarpara were in a slightly similar position to the Baghdadi pioneers in India, except that in an emergency Calcutta, with its facilities, was always accessible. Gradually they worked hard at bringing about changes which made an enormous difference to the quality of their lives.

AGARPARA

Sunnoo Morris explained: "For example, in the bad old days, and particularly during the war when there was petrol rationing, orders for cigarettes outside Calcutta had to be transported by bullock cart on the seven mile route from Agarpara to Sealdah railway station. The firm had their own carts and bullocks, but it meant that a supervisor and his assistants had to be at work at four o'clock in the morning. The bullocks had to be fed and watered, the carts had to be loaded, the cases had to be checked by the gatekeepers. The early start was necessary to avoid the traffic congestion which built up in the city as the morning wore on. However, there was a snag. The distance between the horns of the bullocks was regulated in order to make them road-worthy and any policeman who was diligent about enforcement could make life difficult for the cartmen. Unfortunately our bullocks had fine, and widely extended pairs of horns, so we always had to set aside cigarettes to appease the policemen. Eventually we got fed up with this and decided to trim the horns of the bullocks. This did not cause any pain as long as we were careful not to saw too near the roots. Then we came up against another snag. The carpenters' department was managed by an Austrian refugee. When he saw the docket for the job to saw off horns he was furious because he thought this was a practical joke, and a practical joke at work was just not in his book! Everything was explained and sorted out eventually, but not before there was the most awful row."

Until 1945 everyone - mill hands, factory hands, and supervisors, all worked a six day week, alternating night and day shifts from week to week. In addition, the supervisors had to do fire duty, which meant that they could not leave Agarpara every third or fourth weekend in case of a fire alarm. "In the late 1930s and early 1940s we had fire practice every single weekend. The firm bought a fire engine for the factory and the supervisors had to operate the hoses. There were certain check points in the factory which had to be inspected and logged every two hours. This took all day, and as it was done at weekends, it was done in our time. However, after the war, conditions gradually improved."

On the domestic front, Mozelle Twena employed a servant just to take her sons to school and bring them back. The journey each way was at least an hour with all the bus changes, so there was no question of the servant returning to Agarpara to do a good day's work. "He had plenty of time on his hands in town all day but my husband and I had peace of mind. Gradually things changed for the better and by 1947 we had a school bus which made a great difference to us and to our children. More and more children were around by then and you can imagine how tiring it was with the travelling, especially in winter when they would set out

AGARPARA

in the dark and return in the dark." Sunnoo Morris was very effective in persuading the directors to let him have a vehicle which was converted into a school bus, and which covered about half a dozen schools in the city. Eventually all the children were able to travel in comfort and in safety, free of charge. They were even supervised by a teacher who lived in Agarpara and who worked at the Jewish Girls' School.

The supervisors, predominantly Jewish, in the mill and in the factory had "an automatic right to a flat, rent and all expenses free" said Joe Isaac. Diana added: "Most families had a two bedroom apartment. As in Calcutta, there was usually a through drawing room and dining room with the bedrooms off it, and each bedroom had an en suite bathroom. A covered verandah spanned the length of the living rooms and faced the gardens. The rooms had high ceilings and were cooled with electric fans. There was a separate entrance at the back of the building with a spiral staircase which the servants used. All the fittings were modern for those times, for example, there were no zinc tubs or *choolas*, and everyone had a fridge and furniture supplied. In fact the more senior the position, the greater the perks and eventually we only paid for our food and the children's education. Everything else was provided, the salaries of all the servants, car, petrol, cutlery, crockery, saucepans, the lot."

Joe continued - "As families started moving in, the jungle had to be cleared for building and gradually Agarpara was transformed into a garden city. It became a pleasure for our relatives to visit us, as much as it was a pleasure for us to go to town." Noreen David, whose husband Bernard, was manager of the jute mill from the late 1950s until the early 1960s said "My mother would come to visit me for a week to start with and she usually ended up staying three months." Sally Morris added "when the jungle was being cleared and the monkeys lost their shelter in the trees they used to raid our gardens and even when shooed off, they never scarpered without pulling up vegetables."

Mozelle Twena elaborated on the picture of a garden city: "There were three or four gardens together, for flowers and vegetables, so it was a lovely sight. The soil was good and there were *malis* to keep the lawns and everything in good order. We grew our own corn and a variety of vegetables, and it was good to have everything so fresh."

Noreen David describes the gardens surrounding the house of the jute mill manager: "The house was surrounded by gardens which required six gardeners to

AGARPARA

keep well maintained. There were many fruit trees and there was an abundance of vegetables in season. We had everything fresh for ourselves and our families and the servants took whatever they wanted but there was still so much left over I used to have them load it on a lorry for distribution to the Jewish free schools."

Sunnoo recalled an incident concerning the gardens. "The gardens, and all outdoor maintenance was in the charge of a Muslim. There was a Hindu in charge of chemical research. One day I heard a devil of a row going on outside my office and asked what was going on. The Hindu wanted guinea pigs housed in Alpine Dairy, which was within the B.N.Elias complex, to be brought over to the factory and the Muslim refused to oblige. 'Why, what is your objection?' I asked him. He replied with great emotion: 'You know very well that as a Muslim I will have nothing to do with pigs - it's against my religion'. 'We are talking about guinea pigs, not pigs' Sunnoo argued. 'Pigs is pigs!' came the indignant reply. 'Let me show you' Sunnoo suggested. 'That's funny' said the Muslim. 'These pigs look so much like rats'. The Hindu got his guinea pigs without another murmur."

In 1945 a *shohet* was appointed by the firm. This meant that the Jewish community in Agarpara was able to eat *kasher* chickens whenever they wished rather than having to rely on transport from Calcutta, which could have meant no more than once a week.

By 1948 there was a tailor-in-residence, persuaded to live in accommodation provided by the firm, because of the promise of being kept busy full time by so many potential customers. He came with a resident *dhobi,* and someone's favourite bread man was even willing to make the eighteen mile round trip from Calcutta almost every day to supply the growing community.

But the greatest boon of all was the purpose-built club house. Joe recalls: "In time, this was surrounded by hard and soft badminton and tennis courts. There was a natural pool nearby which was used for swimming, with a shallow area for beginners. Two billiard tables, two table-tennis tables, and a piano were installed. Almost every evening people would drop in for a sing-song. Someone would start tinkling on the piano and before you knew it there would be a crowd of singers." Joe was sports secretary of the club, then general secretary, and was assisted by his wife Diana, who said: "We all enjoyed ourselves every day at the club. The men left the tensions of work behind them. Even if they were having problems between themselves in the mill or in the factory, you would never know it once they entered the club. The men enjoyed the relaxation, the women enjoyed each other's

AGARPARA

company and the support they gave each other, and as for the children, it was just wonderful."

Sally Morris agreed: "Every main entrance and exit had security. There was a *durwan* in post at each point, who knew the children and had affection for them so that they could go around in safety. They did not have to be trailed by watchful servants, they could roam around where they pleased within bounds which gave them all the freedom they wanted, they could organise their own games or take part in the sporting activities in the club. Joe Isaac was very keen to encourage youngsters and was forever organising competitions, between the children and between adults." Sunnoo Morris said: "Mrs Twena's son summed it up when he said he felt sorry for children who were not brought up in Agarpara." The open life there, the easy access to sporting facilities, the feeling of belonging to an extended family and the security it brought, contrasted sharply with the situation in town, amongst flat dwellers.

Noreen David and Diana Isaac's eyes lit up when asked about life in Agarpara. "We really loved it there", "those were really happy days when great friendships developed among most of the women, and even now we have warm feelings for each other. It was very important because we supported each other in times of trouble." Noreen remembers that when she had a sick child, a neighbour volunteered to sleep in to give her and her *ayah* a break. Another neighbour "mothered me; she was an excellent cook and made delicious dishes which we didn't cook everyday because the preparation was tedious. I spent practically every afternoon in her house, chatting and passing the time pleasantly. Entertaining was a very informal business in Agarpara or in Calcutta, only in Agarpara it was so much easier because we were all nearer to each other. If someone was doing something when you called, she simply carried on while a visitor was there - it didn't matter. Women had a great deal of time for leisure. If you liked people then Agarpara was the right place for you. I enjoyed playing cards with my own crowd, particularly at weekends. One day the card party would be at my house, and the next time at someone else's house. Mah jongg was a popular game and we played once a week in each one's house; among closer friends, I mean. I was very keen on sport and the facilities at the club just suited me down to the ground. Tennis, badminton, table-tennis - it was wonderful to have it all at our doorstep. We played almost every evening and not only the adults but also the adults and children. In this way they learnt from us and the fact that we played made them keen on sport. Some of the women liked needlework and knitting. From time to time we did needlework together - one of our neighbours was very good at

AGARPARA

embroidery and she guided and encouraged us". These pastimes were all influenced by the British and far removed from that of previous generations who got together (both men and women) to socialise whilst they smoked hookahs (A) or the "hubble-bubble". Servants prepared the burning coals, tobacco, and added molasses, which was said to have a mellowing effect.

Noreen continued: "During the war the firm paid for a high tea once a week for the British and American Armed Forces and the women would supervise the preparation of the food and entertain the men. It was all good fun - we had to make life interesting and entertaining for ourselves and most of us did just that."

Benny Isaac, who grew up in Agarpara, says: "We spent all the time we wanted out in the open, and there were always other kids to play with just outside the house. We also enjoyed the cinema shows at the club once a fortnight. It's true we had the older films but they were the popular ones and we looked forward to these evenings. Every month there would be a dance and a very special one on New Year's eve. We weren't allowed to go as kids but we used to hide outside and it was exciting just to peek as people were going inside, and to hear the band playing.

"Growing up in Agarpara was something special. As a child I felt the closeness of a small community and it was a good feeling to know that I was a part of this group which seemed to me to be like an extended family, and I felt secure. If there were rows amongst the adults we never seemed to notice it - everyone got together in the club in the evenings - adults and children. The friendships we made among ourselves as children in those days have lasted up to now (after about forty years) and perhaps that was the best part of it. We may not see these people very often, in fact we see those who live in Israel only once in two years or so. But when we get together it is as if we had never been apart.

"Another good thing which I didn't realise at the time, but which I value now, is that I saw much more of my father while I was growing up in Agarpara than my cousins did in town. There, their father would go off in the evenings and they would be indoors with their mother doing homework or playing amongst themselves. Since entire families went to the club in Agarpara, we were around with our parents in the evenings. It didn't matter if we were doing our own thing, playing our own games, while our fathers were playing billiards or tennis, for example; the club kept individual families closer together.

AGARPARA

"It is true that we were probably far more protected and sheltered than the kids in Calcutta. For example, when my cousins were able to find their own way around town in buses and rickshaws, I hardly knew how to cross the street! Nor were we used to the big city and the coldness of it all and I was at a disadvantage here in my mid-teens. But these things sort themselves out with a little time. The important thing is that the benefits of having grown up in Agarpara have stayed with us all our lives."

Agarpara was also a place of social levelling which was rare, both within the Jewish community and in the wider society. There was a hierarchical system in employment, and the jute mill employees were said to have been generally better paid than those in the cigarette factory, but when it came to socialising, there was no disparity. However, not without a fight, according to Sunnoo Morris. In the early days, just before the war, the club house was for the exclusive use of families who worked in the jute mill. It was their idea, their resolve, their efforts, which brought it to fruition, and they were going to keep it for themselves! The factory faction did not see the justice in this and took up the matter with one of the directors, J.R. Jacob, who did not see the justice in it either. He therefore decided to have the club shut down until the two sides could come to some arrangement. After a month the mill faction relented and from then on it was open club for everybody.

The social levelling refers largely to the Jewish community. The Bengali men and women did not attend the club, and those familiar with the Indian scene would not find this surprising. They too had their taboos; food taboos, caste taboos, social taboos which made it difficult for women to socialise freely with men.

The firm provided transport for families to attend services in the synagogues for the High Holidays, but the festival of Tabernacles, *Succoth,* was a time for community celebration in Agarpara over the eight days, when they built a communal *succa*. It is customary for us to eat all our meals in this booth or temporary dwelling throughout the festival. "You shall dwell in booths ... that your generations may know that I made the children of Israel to dwell in booths when I brought them out of the land of Egypt."[3] Diana Isaac recalls: "This was a busy time for the gardeners who did all the hard work, including the weaving of palm leaves to make a temporary cover, and the decoration with fairy lights and fruit. Each family would have their meal brought over in tiffin carriers and everyone shared their food. The ladies would take turns in lighting the *tiryah,* and the men took turns in saying *kiddush*. Those who wished, sang *pizmonim*; (H) festival songs, after dinner."

The other red letter days in the calendar of the Agarpara community were the dances twice a year, the fancy dress parties for the children, and their annual sports day every winter. The dances, particularly on New Year's Eve were very well attended. "All our relations and friends in town would come up as transport was laid on for the occasion" Diana recalls. Again, the hard work in decorating the hall, and in making the preparations would fall to the factory and mill workers, but the members all helped and took responsibility for the organisation of the function. Sally Morris said: "There was always a fine buffet of *kasher* and *non-kasher* food and Lorna Chew, who was not Jewish, was very active in making the arrangements together with Rachel Jonah, particularly during the war." It was at this time that the American Army had a base at Titaghur and Barrackpore a few miles away, and many of the wives from Agarpara worked for them as secretaries and in general clerical jobs. Sally continued "they always came to our dances and enjoyed themselves thoroughly. "Diana added: "People came dressed to the nines, at last they could show off the dresses they had been preparing for weeks. The charge for these functions was very modest as we wanted no more than to cover costs."

Many of the workers at the mill and factory were Hindus, and when it was their turn to celebrate festivals, *Pujas,* (Hi) they were eager for everyone to join in. These celebrations are usually communal, and are public affairs. On *Diwali,* Hindu festival of lights, little clay oil lamps, *chirags,* (Hi) illuminate the outlines of their homes. In each locality residents make a contribution towards the purchase of an idol, representing the god or goddess to be honoured on that particular festival, which is set up in a tent, on a street corner, or a convenient open space. While priests and devotees pray, burn incense, and make offerings of food and flowers in the *pandals* (Hi) special tents for the occasion, others enjoy the fireworks, and the sweets which are distributed. There is music, dancing and the performance of tableau connected with the story of the festival. It is customary for people to move from *pandal* to *pandal*, spinning out the celebrations. At the end of the festival the idols are carried through the streets in procession, with chanting and dancing, accompanying the playing of drums and the blowing of conch shells, and then finally sunk in the river. The River Hooghly, which flows through Calcutta and the surrounding area, is a branch of the Ganges, and as such is a sacred river. This is why it is fitting for idols to be finally immersed here.

The Jewish supervisors in Agarpara were always invited and made very

AGARPARA

welcome at the *Puja* celebrations. There were some, however, who had qualms about attending because this could have been indistinguishable from participating in idol worship. In the end people realised that to stay away would hurt the sensibilities of those who had invited them. Sunnoo Morris says: "When I was manager, I never objected to their placing an idol in one corner of the factory. As a matter of fact I myself contributed to their celebrations and persuaded the directors to do so as well. All the Jews also made a contribution. Their most important *pujas* were *Tool Puja, Saraswati Puja* and *Durga Puja. Tool Puja* was celebrated to honour the machines from which they derived their daily bread. They would decorate all the machines with little paintings of fruit and flowers, and tie ribbons. It was also a festival where they drank sherbet laced with *bhang*, (Hi) derived from the *dathura* plant which has a similar effect to LSD. Two glasses of sherbet and you would really get high!" *Saraswati* is the goddess of learning, and as there is great value placed on culture in Bengal, this is an important regional festival. *Durga,* a benign manifestation of the mother goddess, is also particularly venerated in Bengal. "The men in the factory always gave us *prasad*, (Hi) food where a token offering was first made to the gods, as this was considered an honour. The Jews would accept, but not eat it, and the Hindus understood this but we went through the formalities. We often invited a local dignitary to the celebrations in the evenings when there was a fireworks display, or a tableau. Dr. B.C. Roy who was a Bengali and Chief Minister of Bengal, was also a great friend of the Jewish community, as I believe he was brought up by a Jewish woman. He was always happy to join us. As for the children, they never needed persuasion. The promise of fireworks and sweets was enough for them." Socialising between Jew and non-Jew was therefore reserved for special occasions and this became possible because of connections built up at work. It was the Hindus who showed the way by their offers of friendship and their willingness to share their festive celebrations.

The story of Agarpara and the good times connected with it cannot be complete without mention of Riverside. This was the home of one of the directors, J.R. Jacob, and his family. It is a beautiful villa, built on the banks of the river, a distance of about a mile and a half from the mill and factory. During the war the family moved into town, and subsequently the swimming pool, changing rooms, and the gardens, were made available to families and friends of their employees, for picnics and other social events. There can't be too many among these people who wouldn't have photographs of themselves and their friends posing around the swimming pool, or playing *towlee* under a brick built canopy in the gardens. There were other attractions, like admiring the birds in the aviary, or gazing across the

AGARPARA

river, watching boats come and go, some heavily laden with cargo, others with boatmen preparing their meal, or gently rowing towards their destinations.

Joe and Diana Isaac, and Sunnoo and Sally Morris, calculate there must have been at least sixty Jewish families living in Agarpara in the period immediately after the war. In addition there were several Jewish refugees from Europe working in the factory and the mill. They had come from Poland, Hungary, Austria and Czechoslovakia. There were also Jewish refugees from Burma, so that the total number of people - toddlers, teenagers, and adults - could not have been less than two hundred. This was the time when the Jewish community in Calcutta was at its peak, having been joined by the majority of Jews from Burma. Those in Agarpara represented about four or five per cent of the total.

These numbers could only have been sustained from steady growth and development in the jute mill and cigarette factory. As Sunnoo Morris says "production and people go hand in hand." B.N. Elias & Company had diversified into several other fields in the 1930s and early 1940s. Ezra[4] discusses their expansion, *inter alia,* into bone mills, electricity supply, jute baling, a saw mill, machine tool manufacture, advertising, printing and dairy farming. A small maintenance depot for the repair of vehicles belonging to the mill and factory gradually developed into a garage fully equipped for all mechanical repair and a petrol pump. These diverse business interests made for a network of interlocking support among the employees. If someone from the mill needed a small printing job it could be done at the factory; if an employee at the factory had a problem with his cow he could call in the vet from the dairy; if someone from the dairy needed his car to be maintained he could make use of the garage. In this way the community in Agarpara gradually moved towards self sufficiency.

The diversification in the business interests of B.N.Elias & Company from the 1940s was, to some extent, based on the innovation of their employees who were encouraged by the directors. Sunnoo says that a case in point is that of Sidney Moses. "He manufactured local herbal products and set up his own machinery to produce tablets which sold very profitably to the army. He also manufactured metal buttons for the army and although all these projects were modest, they were nevertheless lucrative, and it was encouraging that if a man had a proposal for a project which was feasible and potentially profitable, he could expect to have a sympathetic hearing."

Joe Issac and Sunnoo Morris talked of progress in the jute mill and the cigarette factory. The success of the jute mill in the pre-war years offset the difficulties experienced by the cigarette factory. But it was in the post war years, in 1952 -53, that Joe talked of a significant change in the jute mill. A shortage of foreign exchange after Indian Independence meant that only specialised machinery, which could not be produced locally, was imported. The entrepreneurial skills of Adrian Gubbay at Head Office in Calcutta and the technical skills of Joe Isaac in Agarpara, were combined in the manufacture of looms at the jute mill. Not only did they meet their own needs, they were able to supply mills extensively in India and Pakistan. Joe had no technical training, but machines fascinated him. "I redesigned the imported loom and designed entirely new ancilliary machinery. Eight looms were built initially in the mill and proved to be of higher efficiency, at half the cost, with lower maintenance requirements. A foundry and factory was built from scratch and we began to produce a loom a day, and offered after-sales service and maintenance. Adrian Gubbay invited government officials to inspect the machines and they were so satisfied, a ban was placed on imports." This is remarkable, because what happened here reflects the national situation. India was forced, by circumstances, to develop her own manufacturing base very rapidly to compensate for the neglect in this area during the period of the Raj. It is remarkable, also, that this challenge was met by self-taught and imaginative engineers like Joe who were entrusted with the responsibility of bringing about this change. By 1965 other mills in India and Pakistan were manufacturing their own looms.

The war years saw considerable changes for the better in the National Tobacco Company, according to Sunnoo Morris. In 1945 he became Factory Manager and in 1946 General Factory Manager, which means that he had overall responsibility for printing, paper laminating, the saw mill and the engineering works. "Modernisation in methods of manufacture and the growth in demand from army contracts saw a switch in the fortunes in the 1940s for the cigarette factory. The monopoly previously enjoyed by the Imperial Tobacco Company was broken. An improvement in the quality of cigarettes, brought about by air conditioning, methods of drying the tobacco leaf, the methods of blending, and control of the physical environment, were all very significant. After the war the firm was exporting high grade cigarettes and pipe tobacco to the U.K., to Singapore and Australia, using a blend of American and Indian tobacco. I would go to Guntur in South India, which was the centre for purchasing tobacco, for a few weeks every year to inspect tobacco, to see for myself what was going on in the laboratories, and to ensure quality control. We introduced new blends and extended our packaging. I was really self-educated in management and in understanding tobacco quality. I bought what books I could in India, and the rest I was able to get from abroad. In 1949 I went on leave to the U.K. and took the opportunity to visit factories, plants for production of cigarettes and all allied products. Subsequently I also visited the United States and several countries in Europe to widen my knowledge of the industry. Time and motion studies enabled us to cut costs and reduce labour, to the extent that we doubled production and reduced our labour by half".

Unfortunately, this brought problems with the unions at a time when there was a great deal of political unrest. During the Great Calcutta Killing and the communal troubles which came with Partition, people were in a state of heightened anxiety. Sunoo said: "It was a dangerous time with 150,000 workers on strike in all the factories around, and it was extremely stressful for the managers, supervisors and their families. Extra gurkha guards had to be called in. I had a narrow escape myself one day when I was cornered by the workers on my way home from work. Luckily someone from the factory spotted the trouble and phoned the police who rescued me and dispersed the crowd." Like Sunnoo, Joe also remembers unrest with the unions, their occasional resort to force, and the period in 1946-47 when "the factory was closed for three months when both Hindus and Muslims went back to their villages" as everyone feared for their lives.

The worst problems with labour abated by the early 1950s and both the jute mill and the cigarette factory were operating successfully. However, by this time the exodus of the Jewish community in Calcutta was gaining pace, and this was reflected in the situation in Agarpara. In 1954 Sally Morris took her children to England to be educated and she returned to India from time to time to be with her husband. In 1958 she settled in London but he was persuaded to stay on for two years to train another General Manager. Joe's wife and sons went on ahead of him to the U.K. and he joined them in 1965. The decline in the number of Jews in Calcutta and Agarpara continued right through the 1950s until the mid 1970s. B.N.Elias & Company and the interests it represented were all sold by 1975 and today there is not a single Jewish person left in Agarpara to recount the fifty year period of settlement there.

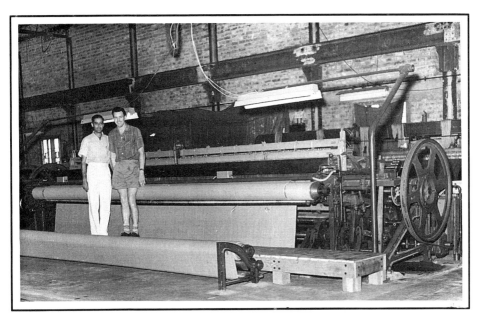

Joe Isaac and Werner Dietz, visiting engineer, the Agarpara Jute Mill. The loom was designed by Joe Isaac.
Courtesy: Joe Isaac.

Celebration of *Saraswati Puja*, Goddess of Learning, who dominates the dieties shown here.
Photo: Cheryl Isacc.

Left: Enjoying the swimming pool in Riverside, Agarpara. F. to B. Matilda Ezekiel, Israel Sopher, Ernie Twena & Eze Silas.
Courtesy: Florence Benaiah.

Below: Celebration in the *Succa*, Agarpara. A number of candles have been lit (table at extreme right) and prayer books are on the table. This suggests it was the seventh night of the festival of *Succoth, Hoshanna Rabba.* L. to R. Diana Isaac, Ernie Twena, Sally Rodda, Sarah Judah, David Judah, Daisy Judah, Seemah Duke, Yvonne Hillel, Rachel Jonah, Barry Cohen, (in front) Mozelle Twena, Clara Abraham, Abe Sargon, Esther Levy, Raymond Levy. Sitting: Elias Judah, Abe Ezekiel, Naji Ezra, Benny Judah, (child) Benny Isaac, Ramoo Abraham, Unknown, Al Levy, Ralph Twena, Ezra Abraham, Judah Judah.
Photo: Joe Isaac.

Chapter 8

AN AFTERNOON AT THE RACES

There is a beautiful race course in Calcutta, right in the middle of the city. The yellow-green turf shimmers in the light of the sun on a winter's day, and the freshly painted white rails add line to the green mass of turf. Flags fly, and banks of potted plants make splashes of variegated colour. In the background looms the massive Gothic outline of the Victoria Memorial, built in pure white marble, looking slightly mysterious through the winter haze. Both the race course and the Victoria Memorial are legacies of the British Raj.

"The sight of the Calcutta Race Course on a December morning would be quite tremendous ... All the main princely houses, Kashmir, Jaipur, Bhopal, would have their strings of polo ponies and they would be ridden round, each one with his *syce* (Hi) groom on, each one with (his) distinctive *pugree* (Hi) turban of the prince concerned."[1] The course itself is so designed for all spectators to be able to see almost the entire circuit of the field. Waiters, impeccably dressed in white trousers and *achkan* (Hi) long fitted jacket, with elaborate red turbans, serve drinks and cucumber sandwiches on silver trays, wearing white kid gloves. The band plays military marches and old favourites to entertain ladies in colourful dresses and hats, or in flowing saris, and men in fine tailored suits, or traditional Indian dress. Every- thing is aimed to be grand, in scale and in detail. This is how it was designed by the British, and this is how it was intended to emulate them.

Winter is the time of the racing season as the weather is cool, fine and dry. In between Christmas and the New Year there are special race meetings during the week, and not on Saturday afternoons, as usual. Members of the Turf Club have badges for themselves and for a guest, and young women such as myself, eagerly sought out members who did not have a regular guest for the special meetings. My friends and I were young and carefree, earning reasonable salaries, most of which was saved as we lived with our parents. The race meetings were full of promise and excitement. Everyone dressed up to be seen, to meet friends who gave tips and took them. I don't know about other people, but the Jews exchanged a great deal of information on dream interpretation, which seemed to convey much more information on the outcome of a race than the run-of-the-mill notions about the form of a horse, the dexterity of a rider, or the reputation of a trainer.

AN AFTERNOON AT THE RACES

Silas was my uncle's friend going way, way back. For this reason, if for nothing else, I could usually rely on him for an invitation to the Members' enclosure and for his protective interest in my gambling for an afternoon. Silas had been a member of the Turf Club since his youth and he never missed a meeting except for illness or a death. As he wasn't a heavy gambler he was able to enjoy the races as much for the beauty of the surroundings as for the enjoyment of meeting friends and the opportunity for a flutter. He was full of *joie de vivre* and goodwill, and knew, either personally or by sight, everyone who was worth knowing on the race course. This, I discovered, was not an advantage at all times, and even I had my uses. "You see the thin tall chap with the Kaiser moustache, leaning against the *neem* tree on the far right? He owns a young horse Honeybee, running in the next race. So far Honeybee is an unknown quantity, so what will his owner do? Back his horse or some other - that's the question. I'll tell you what. Why don't you follow him when he goes to place his bet, and if you can get near enough, you can hear him call his bet. Just concentrate on what he bets to win, never mind about place. Then you can bet the same for yourself, and while you're at it, put on something for me" said Silas, pressing a few crisp notes into my hand.

There is so much to learn on the race course. One thing is that you don't place a bet in every race. This is as much for the good of your blood pressure as it is for your bank balance. It gives you time to pause and relax and enjoy some of the other pleasures of the afternoon. It was at such a time I thought I ought to try my hand at using binoculars and Silas readily handed them over. The horses lined up and then they were off!

"What a shame" I cried "one of the horses has been left."
"That's funny" said Silas. "There are seven horses in this race and I can see seven jockeys' heads bobbing up and down even without binoculars."
"I assure you, one horse is still standing at the starting line."
"What are his colours?" asked Silas, testing me.
"Red cap and white sleeves" I replied with confidence.
He began to lose a little of his self-assurance. "Let's have a look then."
I handed back the binoculars with an air of triumph. Silas peered through them and crumpled with laughter. "You silly goose, can't you recognise a mounted policeman when you see one? He's not *in* the race, he's just there to oversee it!"

Although Silas was an old hand on the race course, he was wise enough to know that jockeys had bad days no matter how well they could ride, and the

AN AFTERNOON AT THE RACES

finest horses were known to fall at the last fence. When he met his closer Jewish friends, after the usual exchange of pleasantries, Silas would usually open up the way to non-rational thoughts. "Had a good dream last night?" he would ask in hushed tones. A "good" dream meant the clear disclosure of a winner. Although it might have seemed amazing how many Jews had dreams the night before a meeting, how well they could recall the details, and how adept they were at interpretation, this was not left entirely to chance. Good luck charms, a talisman, and even open letters addressed to any benevolent passing spirits asking for clear forecasts, would be tucked under pillows to assist in picking winners. These dreams had to be kept more or less secret, for to reveal them to all and sundry would risk shortening the odds, yet not to reveal them at all meant being deprived later of sharing in pleasure or pain. Perhaps most important of all was the danger of being excluded from the confidence of others. I got the impression that a good measure of friendship among the Jews was the extent to which these dreams were shared or withheld. The ones I had little patience with were those who would say "Yes, I have something but not for the next race; I'll tell you later." Or worse still, those who would merely smile a knowing smile and say nothing.

I was Silas's guest at one of the special meetings. It was a beautiful afternoon and everyone was agog with anticipation as they moved about the Members' enclosure where the horses were paraded before each race. This was the time, not just for pleasantries, but for summing up all the signs for the winner of the next race. There was much talk, heard and overheard, about form and other sensible facts, but in spite of the logic there seemed to be a great diversity of conclusions about the winner. Then there were tit-bits of rumour and counter-rumour from the in-group; the owners, trainers, jockeys, grooms and their bosom friends. In this climate of uncertainty, there was plenty of scope for the non-rational.

Silas turned round to see Moses waving frantically in his direction. This was auspicious, surely.
"Silas" he panted, with great excitement "what a dream, what a dream to tell you!"
"Oh yes" said Silas, lowering his voice and stepping closer to Moses.
"Last night" began Moses, and then looked suspiciously in my direction, delaying his coveted news.
"She's O.K. She's E.M's niece, just here for the big meets."
"Right!" Moses seemed satisfied "but you *do* understand, don't you, that we must keep this hush-hush because if everyone backs the winner it will play havoc with the odds and we don't want that!"

AN AFTERNOON AT THE RACES

I reassured him, impatient to share in the confidence.
"Last night my Uncle Nissim came to me, may his soul rest in peace. I dreamt I was in my father's house, chatting and laughing with friends and then my Uncle Nissim came in, carrying a basket of bread. He took me aside by the arm, picked out a nice large loaf, and said "Moses, my boy, I came all the way to give this to you." Then he smiled, turned round and went off, not saying a word to anyone else who was there. "I ask you Silas" said Moses "what can bread mean if it doesn't mean money? And if you give a numerical value to the name N-i-s-s-i-m, (in Judeo-Arabic,[2] of course, which is the language in which he used to calculate), it adds up to 50. The zero has no value, so we are left with 5. That means the fifth horse. The fifth horse must be in the first race as there are eight horses running in it altogether. So, look in your race book and what do we have? Troglodite!"
"Hmm" said Silas. "I don't deny it. Troglodite is a good horse, Moses, but you must admit that recently she hasn't been on top of her form and look, Butler is riding her today. I don't care for Butler very much."
"Hang Butler!" cried Moses "What you want is the right horse. I'm glad she hasn't been on form recently because she'll be an outsider and there's nothing I love more than backing an outsider. You see, today the tide will turn for her!"
"I understand what you are getting at" mused the reluctant Silas "but maybe the five means the fifth race and not number five in the first race. Now today's the first, so maybe we should back number one in the fifth race. Let's see ... Mother of Pearl, now that's a possibility especially as Moffatt is riding her."
"Mother of Pearl is the favourite for that race so there's not much money to be made there." Then Moses' eyes lit up. He had the perfect compromise solution. "I'll tell you what we can do! Back Troglodite for the first race and if she loses, we can try our luck with Mother of Pearl in the fifth!"
"Yes, why not?" said Silas. "Let's all put our money on Troglodite."

Everyone assembled on the stands. The horses were under starter's orders for the first race, and they were off. Silas's eyes were glued to his binoculars. It was then that I heard a familiar chanting beside me. It was Moses. He was singing Psalm 118. "O give thanks unto the Lord, for He is good, For his mercy endureth forever." His lips were moving faster than the horses hoofs, I felt sure. The horses were momentarily out of view as they galloped round the bend and passed the third enclosure. The names of several horses merged into a great roar and this became deafening as they raced through the second enclosure. By this time Moses had reached verse 25 "We beseech Thee, O Lord, save now! We beseech Thee, O Lord make us now to prosper!" Faster and faster came the words of the psalm. The names of the horses seemed to separate "Psyche!", "Man of War!" yelled two

AN AFTERNOON AT THE RACES

factions in the crowd, and then almost at the post I heard "Troglodite!" She came up from the outside to outstrip both Psyche and Man of War who were battling it out in the last furlong. Troglodite was no more than half a head in front of the other horses at the finishing line. Moses had all but collapsed with relief and the energy he put into his psalm reading deserved to be rewarded, surely? Silas and I had the strength to whoop. "Troglodite, Troglodite, you little beauty!" "What a dream" said Silas, shaking his head, almost in disbelief. "What a horse! Well done Moses, well done Uncle Nissim."

We collected our winnings and it was time to debate again. Was the dream open to further interpretation? Silas argued that it was quite reasonable to focus on the number five. If the fifth horse could come up trumps, what potential might there be in the fifth race? What about horse number one? It was, after all, the first of the month. Moses could not improve on Silas's reasoning and although Mother-of-Pearl was the favourite and the odds were getting shorter by the minute, our pockets were jingling and we felt lucky. Silas had noticed that Moffatt was riding Mother-of-Pearl and he knew a friend of Moffatt, so off he went to look for this friend. Nobody could be accused of not doing their homework on the race course. "What does Moffatt think about Mother-of-Pearl today?" asked Silas. No point in beating about the bush. "Dead cert, he's going for a gamble" confided Moffatt's friend.

That seemed to settle it for Silas. With money on the favourite we didn't expect to make a great deal, but we weren't likely to lose either. Moses was very much at peace with the world and was ready to go along on Silas's inside information. After all, Silas had been willing to go along with him and one show of confidence deserved another.

We put our money on Mother-of-Pearl for the fifth race and took our place on the stands. I wondered if Moses would call for heavenly support, and if so would he repeat the same psalm because it brought him luck, because it was his particular favourite, or because in his opinion it was the most appropriate? Or would he choose a different one?

The horses were off. Moses' lips moved, but I couldn't hear the words. I strained because I had to know for the future. Then I heard "out of my straits I called upon the Lord; He answered me with great enlargement." The same psalm, I might have guessed!

AN AFTERNOON AT THE RACES

"Its a one horse race" said Silas, training his binoculars closely on Mother-of-Pearl. This time we could hear the name of one horse only as they turned the bend. We held our breath. The horses were coming into view and as they did so, either Mother-of-Pearl began to tire or the other horses were trying harder. The race was open, every horse seemed to have an equal chance of winning, and everything seemed confused to me as the horses galloped towards the finishing line. "Which horse won?" I had to ask. Then I saw the looks on the faces of Silas and Moses. It wasn't Mother-of-Pearl.

But the meeting was not over yet, so all was not lost. Silas and I sauntered off to look at the horses for the sixth race. "This is an important time to meet people" said Silas, teaching me the ropes. "You never know who you'll run into with a hot tip." Sure enough, we spotted a small group of Jews talking with great animation. Although this was not unusual, as we used to laugh at ourselves for talking with our hands, at the race course it was a different matter; it had to be investigated at any cost. Silas knew them well enough to join in.

"What's all the excitement about?"
"We've just won the double!" one of them said triumphantly. "What do you think about that?"
"Marvellous!" said Silas "how did you manage it?"
"We got the numbers from that *sadhu,* (Hi) Indian holy man, in Kalighat. You know the chap - he's getting quite famous now."
"Famous for what?"
"Race tips, of course."
"Race tips! What would a *sadhu* know of race tips?"
"Nothing, he knows nothing about the races at all, but he does know about numbers. I'm surprised you haven't heard about him. He is covered in mud up to his armpits by the river bank and people go to see him. They throw money and fruit in his direction and just ask him for numbers. The numbers he calls are all race winners."
"Is this the first time you've won on his numbers?" Silas' curiosity had obviously been aroused.
"Oh no, this is the third week running."
"Really? Three weeks in a row can't be a fluke, I'm bound to say."
"No fluke at all, Silas. The man is famous after all. I can't believe you haven't heard of him."
"Do you have anything for the next race? From *him,,* I mean?" asked Silas, hopefully.

AN AFTERNOON AT THE RACES

"I'll tell you what Silas. Why don't you play safe? Back number three win and place to hedge your bet. That way you simply can't lose."
Win and place on number three it was to be. Black Beauty. We went to look for Moses to cheer him up with our news.

Once again we took our places on the viewing stands with great hope and expectation. The horses were under starter's orders and Silas raised his binoculars. They were off! That is, they were all off except Black Beauty. "Oh no!" groaned Silas. "Black Beauty is left."
"Left" I cried. "That's impossible!"
"Nothing is impossible here. Black Beauty won't budge from the starting tape."
"Well, so much for your famous *sadhu*" said Silas jokingly, to his informer. But his informer didn't feel a bit good-humoured. He had put all his winnings from the double on Black Beauty. "I'll kill that so-and-so *sadhu*. I'm going to Kalighat to denounce him to his face and make sure everyone knows the man is a fake! Goodness knows how much money and fruit he's raked off innocent people for his phoney numbers".
"I should have known better, I should have known" groaned Moses.
"Oh come on Moses, it's only a race, not the end of the world" said Silas.
"No, no, you don't understand. I should have known better."
"What do you mean?"
"Well, there's this guy, this very poor Jew, the Halawi chap. Large family and all that. He got desperate so he went to the *hazan* of such-and-such synagogue and asked him to write a prayer which would bring him good luck and help him to feed the family. The *hazan* felt sorry for him and wrote a prayer. Halawi put the prayer paper in his pocket and the following Saturday went to the races and backed no less than four winners. The trouble is, when he emptied his pockets of all the cash, he couldn't find the prayer paper. It had vanished! He went back to the *hazan* and explained what had happened and begged for another prayer paper. "You used my prayer for gambling, and broke *Shabbath,* (H) sabbath, too?" thundered the cantor. "Is it any wonder you've lost it?" "So you see" concluded Moses "I should have known better than mixing up holy men with gambling." Clearly his recitation from Psalms was not in the same category.
"I should have warned you Silas, I'm sorry."
"Well, at least we'll know better for next time."

I sometimes wonder whether he did. When it came to picking winners at the races rationality was completely suspended. Desire to make money in this way was a compulsion. I know for certain of fortunes lost on this race course as they

AN AFTERNOON AT THE RACES

must be in others all over the world. Where there are so many imponderables, and when the atmosphere is pervaded by anxiety and superstition, how are people to make choices? Perhaps once the first step is taken to enter a non-rational world, that world is bound to be full of surprises. Not all of them pleasant ones. But the very anticipation of surprise must be so alluring to some that it becomes quite irresistible.

The Turf Club, Calcutta. The paddock in front of the Members' Enclosure.
Photo: Cheryl Isaac.

Chapter 9

SPORT

Photographs of men from our community at the turn of the century show that they wore baggy trousers, loose shirts, and *sidarya,* (A) embroidered waistcoats, fastened with a set of removable silver buttons threaded at the back with a silver chain. A *dagla,* (A) or long coat, worn outdoors, was fitted, but not too closely. Braid extended across the chest and along the sleeve ends which widened at the wrists. Goitein[1] explained that in the Middle Ages the wide sleeves "served as receptacles ... Men and women kept there a sleeve kerchief, in which money and a wide variety of other objects could be stored." Men covered their heads indoors with shallow crowned black or red velvet caps, some of which were embroidered. A popular outdoor headgear was the fez, which was worn with pride because as Rejwan notes[2] - "One of the innovations which had a bearing on minorities (in Iraq) was that the various types of headdress used at the time (mid nineteenth century) were to be replaced by one uniform headgear - the fez. (This was significant because) it stressed the sultan's desire that his subjects of various faiths should no longer be distinguishable by their attire."

Women wore wrappers indoors; loose cotton gowns flowing from the shoulders to the ankles, with wide gathered collars and elbow length sleeves, often trimmed with lace. When they went outdoors the wrapper was covered with a black shawl embroidered with deep red roses, or a waist-length, lined cotton cape, buttoned at the throat. Married women covered their heads with *yasmas,* (A) scarves which were fastened round their buns or knotted at the forehead. On special occasions such as festivals, weddings and other celebrations, women wore *qussah,* (A) made of rich fabrics such as tissue or silk brocade, which was "full length, fitted to the figure, with a low cut neckline and long sleeves widening to the cuff, where there is a slit. The waist seam and the skirt are gathered at the centre back. A front panel is shaped to the breast"[3] covered by a *zig* (A) bodice, made of fine cloth such as muslin or net, elaborately embroidered, and fastened with straps. Locally, this outfit was called "gawon" and is very likely to be a corruption of the word "gown". This was the traditional dress of Baghdad and neighbouring districts which the Jews of the Raj continued to wear until the end of the nineteenth and into the twentieth centuries, when they gradually changed to

SPORT

European style clothes. Unlike other Jewish communities in Bombay and Cochin, the Jews of Middle Eastern origin never wore Indian dress.

Sport played no part in the lives of people who wore *dagla* and *qussah*. The men, occupied mostly in trade in a multi-cultural society, dressed as they pleased and if they were identified as Jews by their Baghdadi dress, this presented no problems. They married in late adolescence and their youth was spent in providing for their fast growing families. Social life centred round family and community, and the manner of dress within this circle was fairly uniform. Girls generally married while they were of school age and became absorbed in child-bearing and child-rearing while they were still in adolescence.

The turning point for young people came late in the nineteenth century when most Jewish children went to school and where they followed a predominantly British system of education. Their parents began to dress them in European style clothes, and since the eyes of the community were focused on the British model in all matters which did not impinge on religion, sport gradually began to feature in their lives. So far as the British were concerned, "sport was an obsession in the old India that had its roots in the dread that unless one kept fit one would catch some dreadful disease or other."[4]

David Einy grew up in the 1930s and says that there were many parents who were dubious about sporting activities. "You were told that you couldn't swim because you could drown, you couldn't roller skate because you could break your back, you couldn't go horse riding because you could break your neck. With these ideas in the heads of our parents we were left with no alternative but to go behind their backs, and by doing so we were taking greater risks than necessary. My passion was for horse riding. It all started from the time I was in my mid-teens when I began to follow the *syce* (Hi) grooms, trotting horses past our house on the way to the *Maidan*. They would exercise the horses there and I discovered that if you paid a *syce* a little money he would let you ride and save himself the trouble. That is how I learnt. Of course I fell off several times but never suffered any injuries so my parents didn't know what was going on. They were under the impression that I was out on a cycle ride. When I was seventeen years old or so I heard that Charlie Ezra (from the community) was riding in Tollygunge. They were all gentlemen riders at Tollygunge, which means they were not professional jockeys in the official sense, in that they got no fees for riding. It started as a sport but developed into a big gambling attraction. Charlie showed me the ropes, how to proceed for taking a test, and how to apply for membership. You had to prove

SPORT

gentleman status by showing that you were financially sound and had two referees. But you needed a horse to take the test and I learnt that you could pay a *syce* to bring a horse to exercise in Tollygunge instead of the *Maidan*. Six stewards judged whether you could canter and gallop at a reasonable pace and with all the practice I'd had, there was no problem. It was then that I told my parents for the first time what I'd been up to. They were astonished to hear that I had gone as far as passing my riding test in Tollygunge and gradually began to take an interest in the racing events there. When I was eighteen they became enthusiastic enough to help me to buy a horse for a thousand rupees, which was an enormous sum of money in the early 1940s. There were at least ten to twelve young Jewish men who rode in Tollygunge at the time, including Haskel David who is still a top professional trainer at the Calcutta race course. Several Jews owned horses and were well connected with the racing world. In time I trained my own and other people's horses. However, as we were non-professional, we could not ride in the Calcutta Race Course but our horses would run there for all the races except the top events.

"When it came to swimming, there was the same problem about my parents' fears so I used to bunk school with some of my class friends to go swimming in the Dakhuria Lakes. We took it in turns to keep guard over our clothes and watch out in case someone happened to be about who knew us. It was a question of teaching ourselves and each other, starting off at the shallow end and gradually progressing into deeper waters."

In the late 1920s, Moshe Lanyado, a strong swimmer himself, taught a great many people in the community to swim. He inspired confidence in both young people and in their parents, and those who wished to learn knew he was always willing to oblige without any payment at all. He had a beautiful physique, and crowds would gather to see him give diving exhibitions blind-folded, or watch him play water polo, and his impressive collection of medals tells its own story. His wife, Seemah, explains the origin of his interest in sport. "Moshe's mother was widowed when her four children were very young and she had a hard time trying to provide for her family. He longed for a bicycle as he grew into his teens but it was out of the question to expect his mother to be able to pay for one. However, bicycles were given away as prizes in swimming competitions and Moshe saw his chance. He persevered, and after eighteen months won the bicycle he longed for.

"People swam in tanks in those days as there were only a few swimming

SPORT

pools which were quite far out of town, such as the Cossipore Club, the Ordinance Club, the Marine Club and East Park. Moshe swam in the Wellesley Square Tank, which was clean, unlike the Cornwallis Street Tank and the College Square Tank, both of which were full of weeds. I'm certain that there were people who had drowned there, but not from our community. Moshe also swam in the Hooghly, where the currents are very strong, and took part in a twenty-four mile swimming competition in the river. His great ambition was to swim the English Channel, but he didn't know his way about getting sponsorship for this event.

"Exhibition diving at the Wellesley Square tank attracted large crowds and Moshe would dive blindfolded with his hands tied behind his back with string so that he could snap it if he got into difficulties. One day they happened to tie his hands with a handkerchief and the water tightened the knot. On that very day his head got stuck in the mud when he dived and he was in trouble. He even said *Shema Israel,* as he thought his last moments had come, but luckily he was able to hold his breath in the water for several minutes and this kept him going. Eventually he was able to loosen his hands and swim out on the other side. By this time people had become anxious and his mother and sisters were there and were very worried about him. There was a rescue team on standby and they went to help him but he had managed to free himself and as he came out of the water there was a tremendous cheer of relief. After that all exhibitions were cancelled where the diver had his hands tied with a handkerchief.

"A month later Moshe was walking past a photographer's shop in front of the New Market. He saw a photograph of himself in the window taken in mid-dive with his hands tied behind his back and his eyes blindfolded. He asked the manager: "Whose photograph is this?" "Ah" he replied "that's a photograph of a *pagla sahib"*, (Hi) a madman. "That madman" said Moshe "happens to be me!" The manager was so embarrassed he pressed Moshe to accept the photograph without any charge."

Ellis Cohen was one of Moshe's first pupils. He recalls: "When I was about twenty years old, in the early 1930s, I asked Moshe if he had time to go swimming. The answer was 'I have time in the evening but no form of conveyance'. I had just bought a bicycle from my first salary and asked Moshe if he was prepared to sit astride for the four mile ride to the East Park Club. He agreed, and after a year of swimming there at weekends and every morning at the Wellesley Square Tank, with Moshe encouraging me 'come on, you'll get second breath', I became an expert swimmer and a good water polo player too. We learned

SPORT

from the Indian folk who used this Tank that we should rub our bodies with mustard oil and then shower before getting into the water to avoid catching cold, and it worked like a charm.

"Most of the young girls we knew who were keen on swimming asked Moshe or me to help them as they knew we were as straight as a die and would get them off to a good start. We were invited to several week-end parties in Agarpara and Dum Dum, and by the Trivedi family who were Hindus, so the swimming was combined with socialising and it was great fun. Sometimes we would book the Marine Club in Garden Reach and go down in two or three cars early in the morning or in the evenings. On our return we would stop at an Indian sweetmeat shop and buy *kachowrees*, (Hi) spiced pancakes, to slake our hunger."

Other sports were combined with entertainment rather than with socialising, as Joe Solomon recalls. "In 1935 I met Maung Zawiek, a Burmese weight-lifter who inspired me to develop my interests in body building and weight lifting techniques. At this time I joined a club with extensive facilities and excellent coaches, which helped me to increase my power in weight lifting. I then took part in competitions and gave exhibitions in feats of strength. Some were on a grand scale and had never been seen at any one time on a stage in India. The competitions were very serious but at the same time there was considerable entertainment value. For example, the most spectacular was passing a limousine Buick car over my bare abdomen, and to commemorate this and my contribution to record-breaking I was presented with a gold watch and three gold medals which are my most treasured trophies.

"I'll tell you about the car going over my abdomen because this is what people remember most about my exhibitions. First a headband had to be tied tightly round my head to prevent concussion. Then I had to lie down flat on my back, arch my knees slightly and relax my torso. Next it was necessary to exhale completely, hold my breath and contract my abdominal muscles tight against my back. I was asked if I was ready three times, and if I did not give the signal to discontinue the act, the nearside front and back wheels would pass over my bare abdomen whilst the other wheels would pass beyond my feet. The timing had to be very precise in order to avoid injury.

"The truth of the matter is that I was always a little anxious because the timing was in someone else's hands and I wasn't able to get any insurance cover. Physically, however, the strain was no more or less than any other feat of strength,

SPORT

like tearing through a telephone directory with a hard cover, which was less hazardous. But this feat was a great crowd puller and was reported in the press.[5] Among other feats, I performed this one on three separate occasions, and on the last occasion the timing was out by a few seconds so that my breath was not held completely, I lost the full contraction of my abdomen and damaged my kidneys and duodenum. I was in hospital for about two months and had to continue treatment for another ten months before I was able to perform again.

"In 1936 I opened a club for body building enthusiasts and weight lifting in Calcutta with a well equipped gym for weight-lifting, wrestling, boxing, jiu-jitsu, ring and parallel bar work, barbell and body building exercises. Although it was called the Zionist Institute of Physical Perfection, the forty or so members were both Jews and non-Jews, and included women, which was quite something for those days. The most significant event for me was winning the title of Bengal's Strongest Man in 1939."

The sports editor of "The Statesman" reported on October 9th 1939: "Physical Demonstration in Calcutta: India's Best Developed Men." "The Dalhousie Institute, Calcutta, was packed last night for the grand physical display organised by the Bengal Amateur Weight Lifting Federation and the Zionist Institute of Physical Perfection. Rarely, if ever, has such an aggregation of physical talent been seen at one time on the stage in India, and the organisers, particularly Mr J.E. Solomon, the leading light ... has to be congratulated. Of particular interest is that on the programme were the strong men of the Indian, European, Jewish, Armenian and Anglo-Indian communities. An inclusion of an item from the ladies section of the Zionist Institute was very welcome." This was a demonstration of physical fitness exercises and illuminated club swinging.

There was sport purely for the sake of competitiveness in schools and sports clubs, some of which had their own playing fields in the *Maidan.* The Jewish Girls' School started playing competitive hockey in the late 1920s and their Red team, trained mainly by three volunteers, Nat Zachariah, Victor Moses and Ike Hallen, was strong enough to play first division teams in clubs with mature women. Helen Jacob Judah remembers: "Those who played for the School volunteered to do so, but if we didn't turn up for practice or slacked off in any way we lost house points. In the winter months we would have to set out twice a week, at 5.30 in the morning to practice from 6 until 8 o'clock. Luckily I had a friend who lived nearby who was also in the school team and we used to walk together, a mile and a half away to the *Maidan.* People always crowded round to watch us play practice

SPORT

games and cheer us on but the training was hard and made us thirsty. Miss Luddy, our principal, lived near the *Maidan* and sent us a flask of hot cocoa regularly with her servant. It was a relief when we caught sight of him as we knew it was time to relax and quench our thirst. Some of our matches were played in the mornings, but when we had to go outside Calcutta by train, or when teams came from nearby towns to play us, the matches were arranged for the afternoons after school. There is no doubt that while Miss Luddy was principal of the Jewish Girls' School we reached the highest standards in sport and did well academically too."

There were many young Jewish men and women who competed with distinction in a range of sports, either with a team or in an individual capacity. Noreen Ezra David was a member of the Blue Bird Hockey and Badminton Club, which was non-denominational and played in tennis, table-tennis, badminton and hockey tournaments. She won over a hundred trophies over a couple of decades. "Sport was my life" she said, "it just came naturally to me, a gift from God. From dawn until dusk in the winter months, it was one sporting activity after another, six days a week, after I left school. I enjoyed the practice as much as the matches and when I joined the Blue Birds I was lucky to be trained by top players. My mother watched every match in which I played and I can still see her shake her head in disapproval when I made a bad move. I wasn't a fighter; if I felt I was losing I became down-hearted, which is not good for a sportswoman. Even so, I was playing in the Bengal team for the All India Hockey Tournament in 1939 when we won the Championship. I did not go for the honour because I was too young to appreciate what it meant to represent your province in a national tournament. My thoughts were mainly on the fun of living in luxury, away from parents, leading a different life with other young girls. Although I had a healing sprained ankle at the time, I was happy to be selected. It was great fun, all the dignitaries turned out in full force to see us off at Howrah Station. And it was even more fun returning with the trophy."

Rina Einy Margulies competed in tennis in a private capacity. She recalled: "When I was nine years old my sister and I started playing tennis twice a week as an extra activity. My mother played a great deal herself and took us to the Dalhousie Club and the South Club five mornings a week between six and seven o'clock. The intensive practice meant that we were able to play in inter-club matches and then in national tournaments. We played all the year round, even in the hot weather and during the monsoons on a variety of surfaces - grass, red shale and compressed dung, but there were mostly soft courts.

SPORT

"During the school holidays we played in tournaments for two months and travelled all over India and Ceylon. My sister and I played singles as well as doubles, and my parents paid all our expenses. In the age group of the under 21s, it was not unusual for children like us to be playing against young women.

"We often visited the UK in summer when we were in our teens and by the time I was fifteen I was among the top ten women players and represented Great Britain for many years, playing womens' open international tournaments with a world ranking between 250 and 110. I played in Wimbledon for four years and sponsorship from commercial firms helped pay for travelling expenses. Clothing and equipment were supplied by various manufacturing companies, and all expenses for team events were paid by the Lawn Tennis Association. I played for England when I was nineteen in the XXIII Olympiad in 1984, which was in Los Angeles and competed in many tournaments all over the U.S. and Europe. I also took part in the Maccabiah Games, the international Jewish Olympics in Israel, playing tennis in 1984, and squash in 1988. It was really more like a party than a strictly competitive event. During all this time my school work suffered a great deal but I promised my parents I would make up for it, which I did, eventually.

"Playing tennis tournaments in India was a real adventure. Tournaments were often held in rather obscure places, travel was long and tiring, accommodation was very basic and a chaperon virtually always necessary. My mother was very supportive and travelled everywhere with me. As I got a little older, I sometimes went with my older cousin, Enrico, who later played Davis Cup tennis for India. Playing in Britain and Europe was rather different, not only in terms of conditions (travelling and accommodation) but also because there was keener competition and I tended to feel rather less of a "celebrity", though it took time before I felt less of an outsider."

Arlene Einy, who accompanied her daughter Rina on her Indian tours, added: "Every facility was laid on when tournaments were held in the large cities in India, but it was murder in the smaller, more remote places. Sometimes we had to sleep thirty in one room with one toilet. In some places there were no beds, just matresses on the floor, and in winter it was freezing cold. Food was always a problem; it was seldom available in the same building where we slept and everyone would have to get into trucks early in the morning to go to town for breakfast. Indian food only was available, *chappatis, bhaji* and tea. Medical treatment was also a problem. There was an occasion when Rina was playing in Ceylon and she got cramps. I went to the nearest doctor for help but he just shook

SPORT

his head and said 'it is not my business to assist anyone from the Indian team!'

"You could hang around all day and even for two days before you could get a single match in the tournament. Local players usually got preferential treatment. In some places the courts were open to the street and not fenced off because they were not part of a club. Anyone could walk in, and these young girls in their shorts and skirts attracted crowds of men who would distract the girls with loud remarks and I have even seen them throw peanuts at the players. On one occasion the crowd got completely out of control and the riot police had to be called in. Everything was done on a shoestring budget so all the arrangements became a problem."

Sport was often combined with socialising, or seen as a means of enjoying a social gathering. Aaron and Sammy Arakie were excellent tennis players and both brothers won the Bengal Junior Championship, thirteen years apart. In the early war years Sammy was selected from the South Club to go on a training programme of top Indian players with European coaches. The Arakie brothers were fortunate in having a grass court at their house and every weekend, during the winter months, they would have tennis parties. Marianne Arakie, Sammy's wife, recalls: "The brothers organised the programme; mostly doubles, so that as many people as possible would get the chance of a game. Large jugs of *nemboo pani,* (Hi) iced lime and other fruit juices, such as *bael ka sherbet,* were at hand for thirsty players. There were a few spectators, but mainly competitors of a high standard, both Jews and non-Jews. Twelve to sixteen people were invited on each occasion and there was a hard core of regulars but otherwise different people were invited at different times. The games were followed by tea and a sing-song so there was a wonderful balance between sport and socialising. In the course of time, when the Maccabi Club got going the Arakie family and others, such as the Braham family, would lend their courts to the members, because the Club did not have courts of its own."

Reverend Abraham Silas also thought that balancing sport and socialising was a good idea, and as he had four young sons, he fostered this among the age group of eight to the late teens. His youngest son Eze remembers: "My parents were always concerned about the people we mixed with and my father realised we needed to combine our studies with a social life, but one over which he could keep a discreet watchful eye. At this time, in the mid to late 1940s, I was no more than seven or eight years old and my eldest brother was about thirteen. We had a large front garden which my father had cemented over and marked out a badminton

SPORT

court. We put up floodlights, bought a few shuttlecocks and badminton bats, fixed a net and we were in business! Our house became a budding club.

"We had many friends who lived nearby who were only too pleased to have a game two or three times a week, especially on Saturday nights after *Shabbath*. Twenty to thirty kids would turn up, including a few non-Jews who were very much a part of the Jewish scene. They were Anglo-Indians, Indians, Armenians and Parsis and were mostly kids we knew from school whose whole social life was bound up with ours. We mixed very readily at school - even on the social side, so it was part of life. We had a Jesuit education, along with so many boys from the community and I think we have all benefited for this as it gave us a wider and better perspective of life. We weren't worldly, in fact we were very naïve, very protected, but fun loving all the same." Marianne Sadka Arakie agreed. "My sisters and I went to a convent school as boarders since we were five years old. We had no alternative, we had to fit in. But I'm sure Eze is right, it taught us to appreciate what other people believed and to respect their beliefs. It certainly prepared me for later life when Sammy (her husband) and I had to live in Pakistan where we felt at ease with Muslims and Europeans."

Eze continued: "My father was a busy man but always found the time and energy to organise the games; singles, doubles, mixed doubles, handicaps, the lot." Marianne was a regular player, together with her sisters. She says: "I really enjoyed the tin and bottle tournaments because there was such excitement to win as it was all done in one evening - a knockout competition. Each one brought a tin or a bottle of something tasty and the winning partners cleared up all the tins and bottles."

Helene Sopher added: "It started off with badminton but very soon we had jam sessions in the house - dancing to gramophone records. (This is the way the term was used locally). Sunday mornings were special jiving sessions and any other time which could be managed." Eze said: "Both my parents were at work all day and we had the run of the house. The kids used to bring a change of clothes, we would get so hot with hours of dancing. My brother Aaron gradually started up a band. He played the saxophone and three of his friends played other instruments so we began to jive with live jazz music, and our house became a club-house!"

Reverend Silas' ambitions grew with the enthusiasm of the youngsters. He began to organise picnics. Every *Isrohag*, (H) day following the three festivals of

SPORT

Passover, Pentecost and Tabernacles and also on *Lag B'Omer*, (H), in between Passover and Pentecost, were popular days for picnics in the community, probably a custom which derived from Baghdad. Eze recalls: "Mum would organise the food as my father was very strict about what we ate, because it had to be strictly *kasher*, and Dad would arrange the transport. Twenty to thirty of us would pile into a lorry and go out for the whole day. We sang songs, played games and just enjoyed the places we went to - the Botanical Gardens with the famous banyan tree which spread its roots from the branches endlessly, the Zoo, the Dakhuria Lakes, and Agarpara. If the venue was suitable we took a wind-up gramophone and danced. We could never have too much dancing.

"Our house was in a very central spot so it was a convenient place for meeting. My father made Purim a really enjoyable festival for us all as he was the mainstay of all the activities and celebration. He was also banker in our card games on Purim. As soon as the fast (of Esther) was out everyone read the *Megilla* (H), Book of Esther, and then we started to play card games." It was customary for children to be given small gifts in cash from all their relatives on this festival and was the one time in the year when youngsters were allowed to stay up until they dropped while playing cards. Musleah explained[6] "... it is the name of the festival (Purim = Feast of Lots) that has given the association with games of chance and in some families card games are exceedingly popular." The next day we read the *Megilla* in the morning and then we gambled again. As we had a really big compound we were able to have races in the afternoon. In the evening we had fireworks and burnt an effigy of Haman, very much as they do here on Guy Fawkes night.

"Kite flying was a great sport for the boys. We had a large flat roof where the servants had their *godowns*, (Malaya) small rooms. There was a parapet, but rather a low one so whenever our parents were out we enjoyed flying kites in the hot weather. We were really not supposed to do this because the low parapet was potentially dangerous as we could have got carried away in our enthusiasm to cut someone else's kite or to defend our own ones. But when everyone was flying kites and all the multi-coloured squares filled the sky, it was irresistible.

"After five or six years of our house being the social centre for so many youngsters, the Jewish Girls' School moved to Park Street. The school grounds made our compound seem quite small. There were three badminton courts plus space for football and an indoor area for table-tennis. The Maccabi Club, using the grounds and part of the premises of the Jewish Girls' School for sport, became the

SPORT

new centre of gravity and it is here that so many of us have the happiest memories of our youth."

Eric Sopher explains how the Maccabi Association of Calcutta was established. "In 1949 Israel announced that she would stage the Third Maccabiah the following year and Jewish organizations from all over the world were invited to send teams to compete in all types of athletic events. The Maccabi Club in Bombay already existed and decided to send a water polo team, and at that time Nat Zachariah and I got together, called a meeting with a number of men from the community who were hockey players from different clubs, to see what interest they had in forming a Jewish team. It was decided that Calcutta should be represented by sending a field hockey team to Israel for the Games. Nat and I took upon ourselves the task of forming the Maccabi Association of Calcutta, organising training, team selection, transport, uniforms, funds and various other details. In this Robin Shellim and David Nahoum were most helpful. Our meeting place was the Judean Club in Madge Lane and Lady Ezra agreed to be our Chairwoman, Nat Zachariah was elected Honorary Secretary and I was elected President. The team was captained by Sam Luddy.

"Nat was an excellent coach and worked tirelessly to mould a good team of hockey players. The visit was a great success." Sam Luddy picked up the events in Israel. "We stayed in the Maccabiah Village and made friends with teams from several other countries. The atmosphere was great. In 1950 food was rationed in Israel but they did us a favour by giving us an egg a day and meat in our diet. The opening ceremony in the beautiful stadium in Ramat Gan was tremendous and very moving. Our team wore green turbans and white flannels and blazers. We played several friendly matches but in the Games we were beaten by Israel - 1:0. I still have the commemorative medal they gave all the athletes who participated in the Games. We didn't really have the time for very much practice before we left but we were all friends and played quite well as a team, having most of our practice sessions on the *Maidan*. Apart from enjoying the Games, we managed to fit in some sight-seeing in that week and had a lovely time."

Eric Sopher continued: "After the team returned from Israel, a dance was organised to raise funds to pay for the debts that remained. Although most of the players paid their own fares there were several other costs to be met. The dance was very successful but it did not clear our entire debt and Lady Ezra volunteered to pay the balance at our Maccabi Board Meeting.

SPORT

"Perhaps more important than the Games itself, was the fact that the Calcutta organisation continued. We were able to use the grounds of the Jewish Girls' School and Hostel in Park Street and built flood-lit badminton courts where increasing numbers of our young people spent many happy evenings."

Marianne Arakie and Helene Sopher picked up the description of events at Maccabi. Marianne said: "Everything in our lives revolved around Maccabi. We never missed an evening if we could help it. There was basket-ball in summer, badminton and hockey in winter, and table-tennis all the year round." "And don't forget" Eze reminded her "that we could also play football although there wasn't a proper field and it wasn't organised, but the chaps could certainly kick a ball around." Helene added "At first Nat Zachariah was our basket-ball coach. I really looked up to him and adored him because he took a great personal interest in us all. He made each and every one of us feel that we were especially good at sport and brought out the best in us. After a few years Bolek Rembaum took over as coach. He was a first class player from Poland and raised our play to such a high standard, we became one of the top basket-ball teams in Calcutta. We had three divisions, so that everyone got a chance for a game, no matter what their level of play."

David Einy recalled the time when Maccabi challenged the jockeys of the Tollygunge Club for a game of basket-ball. "We decided we would do it in style. So we saddled our horses, wore our racing colours, with our silk caps and riding boots and rode down Park Street to the Maccabi grounds. We held up the traffic and people gaped at us. We even arranged for a photographer at the grounds and hoped that all this showmanship would impress the girls, but they didn't know what on earth was going on and they were more overawed than impressed. Pity!"

Helene said "Maccabi was our life. At least fifty youngsters turned up four evenings a week plus the weekend. When we played exhibition hockey we had to practice five times a week, very early in the morning. We played in tournaments at our club, outside clubs, and on the *Maidan.*" "Come to think of it," Marianne continued "our parents never came to watch us play, nor did they come when competitions were on. They simply left us to it, knowing that we were in 'the right company' which is what concerned them most of all. For our part, all our fun was very innocent, we knew our parents' values and had a strong sense of loyalty and respect for the older generation. What remains in my mind, perhaps even more than the sport I enjoyed so much, was the spirit among us. It was the spirit of fun and good sportsmanship and simply getting together to laugh and talk. Some people turned up just for the company. There was quite a bit of hanging

SPORT

about waiting for a game, so it's just as well the social side was so good." Maisie Sadka Meyer said: "While there is no doubt that the social side was important, the keen sense of competition should not be overlooked." She herself played in Maccabi and won the Bengal Open Championship for badminton in 1959.

Esther Moses Solomon recalled: "An Inter-Club Table Tennis Tournament was organised by the Women's Sports Association of Bengal in 1952. Maccabi won three titles at the finals - the A Division Team Championship, Open Singles and Open Doubles. It was a great and proud day for Maccabi who were represented by Noreen David, Ethel Morris, Marianne Sadka and myself."[7] Esther competed in the 19th World Table Tennis Championships organised by the Table Tennis Federation of India in 1952. "My aim was to be No. 1 in West Bengal for which I had to work very hard. After losing many matches in the Finals, I continued to persevere and in 1952, to my great satisfaction, I beat the then Bengal's number one for the first time. I won several tournaments thereafter and held the title of number one for two or three years."

Eze remembered: "I thought the tournaments between the Old Crocks and the Young 'Uns was great fun. I loved taking part in that." An article in the *Shema*[8] reads: "The finals of the Maccabi Badminton Tournament were played on the 15th February 1956. The most exciting game of the evening was the Ladies' Doubles which was won by Miss L. Lanyado and Mrs T. Zachariah, affectionately known as Tilly, against Miss S. David and Miss F. Sadka. (The winners) proved once again that badminton is not the monopoly of teenagers. (Tilly's) style and play was much admired and although she later confessed that she was rather nervous all through the game, nevertheless she certainly did not show it."

Marianne talked of additional Maccabi activities : "The bike rides were great fun and we arranged this among ourselves. Every Sunday morning we woke at the crack of dawn and hired bikes from the bike shops at Kydd Street and Sudder Street. There was no problem to get out of bed so early in the morning. A few people had their own bikes, but most of us didn't. Sometimes we rode two on a bike. It was quite safe as there was hardly any traffic about at that hour. About twenty or thirty of us between the ages of thirteen and eighteen would be at the *Maidan* by six o'clock, ride to the Victoria Memorial, a distance of two or three miles, and have drinks and take a rest. Then we would head for home and get back by eight for a good breakfast."

Helene added: "Another great pastime was the jam sessions among

SPORT

Maccabi members. Whoever had a gramophone and willing parents had the makings of holding a jam session. They were so popular, we would have them all the time. Sometimes we took a gramophone on picnics and spent as much time as we could dancing out-of-doors."

Helene continued: "Once a year we went to Agarpara to play the team there. They used to come to us too. They were really a crack team because they would play every single day. And the idea of a game and a picnic grew from these visits. When we went as far as Agarpara we made a full day's outing of it and the organisers arranged everything, the fixtures, the transport, lunch, the lot. There was an enormous amount of work which went on behind the scenes and it all went so smoothly we scarcely realised what was going on. Regina Abraham, Bertie Meyer and David Nahoum all worked very hard."

Some of the organisers were characteristically modest about the part they played. Regina Abraham Meir said: "Maccabi was a very important part of our lives, and while it is true there was organisation behind the games, competitions, picnics and special functions, what I remember most is simply having fun. I didn't just get involved with organising, I played too. A lot of people helped; different people at different times, so the load was shared, even from evening to evening. David Nahoum also worked extremely hard to increase our membership and persuaded many young people to join. There was a very small monthly subscription as the idea was that no one should be excluded for financial reasons. It was more by way of keeping a record of our membership than raising funds."

Bertie Meyer agreed. "We relied very much on donations for equipment and for outings. When we were short of money we approached friends and family personally and there were many private handouts. When we went to Riverside in Agarpara for picnics, and this was a very popular spot, Alpine Dairy gave us free ice-cream on the authority of Nissim Elias (one of the directors). Hirsh Curlender's flat overlooked our grounds and our flood lights were connected to his electricity meter. He never murmured about how much we used. Violet and Kitty Mashiah always organised the food. When we went to Riverside, in particular, the cooking facilities there were very useful. All the ingredients were taken down by car and the cooking would be done fresh, on the spot. It was no ordinary meal, it was a feast, with chicken, *aloo makalla,* the lot. We wanted everyone to have a treat - the well-off and the not-so-well-off. When we went out for the day we provided lunch and tea, and the Nahoums contributed all the cakes and pastries. In this way we made the best of the day and returned home by nightfall, most of

SPORT

the youngsters singing all the way back."

A report in March 1956 in the *Shema*[9] describes a Maccabi picnic. "The Maccabi picnic, held at Riverside on February 5th was a tremendous success, enjoyed most thoroughly by young and not-so-young alike, who know from past experience that Maccabi picnics are proverbial perfect social functions.... First mention must be made of those who organised the picnic. Aaron Silas showed great capability with his team of co-workers, in handling the arrangements. Thanks are also due to Misses Violet and Kitty Mashiah who undertook to prepare a sumptuous lunch. These two ladies had a very busy morning but the appreciation was so wholehearted, the effort was really worthwhile. M/s. Nahoum & Sons who catered for a high tea also made an excellent contribution towards the picnic. Transport was arranged to ensure that those picnickers who could not get to Agarpara in private cars were nevertheless assured of a comfortable journey.

"The day dawned cold and crisp, with the sun shining in a cloudless sky. Early in the morning the first busload arrived at the beautiful garden house of Mr & Mrs J.R. Jacob who were, as usual, kind enough to loan their premises for the occasion. The flowers were in full bloom and the various colours splashed amidst the beautifully cared for green lawns. The river, gliding peacefully by, with occasional country craft, added perfection to the setting.

"Everyone was in a fervour of energy and it wasn't long before games and sports were organised ... there were plenty of small prizes for lucky winners. As the sun began to climb higher in the sky, several young people decided the swimming pool was simply irresistible.

"There was one feature at this picnic which was new and creditable. Reverend Silas ... decided that since there were so many young men present it would be an excellent idea to hold the customary evening service. Prayers over, Tony De Souza and his band arrived. Dancing, as ever, proved very popular and this merry-making went on till late into the evening..."

Sport was by no means the only leisure activity enjoyed in the community but was one which appealed to large numbers of people; to those who excelled and who competed for the sake of the challenge, to those who enjoyed the social side as much as the sport, and to those who combined sport with entertainment. Perhaps we didn't realise it at the time but sport, among other leisure activities, opened windows on the wider world in which we lived. Playing with, and

SPORT

competing against, people from other communities enabled us to extend our contacts with them in our leisure hours and the barriers between us became blurred. There were several people who expressed their talents and abilities in drama, dance, music and singing for example and more often than not this meant joining groups of people right across the spectrum of religious affiliation. Occasionally, the Jewish community came together to put on a performance, either at the invitation of an organisation outside the community to promote a multi-cultural celebration, or we pooled our talents for our own fund-raising purposes. Just as the Maccabi was a sports club primarily for the benefit of the Jewish community, there were other small groups set up with different objectives within the community, such as the Over Sixteens where they concentrated on drama.

Once we freed ourselves from being shackled to the world of work and domesticity we began to move away from a lifestyle we had brought with us from our countries of origin. Instead we moved towards a range of activities, following the example of the British. It is from them that we, and other communities of the Raj, came to enjoy so many different ways of using our free time constructively.

Moshe Lanyado at the Wellesley Square Tank, Calcutta, 1933. All his medals were for swimming and diving events.
Courtesy: Seemah Lanyado.

INDIA'S FOREMOST PHYSICAL DIRECTOR

Dr. JOE SOLOMON, D.PH.E. (Ceylon), F.I.C.M., F.I.PH.D. (Delaware), S. G/L. D.O. (Eng.)

Official Holder Of The Title "BENGAL'S STRONGEST YOUTH" (1937-39)
&
Breaker Of Many BRITISH EMPIRE & ALL INDIA Weight-Lifting Records.

ALSO

Director Of THE ZIONIST INSTITUTE OF PHYSICAL PERFECTION, Official Technical And Statistical Adviser To THE INDIAN EMPIRE WEIGHT LIFTERS' ASSOCIATION, Secretary Of THE ALL INDIA STRAND PULLING FEDERATION & Chairman Of The ALL INDIA MEN'S PHYSICAL EXCELLENCE COMPETITION STANDING COMMITTEE.

A noteworthy performance recently accomplished by Dr. Solomon, was the passing of a Limousine (BUICK) Car over his abdomen. A great and unexampled feat, which excited the admiration of an audience well over 5000.

1945. Solly Sopher leads Trickster's Toy owned jointly with the rider, David Einy at the Tollygunj Turf Club.
Courtesy: David Einy.

Rina Einy Margulies. A practice session. Los Angeles Olympics 1984.
Courtesy: Arleen Einy.

Members of the Maccabi Basketball team with their banner. Maidan, Calcutta 1955. Standing: Hanny Cohen, Marianne Sadka, Florence Judah, Louisa Lanyado. Seated: Ramah Cohen, Rachel Silliman, Sylvia David, Fay Abner.
Courtesy: Louisa Lanyado Platt.

PART TWO

Chapter 10

RITES OF PASSAGE*

Religion is concerned with beliefs, values and customs. Judaism, based on monotheistic belief and a revelation of the Law on Mount Sinai,[1] includes a series of customs which punctuate our lives in the cycle from birth to death. These rites of passage reflect, in the main, values and customs which derive from religious belief, but also include superstitions. Our values and practices are essentially about social relationships at different times and in different places and as these have varied, so too has the fabric of life in Jewish communities. Even within the confines of a community as small as that in Calcutta, there were some differences in custom between families, although they were not of particular significance. It is these differences which are fascinating because they throw light, both on elements which are essential to the cohesion of Jewish communities, and on the freedom of individual communities to develop their own *minhagim,* (H) customs and traditional practices, all under the umbrella of Judaism. Although congregational worship is important in Judaism, it is the family that has been at the heart of observance. By watching, hearing and participating, each child in every generation absorbs the customs, not only of the celebration of the Sabbath and festivals but also of personal and family joys and sorrow, the milestones in marking out an individual's passage through life. In this way religious experience, culture and daily life have become intertwined in an inseparable whole.

The Jews of the Raj enjoyed complete freedom of religious belief and practice. Judith Brown has observed[2] "India is a religiously plural society ... the majority of its people are Hindu. Religious minorities originated in waves of migration, in movements of reform or conversion. The largest minority are the Muslims. The Christians were scattered groups who responded to European missionary activity, though there was a far older group ... whose origins were claimed to lie in the preaching of St. Thomas. ... The Sikhs were a sixteenth century reform group, born in the interaction of Muslims and Hindus in the Punjab and North West. Some tiny groups fled centuries ago from persecution or

---

* All those who participated in the discussions here come from families who observed religious practices and customs so that an authentic picture of tradition may be portrayed. They are also affluent enough to show practice unrestricted by financial considerations.

wandered in search of prosperity and arrived in the sub-Continent: India's Jews and Parsis are such. ... (these) minorities tended to be separate social units, following their own customs and marrying ... within their own community ... (they were) separate and closed groups yet interdependent on the rest of society." Beliefs, values and those practices which joined Hindus and other religious groups to their own communities, separated them one from another, in matters of social relationships through the operation of food and drink taboos, concepts of purity and impurity, separation of men and women, and distinctions between the religious and the secular.

Although many of the customs and superstitions from Baghdad stayed with us throughout the nineteenth century and into the twentieth century, our daily lives were lived in a land which was at a confluence of other religious beliefs, customs, and superstitions which were all practiced publicly. In our small community, "nestling among others with varying degrees of sophistication, it (became) necessary to cope with the hazards of everyday life (illness, childbirth, and death for example) in a world where forces impinging on people seem(ed) explicable only in terms of demonic possession. Consequently there are ceremonial ways of dealing with paranormal forces and (which) have been given a vital religious significance."[3]

The first rite of passage came with birth. Sassoon[4] states: "Childbirth (among Baghdadi Jews) is still connected with many superstitions, fears and protections ... from demons and evil spirits... (some of which are) familiar to the reader of the Talmud which suggest that Baghdadians kept these ... rites since ... antiquity."[5] Meyer adds[6] "(During) the first forty[7] days after childbirth, demons and spirits were particularly menacing. Therefore a clove of garlic,[8] (and) strings of amber beads[9] ... were hung by the bedside of the child or mother." In addition an *"Afsa* and *Dahash* (A) nutmeg[10] strung together with a turquoise (coloured)[11] disc, pierced with seven holes or 'eyes' - prophylactic against the evil eye[12], and a symbolic hand,[13] (made of silver with the name of the Almighty engraved on it) for divine protection (was) worn as a charm." There were certain nights when mother and child were said to be particularly vulnerable. Sassoon wrote: "(These were) the night of the sixth day,[14] *sitti,* (A) and the evening before the eighth day. During these nights the child must be borne on the lap and must not be in the cradle."[15]

Ruby Benaiah describes the tradition of *Shasha* (A) distribution, six days after her daughter was born in 1932. This custom is also observed for boys. "We gathered together large quantities of gram (roasted chick peas in their skins), salted and roasted pumpkin seeds and peanuts, all in their shells, almonds and dates in their skins, puffed rice, puffed corn, and wrapped sweets.[16] We mixed this together and put a couple of generous handfuls into paper bags. Then we added small change to each packet. Some people used to put in a little gift instead of money. As usual, the news soon got round to the children in the neighbourhood that there was a *shasha* in our house, and they all came - no invitation was ever necessary. When about twenty-five to thirty children had gathered together in the afternoon, they began to chant *"Shasha Shasha!"* demanding their distribution. The louder the noise the better.[17] The paper bags were then distributed amongst the children and when they got what they came for, they went back to their homes. Later, we heaped portions of *shasha* on to plates, covered with pretty serviettes, and stacked them on a silver tray. We sent a servant round to all our relatives to hand out *shasha."* If the *sitti* was during the festival of Passover, nuts and dried fruit such as almonds and dates, which had no leaven, were distributed.

Ruby continued - "Girls were usually named on the sixth day, but this was not strictly necessary, as it could be done at any time. It was the custom to give the privilege of naming to an older member of the family and we asked one of my uncles to do it. We named our daughter after my mother-in-law, as it was my husband's right to choose a name from his family for the first child. We prefer to name a child after someone who is living."[18] In fact there was considerable flexibility in the community about naming a child after the living or the dead and some people were superstitious about having a child named after them in their lifetime. Elias and Elias Cooper[19] explain further: "Children were never named after their parents, except when the parent was dead before the naming, in which case it was obligatory."

Girls were usually given a single name by saying: "May He who blessed Sarah, Rebecca, Rachel and Leah, bless this beloved child, and her name shall be ......" while the baby was held by the person who named her, and her parents and assembled relatives looked on. The sounds of ululation would then be mixed with jubilant congratulations, *Mazal tov, Mazal tov!* (H) good luck. Ruby said "In the evening after the *sitti* we had a dinner party at home for relatives and friends. It was quite a big affair, going on until about six in the morning.

"When the first child was born, the parents of the mother usually paid for all that was needed for the baby. Clothes, cradle, pram, and anything else they wished to give, each family according to their means."

RITES OF PASSAGE

The birth of a firstborn son was cause for great celebration. Sons were preferred to daughters[20] almost until the time when the exodus from India was in full flood. David and Sophie Elias described the rites when their first son was born. On the eighth evening they celebrated the *Akd-el-Yas*. "We borrowed the Chair of Elijah[21] from the synagogue on which we placed the Pentateuch, opened at the portion of *Pinhas*.[22] This was covered by a richly embroidered cloth, and all those who wished to kiss the book could do so at the proper place, or make a wish, and pick up a sprig of myrtle[23] with which the Chair was decorated, to make a blessing on it." Sophie said: "We applied henna[24] to the palm of a hand, and when the colour had taken, an impression was made on a wall of the house, called *Panja*, which is the number five in Hindi, to safeguard mother and child from the evil eye." David continued, "portions of the *Zohar*, (H) mystical texts were read and afterwards we gave a great dinner party.[25] It was open house, and everyone was welcome. We had a musician to entertain the guests on a harmonium and he sang mainly Arabic songs while everyone was eating, drinking and enjoying themselves. While the feasting was going on we lit candles, one large one in particular which we saved from the celebrations of our wedding dinner party. We lit and placed several little candles on a silver tray together with small silver bowls. It looked really beautiful! The tray was passed round from hand to hand, while everyone was dancing and singing '*El-Eliyahu, El-Eliyahu, Bizcouth Eliyahu*', (H) (God of Elijah, send Elijah to us), while clapping their hands, and people placed donations in the bowls. We gave this money to charity although some prefer to give it to the synagogue, but the candles we kept as souvenirs.

"The next morning, which was the eighth day[26] was the *brit meela*, (H) circumcision, and naming of our son.[27] We had it in our own house although some people prefer the synagogue, particularly if it is a Saturday." David added: "While Sophie was pregnant I dreamt my grandfather came to me so we named our son after him and not after my father, which would have been the usual way. Since my grandfather was dead, we added the name Faraj, (A) salvation, to the first name Ellis. Boys were often given more than one name." If either parent or even a relative or friend dreamt that a certain dead person wished to be born into the family of a particular woman who was pregnant, then the child would almost certainly become the namesake of that dead person, assuming he or she was of the same sex. It was more usual to add the name *Hye* or *Hyeem*, (H) life, to the first name of a boy who was named after a dead person. No similar precaution was taken for girls.

Sophie continued: "We had the *brit meela* early in the morning so that

RITES OF PASSAGE

men could attend before they went to work because we needed at least ten men to be there (to form a quorum). As people came in they greeted us with *Siman Tov*, (H).[28] My mother was the godmother, *takhdumai* (A), (literally meaning, to bring forward) and she carried the baby and handed him over to the *sandak*, (H) godfather, (literally, the child's companion) who sat on the Chair of Elijah with the baby on his lap, supported by a pillow. David was the *sandak*, being the father, although in some cases this honour is given to a grandfather of the baby, or to a close relative. While the baby was brought in the men sang *ben ba lanu* (H) a son has come to us, while the women ululated - *'Killillee, killillee"*. The *Mohel*, (H) man who performs the circumcision, says the appropriate blessing and carries out the surgery: "Blessed art thou O Lord, King of the universe, who has sanctified us by Your commandments and commanded us to perform circumcision." The father responds with the blessing and adds the words: "... and commanded us to bring this boy named .... into the covenant of our father Abraham." [29] In the Sephardi tradition a further blessing is added for having "given us life and sustenance and brought us to this happy season." David continued: "The *Mohel* then made the benediction over wine, dipped his finger into it, placed a drop into the mouth of the baby, and passed the cup to Sophie to have a sip. The custom was to suckle the baby straight away to comfort him."

The *Mohel* blessed both father and son and prayed that the newborn would fulfil the *mitzvoth* of studying *Torah* and performing good deeds. The *Mohel* at Ellis Faraj Elias's circumcision was Sassoon Cohen, a jolly man with a shock of white hair and a flowing white beard. His service to the community over a period of thirty years was exceptional as he performed seven hundred and fifty-two circumcisions between July 1920 and August 1950.[30] David said: "After the circumcision was over we invited all our guests, both men and women, to tea and cakes so that they could make the necessary blessings. That afternoon we had a fish *seyudah*, (H) special meal to honour the occasion, for the family, with *Mogli Roti*, (Urdu) round, flat bread, and chutney. Sophie's grandmother was too ill to attend the celebrations but she asked for food prepared for the circumcision to be brought to her so that she could say the blessings. She waited all day for this because in the confusion of so much going on we forgot to send the servant to her until the evening. After she made the blessings and had eaten, she was satisfied, and passed away peacefully. It was a sad end to a special day for the family."

On the thirty-first day after the birth of a firstborn son there is another ceremony called *Pidyon H'ben,* redemption of the first born son, to Israelite parents. If the father or the mother is a Cohen or a Levi, this is not necessary.[31]

RITES OF PASSAGE

The ceremony fulfils the following commandments: "Sanctify unto me all the first born,"[32] and "... and all the firstborn of man among your sons shall you redeem"[33] The Cohen is a descendent of the High Priest who is God's representative, and is therefore entitled to the redemption money provided he makes sure the ceremony is necessary by first establishing from the mother that she had no miscarriages and that the baby was born normally.

David and Sophie Elias again invited Sassoon Cohen to perform this ceremony. After he questioned Sophie, to make sure the *Pidyon* was necessary, she placed the baby in his arms and David offered him newly minted silver coins, four anna pieces, to the value of five rupees, to redeem their son, saying "Blessed art Thou, Lord our God, Ruler of the universe who has sanctified us with Thy commandments and ordained us to redeem the first born son" followed by the further blessing for having "given us life and sustenance, and brought us to this happy season." Sassoon Cohen then accepted the money and handed back the baby, saying: "This (the money) instead of that (the baby) and now I have received from you five shekels, (silver pieces) the child is redeemed according to the Law of Moses and Israel, and as you have been privileged to redeem this firstborn son may you also be privileged to fulfil all the Laws." The redemption money could be used by a Cohen as he wished, but he usually gave this money to charity. However, others would try to get the money off him to keep for good luck, to make into *tabees,* (A) charms, or simply to keep as a souvenir. This ceremony was held in the morning, and was followed by a customary[34] *seyudah* of cakes and other food to make all the prescribed blessings.

The next milestone in the life of a boy is his preparation for reading *Maftir* (H), the final portion from the *Torah* reading in the synagogue. Ellis Meyer was nine years old in 1925 when he was first called to read *Maftir* on the festival of *Simhat Torah,* (H) Rejoicing of the Law. He says that in those days it was not unusual for boys to be called to read *Maftir* at such a young age.[35] It was customary to choose a festival day when a boy read *Maftir* for the first time and as the synagogue was always very well attended on the the festival of *Simhat Torah* a large congregation was able to enjoy the additional celebration. Privileges of being called to read from the *Sefer Torah,* (H) scroll of the Law, were sold in our synagogues. It was a way of raising funds as there was no membership fee or payment for seats, as in other congregations. "Auctions were conducted in Arabic and the buyer was blessed in Hebrew at the end of each transaction. As in any auction, the highest bidder won the *Mitsvah.*"[36] "As this *Maftir* was so popular, the price rocketed" Ellis said.[37] His *estad,* (A) Hebrew teacher, taught him all the

RITES OF PASSAGE

relevant blessings, and the correct chants for the portions from the Law and the Prophets. He also had some practice reading from the *Sefer Torah* in the synagogue, as the Hebrew script in the scrolls is without vowels, punctuation, or music symbols.

On the morning of his *Maftir*, Ellis went to the synagogue with his family. "I wore a new suit and was allowed to borrow a gold watch and chain to put in my waistcoat pocket like my father and uncles when they dressed up for special occasions. I also had a new red velvet cap for the synagogue with gold *chumkee*, (Hi) embroidered sequins, which I really didn't like at all but it was the fashion at the time." His mother took several pounds of sweets and spices, cloves and cardamom, with her which she mixed and heaped on to silver trays in an ante-room in the synagogue. Shortly before that part of the service when the scrolls of the Law were brought out from the Ark, she gave handfuls of sweets and spices to everyone in the ladies' gallery,[38] while the synagogue *bearer* followed her, holding the tray. She was kissed by relatives and congratulated by all the women individually, usually in Urdu, *"Mubarak"* literally, blessed one. Blessings were showered on her - "may you see him a bridegroom", "may you see him and all his brothers and sisters under the wedding canopy", "may he bring you and your husband great credit ... in good health ... in happiness always." Another *bearer* carried a silver tray piled with sweets and spices for the men and boys, which was handed round by the *Shamash*, (H) beadle. Most of the sweets were sugar-coated carraway seeds, not much larger than a grain of rice. They came in a variety of colours and were delicious, but some of the sweets were larger, as Ellis had reason to remember. The children, in particular, ate some of the sweets, but the idea was to shower them upon the young boy who was to be called to read for the first time.

The reading of the *Maftir* was preceded by *pizmonim*, sung by *mayzamayrim* (H) about six to eight men, who were on the *tebah*, (H) the raised and railed area of the reader's desk in the centre of the synagogue. The more lustily they sang, the better they hoped to be financially rewarded by the family. As this was the festival of *Simhat Torah*, their final song was *Simhona, Simhona, b'Simhat Hatorah,* (H) Rejoice, Rejoice in the Rejoicing of the Law. Even children who were knee high knew this one and could join in while clapping their hands. Then everything went quiet, and the *Hazan,* (H) cantor, called Ellis to the *tebah* by his Hebrew names, followed by the names of his father and paternal grandfather. *"Eliyahu Rahameem, Meir David, Ishaq Meir."* The men called *"b'kabod, b'kabod!"* (H) with honour, while some of the women began to ululate.

RITES OF PASSAGE

Ellis remembers "as soon as I left my place I was pelted with sweets by the men and by the women upstairs; not just the little sweets but some big ones as well, and I had to protect my face with my arms because I was afraid the sweets would hit my glasses. I had to stand on a stool to be able to see the *Sefer Torah,* I was so small at the time but the reading went very smoothly and my *estad*, who was also the *Hazan,* was pleased. When I had finished reading my portion he called my father to read the *kaddish,* (H) mourner's prayer of praise, which could not be read by those whose parents were still living for fear of bringing bad luck, and *hashkabah,* (H) prayer in memory of the dead. My father pledged donations to the synagogue, to the *Hazan* and to the *Meyzamayrim*. I kissed my father's hand, and he blessed me, while placing his right hand on my head. I kissed my *estad's* hand, and he also blessed me. When I went back to where my family were seated, the men called *'Hazak u'barukh'* (H) be strong and blessed and I kissed the hands of my uncles who blessed me. My younger brothers would have been standing while I was reading, as a mark of respect. I then went upstairs to the ladies' gallery and had hardly got there when the older women began their *kileelee*. I kissed my mother's hand, and then all my aunts, and every one of them blessed me and said I had read beautifully." After Ellis returned to his place with his father, brother and uncles, the synagogue *bearers* came in with their brushes to sweep away the sweets before they were trodden underfoot.

The celebrations were continued at home. "We had a big party that evening. There must have been at least a hundred adults and kids rushing about in our house. It was mostly an eating party and the best part was the ice-cream. All my friends were there and I really enjoyed myself." In later years some *Maftir* parties were geared towards children and games were organised, or children were asked to wear fancy dress, but in 1925 good parties usually meant dressing up, eating excellent food, enjoying congenial company, and indulging the children. There was never any question of excluding one or other age group; children, parents and grandparents all seemed at ease socialising together.

The day after a boy's thirteenth birthday he laid *Tefillin*, (H) phylacteries.[39] This marked his coming of age, *Bar Mitzwa*,(H)[40] son of the commandment, after which he could make up a quorum of men for prayer and take on all other religious duties. Meyer [41] states "The injunction that phylacteries be worn by Jewish males on every weekday ensured that their links with Judaism would be maintained." Ellis Meyer recalls: "There was, as usual, a small gathering of relatives at home, early in the morning, because I couldn't have breakfast until I had said my prayers. My *estad* had taught me how to lay phylacteries and I learnt the portion of the

RITES OF PASSAGE

Law which would become part of my weekday prayers.[42] I had new phylacteries which my *estad* helped me to wear that first morning, and I was also given a new *siseeth,* (H) prayer shawl, and a blue silk embroidered case in which to keep them with my daily prayer book. I had to say my prayers aloud, and then followed on with a short *darush,* (H) religious discourse, on the importance of physical cleanliness before prayer. Afterwards we all had coffee with pumpkin and quince preserve, and chocolates, to sweeten the mouth on a happy occasion. This was always a modest affair and quite unlike the great festivities in the West with the obligation to give gifts to the *Bar Mitzwa* boy.[43] We never had any gifts either for our *Maftir* or *Tefellin.* This was our way. However, in later years the food became a little more elaborate and a birthday cake became a special treat." This was another small influence of the British Raj. Nathan[44] observes that in Singapore it was the custom for "the religious aspect of the occasion (to be) stressed throughout and when parties were held, they were usually far from lavish."

It was the girls who took centre stage when their marriage was arranged. I say girls, rather than women, because in my grandmother's day child marriages were quite usual[45] and girls were married in their early teens. In my mother's day they married in their late teens and in the generation after that, the early twenties were preferred. My aunt, Seemah Cohen, became engaged in 1930. "I was lucky to have a love match, having got to know Charlie on holiday in Madhupur at a time when arranged marriages were still common. There were some women who made many matches, some took money but others didn't. It all depended on their circumstances. There was never any question of a fee; people paid what they wished and they were quite happy to be generous if they were pleased about the match and the family into which their son or daughter was marrying. But there were also those who made the occasional match purely out of friendship. They might have known of a young man and woman they thought would be well matched and arranged an introduction - nothing more. There were different ways in which match-making was done, sometimes the parents of the bride and groom made arrangements themselves, without a go-between, if they knew each other well enough.

"A month before our engagement my father-in-law called on my parents to propose formally. Charlie had already proposed himself, but that wasn't really enough. When my parents accepted the proposal it was called *Bath Pucca*", (Hi) confirmation. "It was usual to give the bride-to-be a modest gift on this occasion, and Charlie gave me gold bangles. My mother then offered *misry* to all of us saying, *'Moo·meetha kurow'"* - (Hi) sweeten your mouth.

RITES OF PASSAGE

My Aunt Seemah said: "The *Mileek* (Hi) engagement, took place one month after the *Bath Pucca*. It was an early evening affair and I wore a lovely dress made by a French dressmaker, Madame Vidler, who was the best at the time. It was made of beige silk with appliqué, and was just below calf length. All the women were dressed in beautiful clothes and jewels, and the atmosphere was great. Charlie himself was so jovial, he set the mood for everybody. We must have been at least seventy to eighty people among family and friends. It was not the custom for relatives and friends to give engagement presents as they do nowadays.

"The engagement celebrations usually began at the home of the parents of the bridegroom. Their relatives and friends gathered there for a reception, where they arranged *khoonchas,* which were brought over to our house. When they arrived they were greeted with congratulations and blessings. One of the trays was full of flowers for button-holes which we handed round to all the guests, and another full of *misry*, sweets and chocolates. In those days Nahoums used to import lovely sweets and chocolates from England and Europe; marzipans, sweets with jam centres, sugar almonds, sugar syrup, and chocolates with a variety of centres. These were passed round to the guests to sweeten their mouths.[46] There was another tray with a jewel box where my engagement ring was placed, and I chose a solitaire diamond set in gold. Charlie and I had to sit side by side on a couch. As my mother-in-law had died a few months before, my sister-in-law Rachel put the ring on my finger." Musleah explains[47] "If the .... father (of the bridegroom-to-be) is a widower (he) is excluded from this ceremony, probably to preclude all association with sadness or ill-luck, in which case a sister or a brother's wife or a near female relative fills the role. The fiancée was banned from doing it himself, as it constituted *Kiddushin*, (H) betrothal which, in the event of the termination of the association, required a bill of divorce. The law was stringently enforced in Calcutta." My Aunt continued: "My parents gave a tea party with all the usual Nahoum's cakes and pastries, besides what we made ourselves at home. Sandwiches, *dal sumoosucks, filowrees*,[48] (Hi) the lot. As for the ice cream, it was grand! Everyone enjoyed it. In those days Buchoo, one of our relatives, used to make just two flavours, vanilla and raspberry, and he came with coolies following him, carrying the ice cream churns on their heads. He would make ice cream by hand in his house, in churns centred in stout wooden buckets. (The space between the churns and buckets was packed with crushed ice, saw dust and saltpetre).

"We didn't have the usual *dakaka* (A) because Charlie's mother had not been dead for a year and he was still in mourning; in fact we had no kind of music at all. Frankly, I didn't mind there was no *dakaka* because I didn't care for it myself and it was going out of fashion anyway." Musleah describes *dakaka* "a woman adept in the art of drumming and playing the tambourine. She also displays her expertise in balancing a glass full of liquid or the candy tray on her head."[49] While she did so she sang love songs, and bawdy songs, mostly in Arabic, and the guests gave her small tips.

My aunt continued: "During the period of engagement, the bridegroom sent a trusted servant to the home of the bride with a tray, for every festival. This would contain sweets; *baklawa*, or chocolates, and a trinket, with a few flowers. People sent whatever they could afford. Sometimes it would be a piece of jewellery which had been in the family, sometimes expensive jewellery bought for the occasion, or it might have been an ornament which was not particularly expensive. In *Pesah*, there would be no sweets, just flowers and a gift. At *Hannukah* and *Purim* Charlie sent me a brooch and a ring, and for *Pesah*, a pair of ear-rings."

The *dakaka* came into play again at the next ceremony, the night of the *Khadba*, (A) dyeing with henna. Meyer[50] observes: "Special attention was paid by Baghdadi Jews to the ... eve of the wedding. The groom sent henna[51], sweets, wax candles and shoes to the bride's home where the nails of the bride were painted with henna to protect her from evil spirits [*al kabsa*]. All these ceremonies were accompanied by Hebrew and Arabic songs, sung by distinct groups of singers, each with its own repertoire."

Lillian Abraham describes the scene of her own *Khadba* in 1932 which shows that although we still kept to the old customs of Baghdad, there were signs that in some ways we were becoming Anglicised. "My *Khadba* took place three nights before the wedding, and ten months after the engagement. Invitations were sent out by word of mouth through women who were happy to do this for a small payment. (Casual work like this was given to many people who were glad of it; women in particular were restricted in the jobs they could do). My parents gave a sit-down dinner for about forty guests and I remember we had goose, which was rather special, amongst many other dishes.

"I wore evening dress, green crepe-de-chine inlaid with champagne lace, it was beautiful. In fact everyone was beautifully dressed, as we did for special occasions, complete in our silks, satins and jewellery. People started coming in at about six in the evening and when the boy's party arrived, they came with *khoonchas* made of copper, full of sweets and chocolates, flowers and henna, and there was a gift of a piece of jewellery for me. I had a diamond pendant. This present was usually substantial and the mothers of some brides set a great deal of store by this, as if their dignity depended on it. I have even heard of some men having to borrow money to buy a piece of jewellery for this occasion, it was considered so important. The boy and girl used to sit side by side on a couch and the gift was presented to her. We lit a very large candle, about five inches in diameter, but it was only for decoration and had no religious meaning".

Lillian's family broke with tradition by having English rather than Arabic music. She said "we had a gramophone and so we could have English music. The feasting and music went on until well past midnight. My fiancée wanted to take me for a drive after the party was over, but my father would not hear of it. After our engagement we were allowed out only with a chaperone. He was very strict with us; so strict in fact that I was only allowed to visit the homes of very few girl friends." Lillian's marriage was not arranged, nor was she related to her husband. They got to know each other personally while they both happened to be on holiday at the same time in Darjeeling.

"This was also known as the *Mhendee,* henna night. Henna was applied to the fingernails of the bride and bridegroom, but I didn't like it and just allowed the tip of my little finger to be done lightly." Musleah says[52] "... at such occasions ... hymns are sung in the presence of the bridal couple such as is found in the biblical Song of Songs and the Talmud. Various reasons (for applying henna) are ... warding off the evil eye or producing the hue of royalty. Later, the pulp of ground celery leaves was used when girls objected to the tint left by the henna." The custom of using henna as a cosmetic is prevalent among both Hindus and Muslims in India. Gifts of flowers, heaped on trays, from the bridegroom's party to the bride's house is also a Muslim tradition, but it is difficult to say in which community the custom actually originated.

Lillian continued: "A few days before the wedding it was customary for the family of the bride to give the bridegroom a new *sissith*, made of silk or wool. My family gave my husband a silk *sissith* with blue stripes, and a blue silk case which was embroidered with flowers, imported from Shanghai. They came in two colours; maroon and blue but the blue was more popular. The bride's family also gave the bridegroom a cap. We gave my husband one that my grandmother had made before she died. It was a beauty! and was really the most prominent one in the synagogue. It was made of black velvet with beautiful flowers embroidered in

RITES OF PASSAGE

all colours in chenille work in a classical design. None of the usual *chumki* work. This cap must have been made at least fifty years before our wedding.

"Parents who were able to afford a dowry gave their daughter cash plus a full suite of bedroom furniture, some pieces of jewellery, sets of bed linen, towels, and dresses and nighties."

When Ruby and Joe Cohen became engaged in 1944 they went out to dinner parties, to the cinema, and to social functions without a chaperone. They were fortunate in enjoying this degree of freedom because, as Ruby said: "My sister Flora was certainly chaperoned, and she got married only six years before me." Ruby and Joe fell in love and made their own decision to marry - "arranged marriages were just about dying out by then." They had many opportunities to meet before they became interested in each other because Ruby's elder sister was married to Joe's elder brother and family get-togethers were frequent. Even so, their engagement was a long one for those days; sixteen months, because Ruby was not quite sure of herself, she says, and she also wanted Joe to be certain of his decision. "Girls were never allowed to be independent and we were very protected. My father was old fashioned and strict, and my mother knew what he wanted, so she made sure that we did too." Ruby's precise words are interesting because it reflects a situation which was not uncommon in our community, and that is the chain of command which existed in some families. A father would not dream of disciplining his daughters directly, as this would have been embarrassing for both of them, so the mother usually became the intermediary. This custom is also prevalent in some Indian families. Ruby continued: "Looking back on it, their demands were reasonable, but at the time we were always pushing for more freedom."

The period of engagement was a busy time. Ruby and Joe set up their own household in preference to living in an extended family. A flat had to be rented, which was Joe's responsibility, and furnished, which was traditionally a joint responsibility, the bride's parents providing the bedroom furniture. Before the wedding there was a housewarming and Musleah explains:[53] "Moving into a dwelling place required the friendship of not only human neighbours but demonic ones too. Reconciliation began the night prior to one's moving. The following were ... harbingers of peace - a bible, a mirror, a new pitcher full of water, candy and a green vegetable."[54] *Mezuzoth,* (H) small tubes, containing a scroll with a prayer,[55] were fixed to the doorposts in the house, a universal Jewish practice.

RITES OF PASSAGE

All the household linen was part of a bride's trousseau, and her parents provided clothes to last a long time. Ruby kept several dressmakers busy, including Lillian Abraham and Zon from the Jewish community, and Madam Roshtan, a Russian emigrée who had built up a reputation as a fine dressmaker. The parents of the bride also paid for her dress and those of all her attendants. Ruby had one bridesmaid and two pages. Her wedding gown was bought and shipped by a friend in the United States. "We married just after the war was over and there was still a great shortage of imported fabrics in India. I had something special in mind; a white satin dress which included a satin train in very classical style, with a chiffon yolk. I described all this to my pen friend in the States, and she bought it and sent it on to me. It just needed a few minor adjustments to be perfect. I wore a finger-tip length net veil with a lace border, which was held in position by a head-dress of satin rose buds. My bouquet was also of white roses; they were beautiful, fresh blooms."

The wedding invitations were sent out, as usual, from the parents of both the bride and the bridegroom. Invitations were extended to an entire family, and children were never excluded. Gifts could be sent either to the bride or to the groom, depending on where the greater friendship lay. There was a time when gifts were displayed at the reception, in the style of the British in India, but gradually this practice was discontinued.

At the Saturday morning service in the synagogue, just before the wedding, Joe was called to make the traditional blessings before and after the reading of a portion of the Law. This is an honour for the *hathan,* (H) bridegroom, and before he was called up for the reading of the *Sefer Torah,* the congregation sang a special *pizmon.* As he is a Cohen, he was called for the first portion - a Levi would be called for the second portion. An Israelite *hathan* was called up for the third and subsequent portions.

Ruby recalls their wedding day. "It was a beautiful day, the sun was shining, and it was cool and crisp being mid-winter." Early that morning, Ruby, accompanied only by her mother, went to the *mikwa,* (H) special bath, for a complete immersion[56] which is supervised by another woman to ensure it is done correctly. She said, "Lady Ezra was quite happy for brides to use the *mikwa* in her house because it gave them more privacy than going to the synagogue. In spite of the fact she ordered the pool to be heated, I found it freezing cold."

In the meantime, Joe and his brother Ellis were busy making

arrangements for the reception. These arrangements and costs were traditionally the responsibility of the bridegroom and his family. Joe had a friend from the Marwari community (they are Jains, a sect of Hindus, originally from the state of Merwar), who had a beautiful home and garden in Ballygunj which is still one of the most fashionable suburbs in Calcutta. He gave Joe and Ruby the use of his garden for the reception, at which they had seven hundred and fifty guests, including Jews, Europeans and Marwaris. Joe had to cater separately for the Marwaris as they would only eat from confectioners in their own community. He said "It was one of the largest wedding receptions in the community. Not one of the usual reception rooms in Calcutta could accommodate so many guests at one time, we made inquiries everywhere." There were tables to lay, floral arrangements to be completed, a bar to be set up for soft and alcoholic drinks, a band and dance floor to be organised on the patio, and masses of servants to supervise for all this. Shortages after the war still persisted and whisky was not easily available. Joe said "whisky was controlled at the time. Fortunately I worked at the Bengal Chamber of Commerce and I was able to get two bottles a month. I was collecting whisky for months before the wedding." The requirements of two sets of caterers had to be looked after and Nahoums had to deliver a range of their goodies and put together the 175 pound, five tier wedding cake, which was the centrepiece of the reception. It was a hive of activity and all this time Joe was fasting.[57]

It was the custom in Calcutta to hold the wedding ceremony in the synagogue where the family of the bride worshipped. Joe and Ruby were therefore married in the *Maghen David* synagogue. Ruby's bridesmaid and attendants, together with the immediate family, were waiting on the steps at the entrance. When she arrived with her father, they made their way, followed by all their family and guests, to the far end of the synagogue, in front of the Ark, where the floor level is raised. The *chupa,* (H) bridal canopy, had been set up there. It was made of a heavy scarlet fabric, embroidered in gold thread with the Hebrew words *kol sasson v'kol simha* - the sounds of joy and gladness, which is included in the *Sheva B'rachot,* (H) seven blessings of the wedding ceremony.[58] The canopy was held up by four brass poles fixed to a wooden platform. As soon as Ruby arrived, Joe took his place under the *chupa,* and when Ruby joined him she stood at his right side, while their families gathered together around them. The bride and bridegroom faced their guests, while the celebrant and two witnesses[59] required by Jewish Law to validate the marriage, faced the bridal couple. It was Joe's privilege to choose the witnesses, who were Sir David Ezra and Nissim Elias, and the celebrant. Joe invited Reverend Albert Morris, the *hazan* of *Maghen David*

RITES OF PASSAGE

Synagogue to perform the ceremony. While cantors were often asked to officiate at their own synagogues, this was by no means taken for granted, but regarded as a privilege so a fee was not usually charged. However, sometimes the bride and groom chose to send a small gift of appreciation.

Reverend Morris commenced with two blessings, one over wine, which is usual for joyous occasions and the other over the wedding ceremony.[60] The wedding ring, together with a silver coin and a copper coin, had been put into the wine cup.[61] After the benedictions, Reverend Morris sipped the wine and passed the cup to the bridegroom and the bride to drink. The ring and the coins were removed from the cup and given to Joe. Then followed the reading of the *kettubah,* (H) marriage contract, which included an undertaking by the bridegroom to make provision for his wife, as befits a worthy son of Israel. "The bridegroom must show the witnesses the money (or the ring) which he will use in the ceremony, so that they know it is worth a *perutah* (H) (a coin of modest value in consideration for those who could not afford more). The witnesses must see when the bridegroom gives the money (or ring) over to the bride, as, through this transaction, she becomes bethrothed to him."[62] Joe then took Ruby's right hand in his left and said: "Be sanctified to me with this ring according to the Law of Moses and Israel" after which he placed the ring on her index finger (and then transferred it to the ring finger). This is the *kiddusheen.* By accepting the ring, the bride indicates her agreement to the marriage.[63] A *sissith* was placed over the heads of the bride and bridegroom by their male relatives and Reverend Morris chanted the *Shiva B'rachot* in his familiar rich, deep voice. It was the last ceremony he performed. The *sissith* was removed and Joe smashed a small china cup which he had brought with him. This is done in memory of the destruction of Jerusalem and is in keeping with the Psalmist's verse[64] - "If I forget thee, O Jerusalem, if I set not Jerusalem above my chiefest joy, let my right hand forget her cunning." The bride and bridegroom kissed and were blessed, kissed and congratulated by their relatives before going into the Ark in privacy, to kiss each *Sefer Torah,* known locally as making *zoor* (A).[65] Ruby and Joe then both signed the *kettubah,* followed by Reverend Morris and their two witnesses. *Minha* (H) afternoon service, was read and the bride and groom left the synagogue followed by their family and friends.

In the days of our grandparents, the bride did not sign her *kettubah.* It may have been considered unnecessary for her to have done so, as the undertakings in the contract were the responsibilities of the husband. The wife was bound only to be faithful by consenting, in the presence of two witnesses, to the *kiddushin.* The silver and copper coins used for Ruby and Joe's wedding were defaced beforehand by flattening, suggesting they had intrinsic value only, but this was not strictly necessary. They have been kept carefully with the *kettubah*.

Those who were superstitious, and there were many, would not open their *kettubah* case as long as both partners were alive. Since *kettubot* would only be required in the event of divorce to refer to the details of the marriage contract, it was thought to be unlucky to open the case.

Joe and Ruby's *kettubah* was printed in Bursa, Turkey, in both Hebrew and in English and was a tear-off page from a collection of *kettubot* which had blanks for the personal information to be completed, including the sum of the dowry in cash. Details of the value of the bride's trousseau and other wealth, such as the furniture and jewellery, were also included. This was a far cry from the days when *kettubot* would be hand-written for each wedding by a scribe in Hebrew, and the borders decorated with paintings of flowers, fruit, fish, birds and animals which were meant to be symbols of fertility. Joe and Ruby's cylindrical *kettubah* case of pure silver was patterned and inscribed with their names.

After the ceremony Ruby and Joe went for a drive to give their guests time to get to the reception and find places there. There was no such formality as table places being organised beforehand, no toasts, and no speeches. When the bridal couple arrived, all their guests stood up to welcome them, while the band played Mendelssohn's wedding march, another influence of the British Raj.

Ruby recalls "It was wonderful to be able to have a garden party for our reception. The flowers were in full bloom and everything looked so beautiful spread out on the lawn. We were lucky there was a patio because it meant there was space not only for the band but also for ballroom dancing, which is one thing which is usually missed at a lawn wedding. Joe and I cut the wedding cake, and it was then taken away, cut into pieces, stacked on to trays, and passed round to all our guests. Our parents went round from table to table making sure that all the guests were being properly looked after, and this gave everyone a chance to congratulate them. Then it was our turn to go round to each and every guest, to thank them for coming, for their good wishes and for their gifts.

"After the reception the immediate family went to my parents' house where they gave a dinner party for fifty to sixty guests. Joe and I changed into our going-away clothes as we decided to have a honeymoon rather than stay on for the traditional seven nights of feasting. Instead we had only one night when all the usual festive dishes were served, and we lit an enormous candle which we kept and then used again for our son's *Akd-el-Yas* a few years later. The atmosphere was great and full of excitement. Our wedding presents were all displayed at my parents' house because it wasn't possible to do this at the reception. The Marwaris have a tradition of giving gold jewellery to brides and they were extremely kind to me and gave me some beautiful pieces. After we had eaten and said grace, the *Shiva B'rachot* was chanted again, and then Joe and I went to the station, together with the whole family who came to see us off on our honeymoon. We went to Bombay, more than a thousand miles away, and as we couldn't get a coupé, we had company all the way! We were lucky enough to be able to stay at the Taj Mahal Hotel, just by the Gateway to India and although we didn't have *Shiva B'rachot* in Calcutta, we had right royal treatment in Bombay as we were invited out to dinner every night. Each one of Lady Ezra's family gave us a party and for Sabbath we went to my uncle who taught me to make my first *b'racha,* (H) blessing, over my Sabbath candles."

On the morning after the wedding it was customary for the bride's mother to send a tray to her daughter and son-in-law and to all the close relatives of the bride and bridegroom. This would contain a large piece of wedding cake, *baklawa,* and *misry* coated with *warak* (A) literally paper, or silver and gold leaf. The tray was covered with a beautiful cloth of embroidered brocade kept for special occasions.

On the first Sabbath after the wedding the bridegroom is again called up for the reading of a portion of the *Torah* in the synagogue. Some flexibility was introduced for those who went on honeymoon, and they were called up on the first Sabbath after their return. He was showered with little sweets and spices on his way to and from the reader's desk, as on his *Maftir* day. In the afternoon the men returned to the synagogue for afternoon prayers and Helen Jacob Judah who was married in 1941, recalls: "While the men were away, the close women friends and relatives of my family and my husband's family were all invited by my mother-in-law to her house for soft drinks, cakes and sweets. This party is called *Sabt el Niswan,* (A) the Sabbath for women, and is really quite embarrassing for the young bride because the older women tease dreadfully. Fortunately this get together went out of fashion around the time of the Second World War. The first time a bride visited her parents' home with her husband after the wedding was an occasion for another celebration for the immediate family and close friends, called *Fatah Wooch* (A) literally, the opening of the face, which symbolised that she was no

RITES OF PASSAGE

longer a child but a woman with free access to her parents' home. My mother gave a small tea party when she served much the same things as my mother-in-law for the *Sabt el Niswan*, cakes, *baklawa*, and other sweets. It is usual for parents to give their daughter a piece of jewellery at this party and my mother gave me a brooch; a ruby flanked by two pearls. The *Fatah Wooch* also went out of fashion about the same time as the *Sabt el Niswan*. For every festival in the year following my marriage, my mother sent me a *khooncha*, a gift with sweets, as this was quite usual in those families who could afford to give their daughters such treats."

Most of the rites of passage concern celebration, but as it is written in Ecclesiastes,[66] "To every thing there is a season, and a time to every purpose under the heaven: A time to be born, and a time to die; A time to weep and a time to laugh; A time to mourn ...." There are rites concerning death which are intended to help us cope with bereavement. These rites involve both mourners and the community, placing responsibilities and obligations on the community, and conveying values which suggest that there are many practices through which mourners can be helped in their grief.

Aaron Aaron recalled the death of his father in 1948. "He had been ill for a while and died at home. We shut his eyes,[67] and tied a handkerchief under his jaw.[68] Then we tied his legs together loosely, and his arms to his body. We lowered his body from the bed to the ground and placed a stone under his head as it is our custom to bring the body in contact with the earth as soon as possible.[69] He was covered completely with a plain white sheet and two candles were lit, one at his head and another at his feet."[70] Musleah states[71] "The corpse must not be left unattended (as a mark of respect and for reasons of protection). Psalms should be recited particularly by grandchildren or close relatives. .... All stored water in the household is poured to the ground."[72] Mirrors are covered in the rooms used by mourners as it is forbidden to pray in front of a mirror[73] and see one's own reflection, ie. a graven image. Aaron continued: "The Burial Board, *Oseh Haised*, (H) literally workers of kindness, were informed and it was not long before a few men came to our house to carry out the *rahisa*, (H) washing of the body, as we have to bury as soon as possible.[74]

"*Tahara*, (H) purification, involves cutting the nails, trimming the hair and beard, and internal cleansing. The body is washed with soap in a particular order and a *koolia*, (Hi) small clay vessel, is used for pouring fresh water over each part of the body, after which it is smashed[75] while specific prayers are recited. The water is not dried off so as to retain the condition of purity. I know all this because

RITES OF PASSAGE

I have assisted in this work myself, but in my father's time I had to stand outside the room,[76] and as each vessel was broken the sound went right through me as it was a repeated reminder of the finality of death.

"Although there are facilities for *rahisa* and *tahara* to be done at the cemetery, more often than not we used to do this at home. The *Oseh Haised* people would bring all they needed to the house so that mourners would not be burdened with responsibility."

The shroud is sewn by women[77] who cry *keena* (H) lament, as they do so. The fabric is of fine linen,[78] and was imported from Baghdad at one time. The stitching is very crude and draws attention to the temporary nature of the garment and of life itself. Men are dressed in baggy trousers and a shirt, and a cap is attached to the head. There is a hood and a flap which goes right over the face. A man's own prayer shawl *sissith* is wrapped over his head and around his shoulders but it is first made *pasool,* (H) unfit for holy use, by cutting one of the tassels. Women are dressed in a long shift. Rose water is sprinkled all over the body, to produce a sweet smell and during Talmudic times spices and sweet-smelling ointments were used.[79] The family are then called in to see the face of the deceased if they wish to do so, after which the entire body is wrapped in one piece of cloth and placed in the *aron,* (H) bier. The *aron* has no cover and is usually draped with a plain white cloth, or a *parochet*, (H) curtain or wall hanging, made of fine cloths like silk or velvet. If one has been presented by the family to the synagogue they may bring it back for the funeral. Should time permit in between death and burial an announcement is made in the synagogue because it is a *mitzwa* for people to attend a funeral and comfort all the mourners. However, on the Sabbath and on festivals such announcements are not made.

Sassoon has written:[80] "It is a peculiarity of the Baghdadian rite that a son mourning the loss of his parents ties a handkerchief round his neck." Musleah explains[81] that "this symbolises the shackles of mourning," and adds "At the commencement of the funeral, the officiant performs *kriyah* (H)[82], cuts the shirt or any other plainly visible garment, on the left side for children of a deceased parent, 'bearing the heart', on the right for other relatives. The mourners (men only in some families, men and women in others) tear the slit ... and say: 'Blessed are You, Lord, Ruler of the Universe who, in truth, ordains everything'."

Aaron continued: "We started the funeral service at home. After prayers there was a short *daroosh*, and then my brothers and I read *kaddish.* According to our custom the women in our family loosened their hair,[83] but did not go to the cemetery. They followed the bier for only a few paces.[84] Sons do not carry the bier of their fathers because of a superstition that demons may be up to mischief and make them stumble and drop the bier, but there is no fear about sons carrying the bier of their mothers. In those days there was no hearse and four men took turns in carrying my father's body all the way to the cemetery, reading prayers such as *Shocheneth* - Destiny of Clay by Ibn Gabriol, on the way. Women are honoured by reading *Aysheth Ha'il,* (H) A Woman of Virtue[85] for them, a short distance away from the cemetery. When we entered the cemetery the officiant made *hakafoth*, (H) circuits round the body seven times, (for men only) and those who wished to follow him did so. At the end of each circuit my brothers and I read *kaddish*. Money wrapped in paper was then thrown in particular directions across the body." Musleah states[86] "Two separate bundles, each containing five coins, are thrown across the bier in different directions - West to East, North to South, as the following verses are recited - 'Abraham willed all that he owned to Isaac. But to Abraham's sons by concubines Abraham gave gifts while he was still living; and he sent them away from his son Isaac eastward, to the land of the East'." [87] Dobrinsky explains:[88] "The reference to the 'children of the concubines' is to the *mashhittim* or *shedim* (H), heavenly antagonists, who might come with claims against the deceased man for having sinned. The coins would therefore be offered to satisfy them, so that they would release him from any possibility of justified claims they might have against him."

Aaron continued - "We then proceeded to the grave which had already been dug by Jews. It was only on festival days that we asked Muslims to do this for us and paid them after the festival. The sides of the grave were lined with bricks and clay half way up, say about three feet from the bottom. The white sheet which was covering the bier was spread on the ground, and my father's body was lowered whilst reciting Psalm 111. Friends held a sheet, as a canopy, over the grave. We never used coffins as it was not required by the law of the land and in Jewish Law the body has to be in contact with the earth. As I am the eldest son, I had to go into the grave, lift the flap across my father's face and sprinkle dust into his eyes from the Holy Land.[89] The officiant then addressed my father by name and said: 'Moshe, Ibn Rahael, dust you are and to dust you shall return. Give *mayheela* (H) forgiveness, to all, from big to small'." Family, relatives and friends each took a handful of earth and sprinkled it in the grave. Tiles were then placed over the bricks and across the tomb to form a pitched roof, and when this was in place the upper part of the grave was filled with rubble and mortar up to a few inches from the top, which was covered with earth. The grave was therefore a very solid structure and for this reason we were able to put the tombstone in place after a month.

"Again, according to custom, my brothers and I visited my father's grave on the third and the seventh days after his burial,[90] together with enough men (ten at least) to enable us to read the *kaddish*. If the family could afford it, they left money on the grave for distribution amongst the poor. Those who were able to, came back to our house for breakfast, but before leaving the cemetery we washed our hands but did not dry them,[91] saying: 'May He swallow up death forever and wipe away tears from every face'."

Meyer[92] has written - "The ancient *halakha* required that the mourners be provided with the first meal after the burial of a relative. The obligation rested on friends and neighbours and in this way the community became involved in the bereavement,[93] (they brought) ... hard-boiled eggs (symbolic of silence but also considered a source of life). During the prescribed seven days of mourning the mourners sat on mats on the ground. The usual Services were held thrice daily for seven days and then on Sabbath afternoons throughout the month after the burial. *Kaleicha* (A) flat cakes made from flour, butter and sugar and flavoured with saffron, were distributed among relatives and friends to symbolically release the deceased from obligations he may not have discharged. During the first year of mourning a wick was kindled in a glass containing oil and water. This rite was repeated on the anniversary of the death thereafter." Again, according to the custom of Baghdad, in the first year following a death, relatives of the deceased passed a rosewater bottle, *koom koom* (A) to each congregant in the synagogue to make the appropriate blessing.[94]

In explaining the bereavement custom concerning memorial refreshments, Musleah[95] says - "a *Shulhan*, (H) table, is laid offering odd numbered fruits and other foods ... as a sign of grief over the detachment and disjunction the passing on of the deceased has created in the evenness of the family and community. This is done on the seventh, twenty-second, and thirtieth day after burial and on the eve of the eleventh month and the first anniversay of death. Blessings are recited on the fruits of trees, the produce of the earth, products which do not grow from the earth or drink other than wine, and food other than bread, made from wheat, barley, rye or oats."

Meyer observed:[96] "For some, traditional Jewish beliefs and practices were upheld as personal religious convictions, for others it was a means of association"

RITES OF PASSAGE

between members of a group. The rites of passage described here underline the relationship between individual Jews and the Baghdadi community to which they belonged. This relationship remained unaffected by the slight variation between some families and others depending upon disparity in wealth, differences in countries of origin, influence of schools of thought, for example. However, the fact that most of our customs and practices can be traced directly to the *Torah* and *Talmud* show that the community remained largely endogamous, and the continuity of the community and its ancient faith and traditions is clear. The extent to which superstitions have crept into some customs reflect the fact that Judaism is itself of ancient origin. It has been practised in many lands, and has both influenced and been influenced by many peoples. Superstitions mainly surround the wonder of a newborn babe and the mystery surrounding death. Phenomena which are threatening and not properly understood are likely to arouse fear, and ways and means have been developed to counteract it by trying to regain control over life, often by resorting to non-rational means. Over a period of time magical methods of controlling unknown and unwelcome aspects of life have been imbued with the sanction of religion, which make them respectable and acceptable. In this way superstition and religion became enmeshed to a certain extent, and for many the two became indistinguishable. Rabbis and educators have denounced superstition, even likening it to idol-worship which is anathema to Jews, but their success has been limited and patchy. So far as the Jews of the Raj were concerned, generally speaking many superstitions were practiced until the time of the exodus, if not beyond it. In the main, however, the essential strength of community was in its link with the values of the ancient laws and practices of Judaism.

Above: Naming a baby girl. David Einy holds the prayer book while Aaron Abraham names Rina Einy.
Courtesy: David Einy.

Left: Chair of Elijah, Bombay. c. 1790.
Courtesy: David Elias.
Photo: Saul Einy.

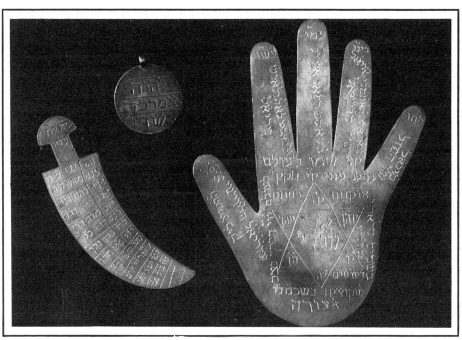

Silver charms for protection against the evil eye. The disc was usually worn by infants. The sword is an unusual shape for a charm. The open palm, *Chumsa* in Arabic and *Punja* in Hindi, means five. *Kabbalistic* inscriptions appear on both sides of the charm. The name of the Almighty dominates the centre of the Shield of David.
Courtesy: Seemah Lanyado.
Photo: John Hyman.

The *Bar Mitzwa* of David Solomon in Calcutta. David Einy helps him to lay *tefellin*, phylacteries.
Courtesy: David Einy.

Silk *sissith* cases with prayer book and embroidered cap. The cases were imported to India from Shanghai.
Courtesy: Eric Morris.
Photo: John Hyman.

Handwritten and painted marriage certificate, *kettubah*, of my grandparents, Meir Ezra and Masooda Musleah, Calcutta, 1887.
Photo: John Hyman.

The wedding of Joe and Kitty Abraham. 24.5.53. The celebrant, Isaac Musleah, facing the bride and bridegroom, chants the benediction over wine and the wedding ceremony.
Photo: Joe Isaac.

Kiddushin. The bridegroom places a ring on the bride's finger.
Photo: Joe Isaac.

A *sissith*, prayer shawl, is placed over the heads of the bride and bridegroom while the celebrant chants the *Shiva B'rachot*, Seven Blessings, over a cup of wine. Close family gather round the wedding canopy, *chupa*.
Photo: Joe Isaac.

The bride signs the *kettubah*, marriage certificate.
                Photo: Joe Isaac.

Marriage Certificate

The voice of joy and gladness
The voice of the Bridegroom and the voice of the Bride

On SUNDAY the FOURTH day of the month of SHABATH in the year 5706 since the creation of the world, the era according to which we are accustomed to reckon here in the city of Calcutta situated on the River Ganges how the Bridegroom JOE COHEN said to RUBY MOSES "Be thou my wife according to the law of Moses and Israel and I will work for thee, honour, support and maintain thee after the manner of Jewish husbands who work for their wives, honour, support and maintain them in truth. And I solemnly undertake to set aside from my own property a dowry in consideration of thy Virginity/Dowry of two hundred silver zuzim to which you are entitled according to Biblical/Rabbinical Law and thy food, clothing and necessaries and to live with thee in conjugal relation according to universal custom". And the said Bride consented and became his wife in accordance with the law of Moses and Israel and the property she brought from her father's house to her husband's house were ornaments, gold, silver, wearing apparel, bed and bed clothes amounting to Rs. _____. And the latter sum of Rs. _____ (promised by the said Bridegroom) and he further agreed to add for her benefit out of his own money to the principal amount of the Kethubbah an additional sum of Rs. _____ making in all namely Dowry, her outfit and addition together with _____ hundred zuzim mentioned above amounting to Rs. _____, and the said Bridegroom admitted acknowledgment of all these sums as having been received by him and he agreed and bound himself to be a debtor to this extent (to his wife) as all these things were in his custody, according to the usage of mort-main property should values depreciate they will depreciate on his own account and should they appreciate they will appreciate for his own benefit and thus the said Bridegroom declared to us "the responsibility and security of this 'Kethubbah' in respect of what she brought from her father's house and the additional sums which were settled on her are binding upon me and my heirs after me and she will have a lien upon all my properties, moveable and immoveable; and my properties will be security and pledge to enable her to realise from my most valuable goods and landed properties which I possess under the sun, what I have already purchased and what I may hereafter acquire and even the mantle on my shoulders during my lifetime and after my lifetime from this day and for ever; and I admit the binding and direct responsibility for all the obligations of the Kethubbah's in respect of her marriage portion and the additions will carry similar responsibility and the importance of all the obligations in respect of the marriage portion and the additions as are customary in all Kethubbah's made for the daughters of Israel acquired by dint of four cubits of ground in accordance with the usage and ordinance of our sages of blessed memory".

This contract is not to be regarded as illusory or as a mere formal document which may be annulled by means of false and frivolous excuses as is (sometimes) known to be done with all sorts of contracts the world over, nor can any circumstance render futile, void or illegal the various testimonies.

And we the undersigned witnesses acquired from the said JOE to the bride RUBY this bride his wife with regard to all that is written and detailed above with a complete and perfect acquisition from now onward by means of a garment fit for the purpose.

All these facts mentioned above are fit, clear, true, firm and established.

I ACCEPT ALL THAT IS WRITTEN AND DETAILED ABOVE.

Joe Abraham Cohen
Bridegroom

Witness

David Ezra
Witness

Reg. No. 104

CALCUTTA,

Bride

A. F. Morris
CELEBRANT
Minister
MAGHEN DAVID SYNAGOGUE

6th January 1946

Marriage certificate of Ruby and Joe Cohen, 1946, printed in Bursa, Turkey.
Photo: John Hyman.

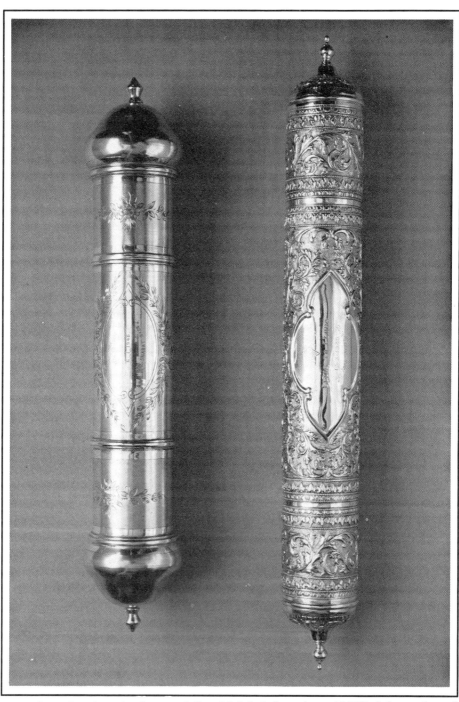

Kettubah cases in embossed and engraved silver. Made in India, early to mid 1940s, belong to Joe and Ruby Cohen and Ellis and Flora Cohen.
Photo: John Hyman.

A Jewish funeral procession c. 1943. The *aron*, bier is carried by men in turn and mourners walk or go part of the way in the cars behind.
Courtesy: Flower Elias & Judith Elias Cooper from "The Jews of Calcutta", 1974.

Chapter 11

FAITH

It is said that anyone wishing to know the traditions of the Jews of Baghdad in the nineteenth century should turn to India and the Far East in the early twentieth century. Linked only tenuously with their parent community, the Jews of the Raj were concerned more with guarding and preserving their religious traditions from Baghdad rather than allowing them to grow and develop locally. What, then, did religion mean to our parents and grandparents? What values did they have which flowed from their religious beliefs? How were these values expressed in their secular and religious activities?

When Iris Moses Ferris said "... and though there may be times when I do not comprehend Thy ways, my faith is unflinching and I bow my head to Thy Divine Will" in a prayer she wrote shortly before her death, she probably expressed one of the essential qualities of faith, and many stories can be told showing action to which it is related. Her friends, Flower Elias, Mercia Mansfield and Michelle Kraft, recall that when Iris was terminally ill in hospital she was still an excellent listener, giving her time and understanding to those who asked for it. Her bed was often surrounded by those who went to visit her with sadness but who left her with happiness. She entertained her visitors rather than expecting to be entertained, she kept their spirits high by remaining optimistic rather than expecting to be cheered up, she gave comfort rather than expecting to be comforted, and in spite of her pain she prayed "let my affliction enrich and not impoverish me and may it never be an excuse for lowering my standards." The whole question of standards or values which flowed from religion was imbibed in very early childhood, and if there was a price to be paid for maintaining them, then it was paid without flinching.

This can be illustrated by countless incidents, and the first I have chosen is one with which I am familiar. We were great talkers, not only as a family, but as a community, and we talked a good deal about times long past. In this way we learnt, through our elders, about our grandparents and great-grandparents, their way of life, the quality of their relationships, their values and mores.

One of my uncles, Isaac Musleah, told me of the days when the family was

FAITH

poor.[1] My grandfather earned a modest salary in a Jewish firm which closed on Saturdays and opened, instead, on Sundays. In this way he was able to observe the Sabbath as a day of rest from work. It was customary at that time to work a six day week, and with the exception of a small number of Jewish employers, Saturday was a normal working day. The prospect of my grandfather finding alternative work was not very bright, and as he had no entrepreneurial skills, the family had to endure difficult times. My grandmother had ten children and modest incomes did not go far, even in those days. The seven daughters had two dresses each; one to wash and the other to wear. There were times when they couldn't afford to buy tea and my grandmother had hot water and a crust for breakfast. There was money for bare necessities, such as house rent and school fees, but it became a struggle to find cash for such things as books and medical expenses, for example. Illness became a time of crisis because my grandmother believed that the higher a doctor's fee, the better the diagnosis and treatment. My uncle was the eldest surviving son, and although he had an older sister, she would not have been expected, as he was, to contribute towards the family income. The family hopes were therefore pinned on the day when he would leave school, and the fact that he was a bright and promising pupil didn't really bear consideration. He had to help support the family, and this he was eager to do to improve their well-being and comfort.

At that time many jobs were available through introduction, and an elderly gentleman who was a friend of the family, agreed to help by arranging a job interview for my uncle in a well established British firm. My uncle described his preparations. He had no suit, but my grandmother arranged to borrow one. He bought a pot of shoe whitener which he used to smarten his *solar topee* (Anglo-Indian) sun hat. He then spent a day polishing his bicycle, not only to make a good impression but to be sure there was no risk of soiling the suit.

He arrived for the interview looking very spruce and his hopes of success were high. The man who interviewed him was well-disposed, obviously impressed by my uncle's enthusiasm for work. A salary was agreed, and they began to talk about holidays when it became clear that the employer had no idea my uncle was not prepared to work on Saturdays. For his part, my uncle wrongly assumed the matter would have been cleared by his contact before the interview. Quite the contrary, the old gentleman didn't dream my uncle would have the audacity to expect any concessions. The employer was puzzled. Why was the young man making such a fuss about not working on the Jewish Sabbath? He was kind but firm, and not prepared to set a precedent. No, there was no possibility of making up the time on Sundays or by working extra hours during the week. The premises

FAITH

would be shut then, anyway. The unbelievable had happened. My uncle turned down his first job offer! His disappointment was great but his faith was deep. He had obviously made an impression on his prospective employer who shook his hand as he left and said "God bless you, son. You will succeed." My uncle went straight to the family friend who arranged the introduction to explain what had happened. The man was bitter. *"Mooth joo!"* he said in Arabic - "Die of starvation." My uncle summoned the strength to say "we may stay hungry for a while, but we won't starve. God will provide." My grandparents were disappointed but approving, for they themselves had imbued in their son the importance of staying true to his faith. Within a few months my uncle was able to get a job where he was not obliged to work on Saturdays. In fact he never worked on the Sabbath all his life, nor did this stand in the way of success, for from the day he started his first job the family never returned to their days of poverty and enjoyed an improving standard of living as the years went by.

Another example of faith put into practice is that of Azeeza Cohen, who trekked from Burma to India in March - April 1942. Her daughter, Renee Moses, kept a personal account[2] of the harrowing experiences she and her family endured at the time. They left Mandalay in great distress on March 8th. Renee wrote: "At last came the painful moment of separation, time to say goodbye to those we had to leave behind, not knowing what would become of them." They trekked through tracks of scorching sand, waded through paths deep in mud by river banks, and then had to face the challenge of narrow, winding ways of rock and stone in the highlands bordering Burma and India.

Azeeza Cohen was the head of a family of eight on the trek, with a baby one month old and two small children. Her concern for each and every one of them muted her care for her own well being. While they were walking in the mountains, less than a week before the journey's end, they "... saw Indian soldiers making *chappatis* and tea, which they very kindly gave to us. However, as it was Passover, my mother refused to eat *chappatis*." It was very rare to find food on the trek, and when it was available the cost was high. To refuse an offer, when hunger and thirst had been endured for three weeks of trekking was remarkable in itself. But bread had not been part of their diet since they left Mandalay, so it was a special treat. To refuse bread when the aroma was actually rising from the cooking required nothing less than deep faith and an iron will. So great was the faith of the people of this generation, and so important the values they attached to religious beliefs, that even in extremity they did not let their standards fall.

FAITH

At the time of their ordeal Azeeza Cohen was a grandmother and her age made her particularly vulnerable to injury and infection. She did, in fact suffer from dysentry in the last days of the trek in the mountains. Renee wrote: "We asked the officer in charge of the camp for medicine or medical advice. He informed us that there was a doctor in the village about a mile away and that we should go to him for help." This was after a whole day's trek! "I really was so tired but went to the village ... the doctor said he had the injection but no syringe, so I asked him what we should do, because we had been told ... that to stay behind meant certain starvation. We were also told that we would have to abandon the sick if they were unable to move. He then gave us two vials of the injection and said "give one to your mother to drink ... and pray to God." Renee comments: "I feel this also constitutes an act of faith on our part as we had to administer orally, medicine which should have been injected, and we had to pray for recovery.

"The next morning I was up at dawn, but was terrified to see how my mother was, because if she could not move we had an impossible choice to make. However, with all the courage I could muster, I walked into her hut and ... she was standing up, dressed and ready. I was thankful to God for his mercy. He had made the decision. I asked her how she felt and she said 'fine, the dysentry is cured'."

It was not only religious beliefs related to a Jewish background which were defended, but also values to be applied universally. Iris Moses Ferris's life personified such values which transcended the boundaries of community and extended equally to every man, woman and child she met, whether it was in a remote village in India or in the highest ranks of the Girl Guide movement in the United Kingdom, where she eventually worked.

Iris's father died when she was a young girl and she spent every weekend with her grandmother and aunt, Rahma Moses, a remarkable woman who devoted her life to teaching and working for the community in many ways. In the years that Iris was growing up and of an impressionable age, Rahma Moses, an essentially spiritual woman, transmitted to her niece a deep faith and a strong sense of traditional values.

Iris became a Guide and very soon after she completed her schooling, took over the running of the Eighth Calcutta Guide Company at the Jewish Girls' School, one of the best at the time, and had responsibility for about thirty girls between the ages of twelve and sixteen. The Girl Guide movement became the channel through which she directed her energies. Ray Shellim, one of her

FAITH

Company, said: "She started with a Jewish group and ended up with the top award for Guiding at state level. When she emigrated to England she joined the World Bureau of Girl Scouts and Girl Guides where she was second in command." Her lifelong friend, Flower Elias, said: "She could have had a teaching job for double the money in London, but with characteristic humility she preferred to join the Guide movement where she started off by making tea. She never went out for praise or put herself forward but her talents and qualifications became noticed and it wasn't long before she became General Secretary. She worked with the Guides in the UK from 1953 until 1970."

To go back to Iris's early days in Calcutta, Ray Shellim remembers: "She was a born teacher, everyone felt they had a direct line to her and she made everyone feel important. Although her weekly programmes were enjoyable and interesting, she made us realise that there was a lot more to Guiding than games, hikes, jamborees and days out. This message came over in a very natural way. Her quiet personality was combined with a deep understanding of human nature and she always tried to divert wrong thinking and action into right thinking and right action by going over the details of a situation and prompting us to pinpoint the negative ourselves. Her great optimism made us enthusiastic about being positive. In this way she guided our thinking so that we could see other points of view and rise above pettiness. In other words she brought out the best in people and because everyone loved her so much in response to her own affection, no one wanted to upset her."

Her friend, Mercia Mansfield, describes Iris as having no taboos. "She was a universalist in her outlook and not hidebound by any kind of orthodoxy." Her son Dan adds "she got on well with people from all walks of life. She was never in awe of the rich or patronised the poor. There was no difference in her approach to children or to the old", and remembers her saying - "if I can help one person it is enough for me." (This echoes the Talmudic saying that he who saves one life, it is as if he saves the whole world). Dan continued: "I was a small boy when we were living in Bandel, a village about twenty miles away from Calcutta, and my mother immediately got into Guiding there. She trained Guides to become trainers. There were some widows in the group who had no chance of any social life whatever and this was a wonderful outlet for them. I remember a great deal of fun and laughter as the women enjoyed the games and got very excited. Eventually my mother became the chief trainer for Bengal. Another thing about my mother; she was always late. Someone was always holding her up. Everyone seemed to know her and wanted to talk to her and she wanted to listen." Flower Elias added:

FAITH

"Her greatest regret about being in the UK was that one doesn't have the time and leisure to listen."

Ray Shellim remembers Iris as "a tremendous organiser. She was also a great delegater and roped in everyone to do their best and in this way every plan went well. She had a great sense of humour which meant she could smooth over disagreements." Iris brought the same charisma and leadership to her activities whether they happened to be at weekly meetings in a small school or at a jamboree in Government House. Her Guides were very enthusiastic because she inspired them to do their best.

In October 1954 there was a short account of the activities of the Guides from the Jewish Girls' School in the news-sheet[3] of the Calcutta Jewish community. Quite spontaneously the reporter added: "We cannot mention the subject of the Girl Guides Association without calling to mind a most beloved lady of our community who has now emigrated to the United Kingdom - namely Mrs Iris Ferris. Her association with the Guide movement has been long and distinguished and of particular significance is the part she played in effecting the merger of the Guides with the Bharat (Indian) Scouts. On her arrival in England just over a year ago Mrs Ferris explained the merger movement to Dame Whateley who represents the World Bureau of Guides and she has since become her personal assistant. The service and value of Mrs Ferris to the Association she so proudly represents have thus been fully recognised. Although we are not fortunate enough to have Mrs Ferris in our midst at the present time we are consoled by the fact that in the position she is now placed, and with her natural gift of deep human understanding, she is bringing sunshine to the lives of her new contacts just as she did here."

Iris died of cancer in 1970. Shortly before her death she wrote this prayer: "... if I must live, help me to live with joy, giving joy.... I am truly thankful for the glow in my heart and the strength ... given me through those who care; for the good days, short or long; for the resilience and renewal of spirit with which Thou hast endowed me; for all Thy blessings, great or small." At her funeral, Sammy Solomon's words were "Your spirit rare that graced earth but a while, Faced death as it had faced life - with a smile."

Iris's life reminds me of a story concerning the great Rabbi Hillel who was renowned for his patience, even in his lifetime. A man decided to put Rabbi Hillel's patience to test, so he intruded on him while he was taking a bath and said

FAITH

"I want you to teach me the whole Law while you are bathing and while I am able to stand on one leg." "Certainly" replied Rabbi Hillel, with complete calm. "Love your neighbour. If you can do that you will understand the whole of the Law and the whole of the Prophets. All the rest is commentary." Loving her neighbour, whoever that neighbour happened to be, was the driving force of Iris's life and in doing so she understood the values which were rooted in her own religion and which could be extended to embrace mankind.

Flower Elias recalls the story of the "vow child". "My mother, Jochebed Solomon, was living with her in-laws at this time. She had a rash and her husband's aunt, a difficult woman, tauntingly told her that it was leprosy. My mother was very upset and, during *Rosh Hashana* the Jewish New Year, at the synagogue, she prayed to the Lord, with tears running down her cheeks. She said 'Oh God, as Hannah prayed to you, so do I. Please give me a son within a year as a sign. I will name him Samuel and I will know then that I have not got leprosy. I will give this son to you.' A few days later, my grandmother told my mother that her younger sister Rachel who was expecting her first child in Ceylon, needed someone from the family to be with her. As my mother was the only sibling who was married and with three children of her own, she was the only person qualified to give Rachel the moral support she needed. Would she go? Jochebed immediately left for Ceylon, where she stayed for three months, during which time her sister was delivered of a lusty son. On her return to Calcutta, her faith in the Lord unshaken, my mother then fell pregnant and waited the remaining nine months serenely until her son was born, just *two days* before the year ended! He was duly named Samuel. My mother did not know how to give her son to God and always felt she had not fulfilled her side of the bargain, but perhaps God looked into her heart and forgave her.

"In the words of Ronald Jacob (himself a B.A. twice over as well as a Bachelor of Music, from three distinguished universities, by the age of twenty-one!) 'Samuel Solomon was the most illustrious person our Calcutta community has produced'. 1904-1988."

I discussed this story with Flower. "Why do you think your mother didn't go to a doctor to set her mind at rest immediately?" I asked. Flower believes that it didn't even cross her mother's mind, because people in great distress at the time would have taken their grief only to the ultimate Source of relief.

Flower thinks that if she had been in her mother's position, she would have

FAITH

had a nervous breakdown in the period of waiting! So, probably, would most of her contemporaries and those of following generations. It is a sign of the times, for we began to lose our innocence. Gone were the days when we no longer questioned. My grandfather would say "*muth poocho*" (Hi) don't question. His son would say "you can question, provided you are doing so in good faith." His son, in turn, would say simply "you can question."

It is interesting to speculate on the change. In the early years of the twentieth century there was an expansion in formal education in our community, and our model was largely based on the British system. Pupils studied in English as their first language, and they began to prepare for the overseas Cambridge School Certificate examinations. This was a far cry from home tuition, common in the nineteenth century, which concentrated on Hebrew and *Torah,* and where Arabic was the main language of instruction, since most of the *estads* would have come from Iraq. Study with an *estad* was generally continued, even in my day, but the time spent with him was greatly reduced. Like most of my contemporaries, as I was growing up I learnt to read Hebrew and chant prayers, but not to translate or understand. I was not alone in my generation to become bored, and endured my lessons merely because my parents insisted on them. I would trudge reluctantly to the home of my elderly *estad* in the middle of a Sunday afternoon and he would rouse himself reluctantly from his nap. My cousins had a different *estad* - a very easy-going man. When he would arrive at their home to teach all three of them, it would be a matter of routine to have long wrangles as to who should go first. This form of instruction did nothing to strengthen faith, renew values, or induce high standards of observance. What really mattered depended much more on what was happening in our individual homes, and standards of observance began to vary noticeably within our community.

By the early part of the twentieth century the men who worked for non-Jewish employers worked on a Saturday which was a normal working day. They could not, therefore, observe the Sabbath day as one of rest. The large Jewish firms such as David Sassoon & Company in Bombay, and B.N. Elias & Company in Calcutta, also began to open their offices and industrial plants on Saturdays, so the majority of working men in the community could not keep the Sabbath. It is possible that as an increasing number of people began to work and travel on the Sabbath the sanctity of the day was lost and it required only one small step to extend the desecration to social life. Some people began to smoke openly, to shop, and to gamble, encouraged by the fact that most race meetings were held on Saturday afternoons. In my generation, and to some extent in my parents'

FAITH

generation, it was not a surprise to hear that the observance of *kashruth* was set aside. At first people began to eat in cafes and restaurants for business and social reasons. This was very different from my grandfather's day when people would not even drink a glass of water outside the home for fear of breaking a dietary law.

A minority of parents sent their children to Jewish schools which were established in 1881.[4] In my generation, and in the generation before mine, a few boys from wealthy families were sent to England for their education. The majority of boys who came from middle income, and even poorer families, went to Christian schools, either Church of England or Catholic schools run by Jesuits, where the standard of education was superior to that in the Elias Meyer Free School for Boys. Many girls like myself also went to Christian schools, in spite of the fact that the education in the Jewish Girls' School, which was mainly fee-paying, was creditable. It was in these schools that I, and so many like me, became aware of another religion and culture which we studied. On the whole parents seemed to have no misgivings about this, although at school many of us joined in the hymn singing which we enjoyed, and sometimes even led, with enthusiasm. We were also impressed by the decorum at assemblies and prayers. However, we were discreet about this at home, perhaps because we felt guilty, or perhaps because we were concerned about the possibility of parental disapproval. In any case, and particularly as we grew older, we began to appreciate that life outside the confines of community could be interesting and rewarding, and many of us were able to look at ourselves more objectively. Some questioned the free and easy atmosphere in the synagogue where, for example, it seemed to be a virtue not to chant responsive prayers in unison, or where people walked in and out, greeting each other effusively and enjoying personal conversations while services were in progress. On the positive side, there was an understanding that the synagogue was not only a house of prayer but also a house of meeting, and that this was just as important in binding us together.

Two major forces were in motion towards the turn of the century. The first was a trend towards secularisation, which was considered desirable because it resembled the British way. Some of the Jews of the Raj sent their children to boarding schools where the value of educational excellence was placed higher than a Jewish environment. Secondly, at the same time, inspiration and instruction in religious education generally began to lack lustre, and the boundaries of observance which had once been universal became blurred and unclear. There was much talk, and some inquiries made, about the appointment of a rabbi following the Second World War, which was influenced by Rabbi David Seligson

FAITH

from the American Armed Forces. However, no appointment was made until 1952, when the exodus of the community was already gaining momentum.[5]

In spite of the changes in the degree of religious observance between members of the community, there were very few who actually dissociated themselves from Judaism. Nor was there any major split between the firm traditionalists and the others.[6] Of course we criticised each other, but the criticism came more with sorrow and resignation rather than with hostility. There was never any thought of praying separately; some dissenters did not attend services at all, or they attended services very late. However, Sabbath attendances were never particularly large and few women, even the observant, went to synagogue every week.

The only times the synagogues were full to capacity were during the High Holidays for the celebration of festivals remained an important part of expressing our faith. This was usually done with different degrees of enthusiasm from home to home but in the more observant ones, all our senses and emotions were thoroughly satisfied. We smelled the perfume of flowers from one end of the house to the other. We smelled the aroma of cooking from the wonderful festive dishes till our mouths began to water, and we smelled the fragrance of rose water as we said the traditional blessing during the festivals. We then tasted the dishes which had been so carefully prepared by our cooks and supervised by our mothers. We ate the nuts which we toasted for our guests and for ourselves, and the goodies which were bought from Nahoums. We heard the sounds of the chants which were sung only on specific festivals, and which gave those days a special meaning. We heard the benedictions, and the sound of the *Shofar* (H) ram's horn, on New Year's Day in the synagogue and rejoiced that we had been "sustained in life to witness the season." We heard the blessings and good wishes of our family as we kissed the hands of our elders after *kiddush*. We enjoyed the congratulations on our new outfits from our friends and relatives.

In those warm and sunny days we wore bright and beautiful clothes "dressed to the nines in our silks and satins, showing off our bits of jewellery" as Flower Elias remembers it. Men and women, boys and girls, spent a great deal of time before the New Year choosing fabrics and being fitted for new clothes. This excitement added to the anticipation of the celebrations.

We watched all the preparations for the festivals with a great sense of joy, particularly when we were children, as there were mainly rewards and few

FAITH

responsibilities. We saw the gathering of the community in the synagogues and looked forward to socialising with our friends. We took great pleasure in seeing the magnificence of our surroundings in the synagogue, particularly on the festival of *Simhat Torah*, when all the silver or velvet clad scrolls were taken out of the Ark and displayed in front of it. And when the *Parokheth,* cloths of silk and velvet, beautifully embroidered in gold thread in memory of those who had passed on, were draped right across the ladies' gallery. For the young, and the less conservative in our community, there was a sense of anticipation, as after the main service was over the women were allowed, just for this part of the festival, to sit with the men who did not join in the *Hakafoth*, with the *Sefarim.* There was singing and dancing, joking and flirting, and the joy of the community was irrepressible.

It is this sense of involvement on an emotional and sensual level, just as much as the religious significance of the festivals, which has left a lasting impression. It is an expression of faith, not only in a spiritual sense, but also in a physical sense, and the combination of the two, together with the unquestionable aesthetic arousal, which made our religion so very meaningful for us.

In spite of the differences between ourselves in the degree of observance, on the whole our fundamental attachment to Judaism remained undiminished. This is interesting because there were no external problems to remind us that we were Jewish. Politically, religiously, and socially the Jews of the Raj had been completely secure for two hundred years. Nor was the attraction to secular Zionism strong enough to provide an alternative path to Judaism in the days of the Raj. It was probably the flexibility of the wider society, and our own live and let live disposition towards observance which was our strength. Our emotions and our sentiments were not exposed to threat from without or within. Generally, our sense of Jewish identity which was our legacy from Baghdad remained intact, our sense of belonging to the community remained strong, and our sense of ease in our environment remained gratifying.

Gathering for prayer before laying the foundation stone of the Maghen David Synagogue, Calcutta, January 1883. Rev. E.M.D. Cohen (seated in the front row) wearing a solar topee and with a white flowing beard, was cantor of the synagogue from the time it was built until his death in January 1927.
Courtesy: Tudor Processing Limited.

Maghen David Synagogue on the festival of *Simhat Torah*. At this time the beautiful *parokhet*, curtains or wall hangings are displayed, together with the silver cased *sefarim*, almost a hundred, which are taken out of the Ark (behind the three arched doorways) and placed in front of it. The ornament over the centre arch measures "seven foot by six foot ... contained 3500 tolas of silver, with portions overlaid with gold and covered with velvet ... was designed by Moses Mayohas, embellished by Ezra Aaron Gareh and (made) by John Boseck & Company." E.N. Musleah. The *ner tamid* everlasting light is at the left of the main arch.

Iris Moses Ferris (centre) with Guides from the Jewish Girls' School, Eighth Calcutta Troop. Early 1930s L. to R. Helen Rassaby, Ramah Luddy, Iris, Sally Luddy, Mercia Rassaby.
Courtesy: Rachel Shellim.

Interior of *Beth El* Synagogue, Calcutta. View from the Ark towards the entrance.
Photo: Cheryl Isaac.

Megilla, Book of Esther in a silver and gold scroll holder made in Shanghai, c. 1910.
Courtesy: Ruby Mordecai.
Photo: Isaac & Anna Mordecai.

Aviva Mordecai, Ruby Mordecai, Tammy Mordecai, Isaac Mordecai.

The *Hannukiah* is in brass to hold oil lamps. Made in Calcutta, Calcutta, c. 1910.
Courtesy: Ruby & Elias Mordecai.

FAITH

My Prayer.

Dear Lord, if I must live, help me to live with joy, giving joy, and if and when I become a misery unto myself and those around me, I pray Thee take me.

If I must suffer, help me to endure. When I falter, I pray Thee lift me up; let my affliction enrich & not impoverish me and may it never be an excuse for lowering my standards.

I am truly thankful for the glow in my heart and the strength Thou hast given me through those who care; for the good days short or long; for the resilience and renewal of spirit with which Thou hast endowed me; for all Thy blessings great or small.

And though there may be times when I do not comprehend Thy ways, my faith in Thee is unflinching and I bow my head to Thy Divine Will.

Iris Ferris
Royal Marsden Hospital
Sutton, Surrey.

7th November, 1969.

Chapter 12

CHARITY

The Jewish community of Calcutta was stratified, like most other societies, by income and status groups. When the first settlers arrived in Calcutta in the late eighteenth and early nineteenth centuries, there were two distinct groups; the wealthy merchants seeking new trade opportunities, and those who served their domestic and business requirements. The first, second, and sometimes third generation of those who had settled in Calcutta from Iraq, came from families who had gained a livelihood over a long period of time through their skills and experience in certain fields; merchants, jewellers and shopkeepers on the one hand, and hawkers, and those who provided special services for Jewish communities, such as teachers, scribes, men who did circumcisions and those who slaughtered animals and birds according to Jewish Law, on the other. Some families became very successful where business acumen supported their mercantile and real estate enterprises, but very few became outstandingly wealthy and only one or two could vie with the wealthiest in the city.

It was not until the first quarter of the twentieth century that employment opportunities expanded for those who were not directly engaged in trade. Until this time higher and professional education was not within the reach of the Jewish community. The Raj did not promote the development of an industrial and manufacturing base in India which meant that employment in these areas was closed. As Jack Raymond explains: "All our raw materials were being exported to Britain and we had to import finished products, which meant that we were paying over the odds for what we had, while being deprived of a whole range of job opportunities. Another difficulty was that of getting your hands on capital. You couldn't walk into a bank and take a loan for starting up a business without collateral and most of us were unable to provide this. So one way or another we were trapped." The quota system for jobs in the public services imposed by the Raj made it very difficult for Jews to gain entry into these fields as they were not classified as Europeans. Directorships in large commercial and financial houses were also the preserve of Europeans, which severely limited prospects for those of other communities. There were two distinct standards of living in India during the Raj; European and Indian, the latter being significantly lower. Many Jews aspired to the standards of the former and achieved their goal, but there were also those who did not have the educational opportunities, or the skills to compete.

CHARITY

The employment situation changed in the first and second quarters of this century. Higher and technical education became increasingly accessible and many Jews took advantage of the consequent expansion in job opportunities. Wealthy families sent their sons to England to get professional qualifications and most of them returned to Calcutta to serve the wider community, mainly in law and in medicine. Gradually the structure of the community became less polarised between the wealthy and the poor, and a middle income group developed and grew into the largest sector of Jewish society.

Until the 1930s many people earned their living from trade[1] directly or indirectly, both on a small and large scale.[2] Those who traded overseas were vulnerable because goods transported by sea were not always insured,[3] and those who "shuttled between Calcutta and Rangoon, Singapore, Malaya and ... Shanghai, Penang and Hong Kong"[4] were at some personal risk of life and limb.[5] It was not rare for these people and their families to experience periods of plenty and periods of want and as one woman said "the house was always full of visitors when times were good but when times were bad no one asked about you. It was then that we had to get rid of the servants, one by one, and this put a great strain on my mother. We had to move to a smaller house in a poorer area. My parents began to quarrel and there were dreadful rows. Eventually my father took to drink with what little money he had, just like the other poor people. He was criticised, but it was his only escape from utter degredation."

A substantial proportion of the poor were low wage earners with large families who were able to manage until the need for occasional, but relatively high expenditure, forced them into debt. A friend who was familiar with this situation said: "We all lived from hand to mouth in our locality, and if the rent couldn't be paid, the landlord would just have to go without his money for a while. He knew the circumstances of his tenants and that he couldn't expect to draw blood from stone. After all, if it became necessary to pay dentists and doctors, or buy a pair of spectacles, that came before paying the landlord. It was simply the way we lived, juggling expenditure all the time."

Widows and their children, deserted wives and their dependants, women with unemployed husbands, were in a very difficult situation. I was told - "My mother used to tell us that our grandmother would leave home first thing in the morning to buy cloth from her meagre earnings of the day before. Then she would go from one Jewish home to another, day after day, in the scorching heat or in the pouring rain, to display her goods and persuade people to buy. In this way she

CHARITY

kept her family together." Another person said: "My mother was working from morning till night, making pickles and jam and then trudging from door to door selling in the community. There was always food on the table, but very little besides."

In the second half of the nineteenth century, "most of the Jewish inhabitants of Calcutta were emigrants from Baghdad, Basra, Aleppo and other cities in the Middle East ... (they) were not literate in English, and sometimes not in *any* language .. The milieu in India classed them as 'non-Indians' which meant they could not become tradesmen or engage in menial work ... some form of petty trade or hawking were the only fields where they could hope to make a start ..."[6]

Housing conditions for the poor were appalling and over-crowding was common. This, coupled with malnutrition, resulted in chronic health problems. A man told me: "The three main killers were TB, cholera and typhoid. When one kid in the family got ill, you could be sure the rest of us would catch the illness. What else could you expect when there were six people or more to a room and about thirty people in one building sharing a communal toilet and bathroom? As for cholera and typhoid, that is not surprising. We all ate food sold at street corners because it was cheap and tasty and filled our stomachs but sometimes we paid the price in lives. My mother had eleven children and only five survived, the others all died of one disease or another connected with poverty."

"We never went without food" one man who had experienced poverty told me "but you have to ask 'what did it mean to have a meal?' Sometimes it was no more than a few spoonfuls of boiled rice with a piece of cucumber, which was the cheapest vegetable you could get. Or we would soak fresh chickpeas overnight to sprout, sprinkle salt and pepper, and that was it. That was a meal. But once a week we had chicken, no matter how poor. Those who couldn't pay for it usually had a chicken meal sent to them by someone who could afford it." Another man said: "Once a week, I remember it was Tuesday evenings, a few of us from school (Elias Meyer Free School) would go to the Baptist chapel near the school. We heard they showed religious slides and sang hymns and then they served tea and buns. We watched the slides patiently and sang the hymns with gusto, waiting all the time for the tea and buns. Can you imagine what it meant having a bun once a week? Normally if we were given a bun once in six months we would have considered ourselves lucky. Our parents had no idea what we were up to, and we had to be very careful they didn't find out in school, or else we would have risked

CHARITY

being expelled. Once you were expelled that was the end of your education because our parents were certainly not able to pay fees and every other school was fee-paying."

Another man who had been a pupil at the Elias Meyer Free School told me: "I can't remember my parents ever buying clothes for me. We were given a complete outfit from school twice a year; just before Passover and New Year. By the time these festivals were nearing our clothes had patch after patch, but it didn't seem to matter to us at the time because most of us were in the same boat. If we did manage to get other things to wear in between it meant that someone would have given them to our family. We had no warm clothes and this was terrible for us on winter mornings. We were obliged to go to synagogue, morning and evening, every single day. It was cruel in short trousers and short sleeved shirts as we shivered through those cold, dark mornings. Did we complain? you ask. Did our parents complain, even indirectly? I'm not sure who would have been more scared to complain - our parents or us. We would simply have been told to leave if we didn't like it, so we were hardly in any position to complain."

An old pupil of the school remembers. "The festival we loved best was Purim. You know why? We were given a silver four anna piece at school, and this would have been worth about four or five pence at the time, but speaking personally, I felt like a king! We had to go to school as usual, and at 9 a.m. we assembled in the hall. We would be kept waiting and waiting for our money but in the end it was worth it."

Life was tough for the hard core of the poor. Despair was often seen as the hardest part of it all. "There was nothing to look forward to - no chance of bettering your circumstances and because people knew your circumstances they took advantage of you. The poor had to know their place and had to be kept in their place. You would have thought there was something to be afraid of if we got above ourselves. In our fathers' generation, people were uneducated and we were born into poverty. At least we got a basic education in the Jewish schools which helped us to get jobs but we were so poorly paid we were just about able to keep body and soul together."

The scars of poverty which remain as raw as if they had been inflicted yesterday, concern the attitudes of some people from the higher income groups. Sometimes help was given with good grace, but not always. "Those who were well off had the habit of speaking to us in a degrading way. Sometimes their tone was

CHARITY

offensive, sometimes it was what they said, but often it was both." A man from an affluent family observed: "Poor people were sometimes treated as if they were sub-human and had no right to any of the joys in life. There was this man, ..., who used to try and make a little money by selling peanuts and other bits and pieces, and in doing so he brought quite a bit of joy to those who were more than happy to make use of him. This man was also getting community assistance and everyone knew it. Then one day he was seen at the pictures with a girl friend. It was a matinee show, so the tickets were cheap. But that was too good for him. 'What' he was asked indignantly 'were you doing at the pictures? If you can afford one rupee and eight annas to go to the pictures you certainly don't need charity!'." Another person remembers that his mother, like many others who had large families, was taunted: "If you didn't bring so many children into this world all of you would not be in such misery today." He went on to explain "the last thing our mothers needed was a lecture. It was they who knew the sorrow of losing child after child. This was always a risk and always a great fear."

How then, did the community take responsibility for the poverty in their midst? There were many who suffered from malnutrition and some who died of poverty-related diseases. But most did survive. The first line of defence, particularly from the early twentieth century, was charitable institutions. In spite of the fact that Calcutta Jewry may have seen themselves as having no particular talent for organisation, it is clear from the discussion on Social Welfare in "The Banks of the Ganga" that in this respect their achievements were significant. This is not to say that the pressing needs of all families were being met, and many cases slipped through the net. There was no such concept as systematic means testing, and no generally accepted guidelines for giving support. Decisions were ad hoc, usually based on conventional wisdom and information received from secondary sources. One of the people responsible for making decisions on the distribution of community funds once said to me: "I feel most sorry for poor people with rich relatives. Everyone assumes that families look after their own, or *should* look after their own, but this is not always the case, and some lose out both at the hands of their relatives and at the hands of the community". One of the saddest cases I know, where community help was witheld, is that of a teenage boy who was suffering from TB while he lived in overcrowded rooms with his family. They asked for assistance to have him sent to a sanitorium, for his sake and that of his brothers and sisters, but were refused. Their despair was made known to a young man with a strong social conscience, who went straight to a successful businessman, well known for his philanthropy. He was given a book of signed blank cheques to be used to assist the family. The young boy was then sent to a

CHARITY

sanitorium but the delay in getting him there did not help his cause. He died shortly afterwards.

In the days before corporate help was available, and even afterwards, Musleah notes[7] - "References to the distribution of 'charity' are common not only at regular intervals (for example, every Rosh Hodesh), (i.e.) the first of the month, but also in answer to special pleas by the extraordinary Ezras and Gubbays as well as by a large number of other individuals. Mozelle Ezra would hand out Rs. 5,000 every month to various individual families. In the mid-twentieth century, the heirs of Benjamin Nissim Elias and his wife, Rahma, would dole out thousands of rupees every month from a trust fund ...."

A man who worked for one of the wealthy families recalls: "They had a statue of an Oliver Twist type of figure on the landing of their home. My boss told me he placed it in a position where he was bound to pass it several times a day. 'I want it to remind me every day that it could have been me'. Whenever he and his wife would see poor, infirm or elderly people come up their garden path they would take their names and addresses and say 'don't worry we will send you something regularly in future so you don't have to take the trouble to come for it yourselves". They would be given money and sent home in a taxi. If people were too shy to call for help and wrote a letter requesting money, discreet inquiries would be made to find out if the case was genuine. If it was, the name would go on a list. On the first day of every month, except Saturdays, all the people on the list would receive envelopes with cash. I would deliver these envelopes myself and was under strict instructions to leave straight away, not even to pause for a glass of water, in case I was seen and the family was recognised as accepting charity. Every *Rosh Hashana* the poor would be given suits, shirts, ties, handkerchiefs, socks. Nothing was forgotten. These people were so poor they couldn't afford to buy a pair of socks, let alone a shirt.

"After my boss died, his wife found a list of people to whom he gave charity privately. It included Jews and non-Jews and the amount he gave out every month was over seven thousand rupees, which was a fortune in those days. I did not like to bother his widow with continual requests for help once he had died. People knew where I worked and they often made approaches through me. As time passed she became aware that the requests were drying up and she asked me if I knew the reason for this. 'I don't like to worry you' I replied. She was furious! 'What right do you have to deprive me of the opportunity of doing charity? I don't need you to protect me from the poor. If ever I hear that you asked my brothers-in-

CHARITY

law for help before coming to me I shall be very upset'."

Everyone, the rich, the comfortably off, and the poor, knew that the religious injunction of *Tsedaka* (H) was of supreme value in their Jewish heritage and a few families set up community institutions to provide for the needs of those in want. *Tsedaka* may loosely be translated as charity, but it is really untranslatable. It comes from the root of the word which signifies justice. Charitable work is therefore a commitment to redressing, as far as possible, the unequal distribution of wealth in society. "The Jewish community of Calcutta, since its inception at the turn of the nineteenth century, had more than its fair share of poverty; about a quarter required the helpful hand of their co-religionists."[8] If about a quarter needed continual help, there were more, perhaps as many as another quarter again, who would have had occasional help. Unfortunately no reliable sources exist about precise facts and figures.

It was probably the middle income group who were most effective when it came to bridging financial gaps on an individual basis. The fact that there was less social distance between them and the poor meant that they could keep their ear to the ground to pinpoint need and to plead the cause of those who, above all, could not plead for themselves. There were a number of people, mostly women, who were virtually self-appointed social workers, reasonably well off, and who had friends among the poor. They took on the role of intermediary, not only to bring material relief, but to do so in such a way as to preserve the dignity of those who received help. This they achieved by eliminating face to face charity. Here are some examples. "My mother was very good at begging for others. There was never any embarrassment because it was not for herself she was asking, so she felt free to be as pressing as the case deserved." "My grandmother was always going out with mysterious packages under her cloak. She thought nobody could see what she was up to." "Mother used to stuff her pockets with cash every morning. She'd say, 'you never know who will need it urgently'. Her sources of supply were her own children and grandchildren who were pledged to make a regular contribution to her private fund from their salaries."

Friends remember that their parents and grandparents used to arrange for provisions to be distributed to the poor twice a year, before the festival of Passover and before the Jewish New Year. Funds for this distribution were usually donated anonymously by the rich. "Baskets with oil, unleavened bread or flour, rice, and even vegetables and chickens were sent out to make sure that as many people as possible would be able to celebrate the festivals."

CHARITY

There were families, mostly in the middle income group, who cooked meals for those who wanted it, either only on the eve of Sabbath, or on weekdays. There was a time when my mother helped a particular family on Friday nights and there was an occasion when our servant could not get into town because of a bus strike. The following Sunday I happened to be with my mother when she explained the lapse to the lady concerned, who had eight children. Her husband had a full time job, but earned a low wage. She said: "We simply wouldn't believe that the food was not coming. Then our youngest fell asleep at the table and we had to carry her to bed. When the next two young ones saw this they burst out crying and went to bed themselves. Gradually the older children began to give up hope and eventually even my husband and I couldn't wait up any longer, so we locked up and went to bed." I was about ten years old at the time and shall never forget trying to imagine myself in their predicament, but it was impossible.

It was not unusual for poor people to go to certain homes knowing they could get a hot meal. Florence Sadka Meyer told me of one such woman who had eaten and showed her enjoyment of the taste of the meal by raising her arms and lifting her eyes to heaven, and exclaiming from the bottom of her heart: *"Abdalakh alla!"* (A) term of endearment addressed to God. This unusual and spontaneous thanksgiving made a lasting impression on the family.

Giving charity was not confined to the rich or to those who were in comfortable circumstances. The poor would share their meal of bread and onions with each other, even if it was done at a high personal cost. One of my friends remembers her mother used to say that when her grandmother sat down to a frugal meal after a hard day's work of selling cloth from house to house, and someone called while she was eating, she shared that meal quite automatically. They gave what they could materially and emotionally, for they did give each other enormous moral support. There was a woman in our community who would go from house to house, begging for money and food. Everyone thought she was doing this for the sole benefit of her own family but my information is that she distributed much of the food to those who were too sensitive to beg for it themselves.

The people who were difficult to assist were those who saw themselves as "respectable", implying that they were "formerly in comfortable circumstances; not given to begging or soliciting for oneself."[9] The more fortunate among them had friends in the middle income group in whom they could confide and who were able to offer relief themselves or get it from others without disclosing the identity of the beneficiary or the benefactor. A stroke patient in need of physiotherapy, a bride

CHARITY

in need of a trousseau, a child in need of remedial teaching, a family in need of clothes, were examples which I came to learn about through the community grapevine.

A considerable amount of charity was given spontaneously. Aaron Aaron, who was a Scout Leader and took about thirty boys to camp from the Elias Meyer Free School told me: "When I took the boys to Madhupur, and half the community were there on holiday, we could be sure of a great deal of goodwill. One year, old Mr S pushed money into my hand and said, 'here, extend the boys' holiday'. Then there were times when we would be invited by particular families for tea. They really laid on wonderful spreads with the best in the local sweetmeat shops and also baskets of cakes from Nahoums. Mrs. A was not a rich woman, but she offered to cook for us for the Sabbath. She only took enough money to cover the bare cost of the food, but I can't tell you the trouble she took over the meal. We had everything you would have found in the richest of homes."

While it was a matter of pride to live up to high standards, it was a matter of merit to give help to those who needed it. This help was given in cash, in kind, and in services, at every level of our small community. Although institutional care came gradually, personal and private charity was an integral part of our daily lives and was something which remained with us throughout the days of the Raj. When we take a glimpse at poverty from the point of view of the poor, it is clear that in spite of the best efforts of the community as a whole we could have been more sympathetic, more understanding, and above all, more effective, particularly by encouraging self-help. This was explored merely at the fringes and contrasts with Sir Victor Sasson's efforts in Shanghai.[10] With hindsight, it seems it was not so much that we were inept in our organisational ability, but in our lack of insight that a range of needs required a range of remedies. Charity, for the Calcutta Jews, mostly meant being well intentioned. It meant reaching into your own pocket, or persuading others to reach into their pockets. It meant giving time and asking others for their time. It meant making decisions for other people from a distance and without consulting them. While this may have been appropriate, to some extent, for the most vulnerable groups such as the sick, children, and the 'respectable' poor, it was not so for the unemployed and the under-employed. It is a sad reflection on our way of thinking that even provision for basic education in Jewish schools started as a reactive measure to missionary activity[11] rather than as a result of foresight and planning, and vocational training and the development of cooperatives hardly, if ever, got off the ground. Events since the exodus from India have shown that the "poor" of Calcutta no longer remained poor when they

CHARITY

settled in Israel and in the West. They made the most of opportunities to improve their circumstances and their quality of life. This was summed up by one man who settled in London. "It was not easy to start with but we knew that we were winning every little struggle, step by step, because there were props rather than barriers all along the line. Within ten years or so most of us have managed to make a good living for ourselves and a completely different way of life for our children."

Although there were some among the poor who seemed content to depend solely on the community for their income, there were many more who should not be forgotten, who did their best to earn what they could, in spite of social and physical disabilities. They bore their poverty with dignity and their self-esteem was high. I knew just such a person since I was a child and I shall refer to him here as Joel.

Joel was there ever since I could remember. He was a visitor at my grandmother's house, every Sunday to Thursday, where he went straight from the synagogue after evening prayers. He was not quite like anyone else I knew. He even looked different, although it took me many years to realise this. He was small and stockily built and was physically strong. Unfortunately his eyesight was so poor he could scarcely recognise people until they were face to face with him. His special spectacles, with small, thick lenses, seemed to make his eyes disappear altogether. He probably shaved once a week, just before Sabbath, because he always had a short stubbly beard, which made him look unkempt. The only features which were visible were a short forehead, a small nose and ears supporting round, black-rimmed glasses, and cropped jet black hair. His head was always covered, in the manner of orthodox Jews. He wore a battered, fawn coloured felt hat, creased down the crown. Underneath there was a cap, sometimes in white cotton crochet, sometimes in red velvet, which he wore indoors. He never went anywhere without his walking stick which he probably used as an aid to his sight rather than to his mobility. All his clothes were hand-me-downs; ill-fitting, frayed, and somewhat grubby.

Joel was a man of few words with adults, although they liked and respected him. He would usually speak to them when spoken to and often in a gruff and dismissive tone of voice. He seemed to be constantly on the defensive, making a rule of never discussing anyone, or anyone's affairs. This was a rare and shrewd strategy for someone who lived in a small, close-knit community, especially as he depended on the goodwill of those he saw frequently. Even innocuous questions about the health of people could bring a cool and abrupt

CHARITY

answer. "How should *I* know?" or "Don't ask *me*!" Things were rather different with the children of the house with whom he must have felt more at ease. One of my earliest memories is of being entertained by Joel. He told fairy tales which were not in books, he made funny remarks, but best of all he could work wonders with his hands. "Got a handkerchief?" he would ask eagerly. I would run to fetch one, full of expectation. He would fold it to make a handbag. Then with a few deft movements he would turn it into a mouse. Or he'd make a hat and turn it into a boat, and so on and on. He could make beautiful objects from candle wax. He collected the wax from candles lit when Sabbath went out, then warmed this over a flame and would mould one animal after another. One day he made a beautiful pair of miniature spectacles. It was pure magic! For a long time I believed he must have been the cleverest of men.

Joel always ate his evening meal before the rest of our family, and he sat by himself, at a small round table on the verandah, next to the kitchen. I don't know whether he preferred this arrangement for fear of intruding, or if it was imposed on him. One of my aunts always served him a hot meal herself rather than leaving it to the servants. She enjoyed piling food on other people's plates, even after pleas to stop, and this was not uncharacteristic of the women in her generation, but she seemed to take special pleasure in doing this for Joel. I remember him saying, "enough, enough, that's enough *please!*" Perhaps she believed that it was the only time of day he ate properly and she might have been right.

I noticed that Joel was very obliging when asked to go on an errand and he knew, with a certain pride, that if cash had to be delivered, he would be the first to be trusted with it. I came to realise that the provision of occasional work was one small way in which self-help was encouraged. No rate was ever agreed for the job, because it was meant to appear as a favour. The reward was always generous to avoid discontent. "Do me a favour" my grandmother would say to Joel. "I owe so-and-so, x rupees for such and such. If you are passing her way, would you give it to her on my behalf? You know how I hate to hold other people's money." This was true. It was part of our value system, certainly in the days of our parents and grandparents, not to let the sun set on a personal debt only known to the giver and receiver, as life itself was uncertain and the debt could remain unpaid, which was seen as a terrible prospect. And so it happened that Joel spent his days either trudging through the streets on errands or visiting those families where he was known and accepted without reservation. He was an eccentric and sensitive man and never went where he thought he might not be wanted. He had a flair for

CHARITY

repairing clocks, in spite of his poor eyesight and from time to time he would ask "got any clocks for me to look at?" Again, when it came to payment, he relied on the discretion of those who brought work his way. The synagogue paid him a small retainer to attend services twice a day, to make up the required quorum of ten men, and this was Joel's only regular source of income.

Many years later I got to know that he gave all his synagogue earnings to his elderly mother. This seemed curious since Joel seemed to prefer to deny her very existence, even though they slept under the same roof, and he spent the Sabbath at home. Obliging as he was to do any odd job, he was never willing to carry a message to his mother, not even if my grandmother said it was important or urgent. "Send someone else to tell her, send one of the servants, send anyone but don't ask *me!*" Joel's mother was also a frequent visitor at my grandmother's house and if she arrived while he was there, he dropped everything instantly, grabbed his hat and made straight for the front door. She would rail against him, and I can still hear her shrill voice, getting shriller by the moment, as she would cry - "he's useless, good-for-nothing, unwilling to do an honest day's work, unwilling to ease our poverty!" Who knows what secret dreams, hopes and ambitions she had cherished for him, and for herself, through him? Who knows what sorrow and despair she might have gone through when these dreams seemed difficult, and then impossible, to realise? Did she make him feel guilty, inadequate, or a failure? Did he feel bitter or rejected? In those days people didn't analyse their feelings, they simply gave vent to them in no uncertain terms.

When Joel had reason to refer to his mother he called her *Nucklee*, (Hi) inessential, or unimportant. His father, whom he adored and who had died many years before, would have been *Uslee,* (Hi) the essential or real one. It is true, people from our community had a particular fondness for nick-naming others, but I've never heard of anyone else nick-naming his own mother! Nick-names for people in particular occupations were as common as anywhere else in the world, but there were imaginative nick-names to describe the characteristics of people such as *Yosef Toffani,* Joseph Tofan. There was a mail train called the Tofan Express, 'storm' in Hindi, and as this man talked and moved very quickly, the description was thought to be well suited. Or, there was simply *Choomti*, (Hi) ant, the name given to a woman who walked as slowly as an ant, without so much as a reference to her own name as well. Lulu Tweelee, (A) or the tall one, was so called not because she was particularly tall herself, but somewhere along the line her family had been given this nick-name and it had stuck, regardless of personal suitability. There were nick-names to reflect resemblances to famous people, like

CHARITY

the King of Abbysinia, quite a mouthful in comparison with the actual name of the man concerned, but far more colourful. And *Melech Habashan*, (H) King of Bashan, although who ever presumed to know what he looked like from Biblical times is anybody's guess.

"What's up between Joel and his mother?" I asked one of my aunts. "Does he really dislike her as much as he says or is he putting on a big show?" "You will have to ask him yourself" she replied. So I did, when I thought the moment was right.

Joel was repairing a clock on the verandah of my grandmother's house. Aunts and uncles were coming and going but nobody settled beside him. I saw my chance and drew up a chair. He was flattered because he had a voluntary audience and began to explain how a clock works and how this particular movement had become impaired. I didn't have the slightest interest in mechanical things but listened in silence, nevertheless. When the clock was being returned to its case I asked Joel -
"Do you really dislike your mother or are you pretending?"
"Don't even mention her name," he said, not looking up, and with obvious agitation.
"But why, what has she done to you?"
"What has she done! What does she do? I'll tell you. Nag, nag, nag. It never stops. She can never be satisfied, so I have to run out of the house first thing in the morning and make sure I don't get back till she's asleep. That is the only way I don't have to hear her shout at me."
"My mother nags me too, Joel," I said, unconvinced, "but I don't dislike her!"
"Don't even mention your mother and my mother in the same breath. Can you compare heaven and hell?"
It was left at that. Perhaps one day I would understand, when I was grown up.

When the Second World War broke out there was a great surge of patriotism amongst the Jews of the Raj. No matter that the battles were being fought far away, and no matter that the only real impact the war made on our lives in those early days was a severe shortage of all imported goods which had previously flooded the market. The wireless bulletins constantly carried news of the progress of the war and this was discussed and debated from day to day in our homes. The newspapers described battles and campaigns, and maps were published to illustrate what was going on. Until this time we had never known Joel to take an interest in world affairs but the war had stirred deep feelings of loyalty

CHARITY

to the British. He stuffed his pockets with maps from the newspapers and plotted the progress of the war. He told me of towns and cities in Europe which I had never heard of before, and nor, I suppose, had he. But times had changed and so too had his interests. He could recount, at a moment's notice, an update of battles on every front. You had only to ask "How's the war going, Joel?" to get a full bulletin. When Japan joined the Axis powers in 1941 his patriotism intensified and his pockets bulged even more with maps on a whole new front.

It was 1942, and the Japanese were advancing into the highlands of Burma. We feared that unless there was a turn-around in Assam, we in Bengal would be next on the battlefield. Many school buildings were requisitioned by the Armed Forces and schools were evacuated further west. This meant that many women and children had left Calcutta. In the winter of 1942 Japanese planes were overhead and Calcutta was being bombed. The war, which had seemed so remote, was now at our doorstep. The servants were frightened and uneasy, but the crunch came on Christmas eve when the Japanese bombed the town for the first time, rather than the docks where they had previously concentrated, in the hope of breaking the morale of the civilian population. It was a long raid by their standards and a devastating one by ours. The main problem was that no proper arrangements had been made to provide shelter from the bombs. At this point the servants had had enough. They came to us on Christmas morning and said: "We have seen death with our own eyes. Pay us our wages if you wish, but if not, we are still off to our villages even if we have to go all the way on foot." Some of them lived several hundred miles away. Luckily for us, our mother knew how to cook, but food was scarce, particularly as we were living in the dock area, five miles from the centre of town, as my father worked for the Port Commissioners. My grandmother became concerned for our welfare as we had no servant to do the shopping or cooking. Then she had a brainwave. Joel knew his way to our house and it was possible he could be persuaded to bring us some fruit and vegetables, and best of all, a *kasher* chicken. Joel readily agreed to help. He knew my mother was always pleased to see him and she would be delighted to have the chicken.

The chicken was delivered. We all enjoyed Joel's visit and he was happy to have been with us. After he had refreshed himself, he set off for town. At this time people were very nervous and when Joel was spotted not far from our house, and taken for a suspicious character, or a Japanese spy, as someone had imagined, the police only had to be alerted to detain him. Joel was carted off to the police station and subjected to long and detailed questioning. The fact that his pockets were filled to bursting with newspaper cuttings of maps on military campaigns did

CHARITY

nothing to help him. However, he had the presence of mind to explain he was on an errand and mentioned my father's name and position. A messenger was sent to the docks to summon my father who vouched for Joel and at last everything was sorted out and he was released. But it all took a long time, and he had been frightened and humiliated. Worst of all, he was offended that his patriotism had been put in question. As soon as my mother was able, she made a special trip to town to find Joel. She found him still in shock and in pain. "Don't ever ask me to come to your house again" he said sadly, and he never did.

Nevertheless, his interest in the war remained undiminished and his pockets were still stuffed with maps and newspaper cuttings. Neither did he alter his way of running errands, trudging miles with the aid of his walking stick. He had a favourite Hindi proverb which he repeated over and over again. *See-r sala-mutt, pagree hazar* (Hi). Peace of mind (enables one to wear) a thousand hats, or become very flexible. His way of getting peace of mind was to distance himself from his mother, while still assisting her and all those who asked for his services. Joel's story speaks of one who lived on the margins of society in a small community. In spite of poverty and disability, he managed to maintain his independence, his eccentricity, his dignity, and his sense of purpose.

PART THREE

Chapter 13

REFUGEES FROM BURMA

It was the 14th of February, 1942. Albert Judah was in Bassein, a half day's journey by boat from Rangoon. He had been employed there in electrical goods supplies since 1933 and after nine years he packed only those few personal belongings which would fit into a small trunk. Albert's parents and his other unmarried brothers and sisters had gone to Calcutta where they decided to settle. Grateful as he was to have the job, he decided it was time to leave for Rangoon. News of the war was disturbing. Malaya had been over-run by the Japanese army and Singapore's naval defences, considered to be impregnable, became ineffectual against a land attack. The "Stay Put" campaign, aimed at Indians and other non-Burmese, became meaningless. In spite of the successes of the Japanese army, Albert Judah, like so many other civilians, believed that Japan was a third rate power and no match for the British forces. This made them complacent and unable to prepare for the invasion, either emotionally or practically. The Japanese army took Victoria Point, in the southern-most part of Burma, on the 15th of December, 1941.[1] At that very time Elmo Sassoon's grandmother in Rangoon was making wine for a wedding in the family which was to take place in February, and he knows of others who were paying wages to their servants three months in advance.

Albert arrived in Rangoon on the 15th of February to hear that Singapore had fallen. On the previous day he decided that as river transport services were still normal, he should join his sister and her family in Rangoon to give them support. Large numbers of Jewish families had already left for Calcutta by boat, particularly women and children. In a telegram from the Governor General to the Secretary of State for India, he said: "Naval and military authorities agreed (to) the use of returning transports for Indian evacuees, provided there was no delay in the turn round of ships. (The boats) would be routed from Rangoon to Calcutta or Madras. The Burmese authorities would take responsibility for feeding arrangements and medical inspection prior to embarkation and during the voyage. Passengers were advised to carry four days' cooked food and were limited to 50 lbs of baggage."[2] Those men who had business interests stayed on in Rangoon in the belief that the reverses of the British army were temporary. There appeared to be

REFUGEES FROM BURMA

some truth in this, Albert thought, because the government was recruiting for the Town (Home) Guard. He found "the city was half deserted. Shops were locked up, doors were cemented in, and many Jewish homes were left unoccupied." He had heard that people were burying their jewellery and precious articles, expecting that these would be retrieved in a short while. What Albert did not know is that "by 12 February Army HQ were dispersing stocks from Rangoon ... and government departments were beginning to evacuate. The banks left for Mandalay on February 20th owing to almost complete desertion of staff. On 20 February ... orders for the first phase of the evacuation of Rangoon were accordingly given ... the government left on March 1st and on March 7th the demolitions were carried out and the military evacuation took place."[3] Since the end of December 1941 there had been devastating air raids on Rangoon and there were heavy fatalities and casualties. In the first raid alone there were estimates of 2,750 dead and 1,700 wounded[4] and an official report at the time indicated "a mass exodus of Indians, with paralysing effects on the city ... public transport ceased to function, bazaars remained closed, shops were shut and trade was at a standstill. Rangoon, the great business machine, had stopped working. The country was cut off from the outside world."[5]

On the 19th February, 1942 Albert Judah, together with his sister and her family, went to Mandalay by train, where they arrived on the 21st. They were advised to go there to register for evacuation as the British Government was organising treks to India. However, at that time no one had the faintest idea what that meant. They stayed in Mandalay until the 8th of March and saw that people were living from one day to the next. Albert said: "Those who wished to leave were trying to convert goods into cash, and there were others who decided to stay, and were gathering stocks in the hope of making fortunes when supplies were cut off, their main interest being in imported goods such as medicines, saccharine and cigarettes." People in Mandalay were buying and selling frantically, while the Japanese army was steadily advancing into Burma.

The news that Rangoon had fallen on the 8th of March did not reach Albert on the day that he left Mandalay. However, he guessed something was amiss because just before he boarded the train he saw the Rangoon Fire Brigade in Mandalay. The train, with an armed guard in every carriage, transporting Indian, Anglo-Indian, Chinese and Jewish refugees including Albert, left Mandalay at 11.10 a.m. and arrived at Monywa at 4 o'clock the same day. They were advised to carry an unbreakable plate and mug for the journey, but otherwise their luggage had to be very light. At Monywa they transferred from the train to a launch, which was packed to capacity - at least 200 people, as Albert recalls. The launch was to convey them to Mawlaik, on the River Chindwin. "The capacity of the Chindwin river steamers (imposed) a limit of about 1500 (people) per diem to the flow into Kalewa."[6] Albert recalls the scene: "There was just enough space to stretch out on deck and people had to sleep on the spot where they happened to be jostled. Water was so scarce, supplies were protected by armed guard, and people carried what food they could; bread, until it turned as hard as rock, tinned provisions, and biscuits. Limited quantities of food and tea were available on board but at this early stage of the journey, many rejected the food which they considered to be inedible".

They left Monywa at dawn the following day and travelled all day on the river until nightfall, when they reached Kalewa, and moored there for the night. Again they slept on deck, and continued their journey very early the following day, the 10th of March, but had to disembark as the water was shallow and the launch was overloaded. In a deciphered telegram (No. 679 dated April 7th 1942) from Maymyo, the Governor of Burma informed the Secretary of State for Burma that the "limiting factor" for increasing the rate of evacuation through the Tammu Pass was "lack of water in the Chindwin." This meant that Albert, and so many thousands in his situation, had to walk along the river bank, as he put it "in the baking heat and on the burning sand" before they could embark again and continue their journey until the late evening, when they moored again. They reached Mawlaik at 10 a.m. on March 15th.

It was in Mawlaik that they heard that the Japanese were advancing north, and although everyone was upset, there was no panic. It was in Mawlaik that they were divided into groups, about sixty men, women and children in each group. Not all the families were able to travel together and this was distressing but understandable because the elderly, the sick and the infirm had to take the least difficult route, mainly on the waterways. The others, like Albert, had to walk. Everyone accepted the situation and no one had any idea what lay ahead in the weeks which followed. They were just anxious to press forward. It was in Mawlaik that Albert, and the people in his group boarded another launch, the "Namtu" and set off at 12 noon. A fire broke out on board to add to their troubles but was brought under control without loss of life or cargo. They went on to Yuwa, stopped there for the night, and continued the next day, March 17th, to Sittaung, where they arrived at 2.30 in the afternoon and disembarked.

By this time the Tammu Pass was the only overland route to India which was still open. Albert and his party headed for Tammu on foot. The luggage was carried by coolies or by elephants. It rained heavily and they made slow progress through the Kabaw Valley. The organisation of evacuation through this route began first as a private enterprise by BBTC (Bombay Burmah Trading Company), but was taken over subsequently by government officers. This was the sole channel through which military supplies could reach the fighting forces.[7] At the time of the evacuation, workmen were trying to complete a military road through the Tammu Pass for the movement of the army and there was a limit of 500 refugees a day on this road. It is estimated that approximately 200,000 refugees crossed to India in safety through the Tammu Pass and fatalities were low. "The known deaths (were) 4,268 (but) the actual death rate will never be known (and) could even be double that figure."[8] In the days of union between India and Burma, the British had neglected to build up communications between the two countries. A railway was planned, chiefly for military reasons, but it was never constructed. Its absence was to have a powerful effect on the shape of the fighting and on the plight of the refugees. "Given any reasonable amount of transport, the death roll would have been significantly lower ... the evacuation problem was predominantly one of transport."[9]

Each group of men, women and children was led by a guide and assisted by Burmese coolies who were taken on locally. While mothers carried their babies, the coolies carried infants and the baggage, and when there was a shortage of coolies, the trek came to a standstill. "When the refugee flow was averaging 1500 a day, porters had to do a minimum of 10 stages with a two day rest for the round trip, and when four and sometimes six carriers were necessary to one sick person in a *dhoolie,* it can be seen how many tens of thousands of porters were required".[10] Aisey Jacob Ezekiel, who was six years old at the time, remembers being carried in a basket on the back of a coolie. She was lucky. Her ten year old sister had to walk like most of the others, including pregnant women. The sick and infirm rode on the back of an elephant, or in a *dhoolie,* (Hi) a crude wooden seat astride two bamboo poles, carried on the shoulders of two or four men.

Albert recalls that he had only one thought and that was to keep together with the group. "We started on treks early in the morning and usually finished around noon because of the intense heat. We trekked six to eight miles on average from camp to camp. We had to drag our feet through muddy ground, particularly after heavy rain." The Administrator General's Report on this is "no survey would be complete without reference to rain and mud. It was a cruel fate that imposed an early and heavy monsoon. (Conditions) varied from mud slides to buffalo-wallows."

By contrast, but by no means any less difficult, Albert remembers: "At other times we had to trek through jungles without any paths, and the ground was uneven and full of stones and rocks which went right through our shoes. After leaving the border between Burma and India we went over high mountains in very narrow and steep places and it was exhausting." A Report on the Burma Campaign 1941 - 42 by Sir Reginald Dorman Smith, the Governor of Burma at the time, states: ".. it was after Tammu that the really difficult part of the journey began ... by footpaths or mule tracks through the Naga Hills, over the divide to Palel."[11] To add to these difficulties Albert had an attack of malaria at this stage of the trek and was forced to walk on in spite of a high temperature. The sick and the dying were being left behind and it was a terrifying prospect. He and his group had been trekking in the Kabaw Valley just before crossing the border into India. It was called the "valley of death because (of) the peculiar virulence of the malaria which could be contracted there."[12] Of this "desert" area the Administrator General has reported: "When the refugees reached the hands of the Indian authorities they were invariably in poor physical condition and at a stage of their journey when the greatest of their physical trials had yet to be faced; the crossing of the 5000 ft - 8000 ft hill barrier ... (which) involved anything from five to fifteen days..."

Albert remembers "the camps were usually very temporary shelters made of bamboo and thatch. The bunks were mere bamboo slats without any bedding and the knots pierced into our bodies. There were seldom any toilet facilities, with no privacy, and washing or bathing was only possible when we were near a river.

"When we reached our destination for the day we queued up with our bowls for food. This was always a bowl of rice with some lentils. The rice was full of small stones, mud and grit, and the lentils were cooked with chillies. This made life very difficult for those with tummy troubles and for the children." This is confirmed by the Report of the Administrator General "... although there was no starvation ... the refugees had been called upon for long periods to sustain life on little more than rice and salt with occasional issues of dal ... (and) it was inevitable that large numbers became debilitated and were attacked by diarrhoea and other stomach complaints before their major physical trial was yet to be faced."

Albert trekked with two nephews who were identical twins. This caused some confusion at the food queues as the organisers thought that one youngster was coming back for seconds. "Didn't I serve you a little while ago?"

A great hardship was the shortage of water, particularly as the trekking made people very thirsty. Albert says "we were allowed no more than one cup a day for all purposes, but there was so much chlorine in it, it tasted like medicine and was difficult to drink. But by this time we didn't care what we ate or drank, or whether we ate anything at all. On the days when we were lucky we passed through villages where they had a little food to sell. Bananas, potatoes, and tea with salt as there was no sugar available; the local people recommended it. It did not taste as bad as it sounds. Sometimes we were able to drink elephant's milk. It tasted extremely sweet, and that was good.

"Of all the memories of the trek, the most harrowing are of the dead bodies, which were collected every day at the camps and of the dead bodies floating in the River Chindwin." Albert also has vivid recollections of disease, swollen feet, ulcers, mosquito bites, and sand fly bites. The sand fly transmits kala azar which affects the spleen and distends the abdomen; untreated, it can cause extreme wasting and death. Malaria, or jungle fever as it was known locally, was common. The Administrator General's Report was that 75 per cent of all refugees were suffering from it. Attacks of ague and high temperatures meant that many people were forced to continue the trek at great risk to themselves one way or another. Trekking in heavy rain meant they would arrive at camps soaked to the skin. They would have to light fires to dry off their clothes. Beetles, insects and leeches added to the general discomfort. There were places in the mountains where the sounds of crickets drowned the silence, and screeching monkeys gazed at the trekkers with great curiosity. It was impossible to avoid contaminated water. Conditions were so insanitary, that the incidence of diarrhoea, and of dysentery, the great killing disease, was very high. Accidents and injuries were common every day but there was no medical treatment, no first aid, and no fresh water to bathe bites, ulcers or wounds. The Administrator General's Report again confirmed "everything meant by medical resources were comparatively non existent."

It was a full four weeks after having left Mandalay, on the 5th of April, that Albert and his group got as far as Palel in Assam. They had trekked for five days in the highlands bordering Burma and India. It was in Palel that he had some medical attention which brought temporary relief from malaria, and they were first welcomed to an American canteen, and given cigarettes. They were also able to wash with hot water, had hot tea with sugar, ate bread, butter and jam, and were

REFUGEES FROM BURMA

served at tables laid with clean linen. "The cream cracker biscuits with butter tasted just heavenly" Albert still recalls with a smile. They then travelled to Imphal by bus, twenty miles away, acutely aware that at last they could rest their weary and painful legs. After an overnight stop at Imphal, where they were given a packed tiffin, they continued, very early in the morning, to Dimapur by bus, and arrived there that same evening. They boarded a train at Dimapur at 11.30 on the night of April 6th, arriving at Parbatipur early in the morning of April 8th, having travelled via Lumding Junction to Pandu, where they crossed by ferry to Amingoan. The Administrator General reported .".. there are thirty-eight active volunteers who meet all trains and give light refreshments to the evacuees, the cost of which is being met by the proprietor of the Setabganj Sugar Mills. Fruit and milk are supplied to sick refugees. Four local doctors have agreed to render any help necessary." The sterling work of the Indian Tea Association in supporting medical care has been commended in the Report. Finally, a train from Parbatipur carried Albert and his co-evacuees directly to Calcutta at 3.30 in the afternoon on April 8th, a full calendar month after leaving Mandalay. He remembers with great appreciation the warmth of the local people who crowded round them at every stop on their long railway journey to Calcutta. They were poor people, who were as welcoming with their words as with their offers of food. *"Rungoonwalla, Rungoonwalla!"* they cried, with gifts of Indian sweets and savoury snacks.

A Reuter's report in New Delhi on June the 3rd 1942 paid tribute to the refugees. ".. the refugees themselves ... displayed a stamina and fortitude without which all that could be done for them would have been to no avail."

It was customary for refugees from Burma to be met at the railway station in Calcutta by relief workers from many groups, including a representative of the Jewish community, to offer food and shelter. But Albert was able to go straight to his parents' home. They had had no word of his whereabouts and were overjoyed to see him. It was the seventh day of Passover but in his honour they went through the entire *Seder* (H) again. The *Seder*, service at home where the story of the exodus is told with dining, wining, and singing, is celebrated on the first two nights of the festival in the diaspora. On this occasion Albert and his family had a very special exodus in mind, an exodus which he recorded in his diary from day-to-day on the trek, and which is still in his possession.

Like most of the people who trekked from Burma, Albert had to go into hospital very soon after his arrival in Calcutta. He had to be treated for malaria and there was an ulcer on his leg which wouldn't heal. He carries the scar to this day.

REFUGEES FROM BURMA

Those refugees who wished to travel to any destination after their arrival in Calcutta were able to do so free of charge. A Reuter report dated the 4th of May, 1942, New Delhi, confirms "all indigent refugees were being returned to their homes free of charge and given a subsistence allowance." The only ones willing to stay on in Calcutta were those who had friends and relatives there, as the others wished to travel as far west as possible since the threat of the Japanese war was too close for comfort in Bengal. For those refugees who decided to stay in Calcutta there were certain advantages. Accommodation was not difficult to find since many families, mostly women and children, had evacuated the city; jobs were not too difficult to find because refugees were given priority; there were no language barriers because those who lived in Burma spoke English, and Burmese was an additional language. A concentration of both American and British armed forces in Bengal created many job opportunities, particularly in the service industries. Albert found work in a cigarette factory - Godfrey Phillips - as soon as he was fit enough for employment, and ready to come to terms with the trauma of the trek.

There can be no doubt that those who trekked to India were the most unfortunate for this was the hardest way to have left Burma. "Evacuation by sea began immediately after the bombing of Rangoon (December 1941) but the numbers endeavouring to evacuate were always greater than the amount of shipping available and, as a result of justified complaint of corruption in the ticket offices of companies concerned, (the) whole question (has been) ... taken over by the government. Indigent persons awaiting passages were provided with free accommodation, food and medical attention."[13] An earlier communication states,[14] "There are something like 40,000 Indians desiring to go by sea but considerable shortage of shipping ... aggravated by Scindia Company withdrawing ships from Rangoon. Naval authorities seem doubtful of allowing deck passengers on the ground of security about information of dates of sailing."

Albert's brother-in-law, Joe Abraham, and his father together with eight brothers and sisters, managed to leave Rangoon by the last chartered boat for Calcutta at the end of February, 1942. Joe was doing voluntary work for the ARP (Air Raid Precaution) when he heard that the s.s. "Chilka" was to leave Rangoon with as many refugees as could be packed on board. There was space for eight first class, twenty-nine second class, and just over three thousand deck passengers.[15] Joe and his family moved away from the centre of Rangoon where they lived, and where the bombing seemed to be concentrated, to the relative safety of the Jewish School which was in the suburbs, about three miles away. He recalls there must have been at least fifty or sixty Jews sheltering there with them. While the air raids

REFUGEES FROM BURMA

were on they took cover in dry, unused concrete gutters about four feet in diameter and covered them over with slabs of stone. No arrangements for shelter had been made and they felt lucky with this makeshift protection. Everyone who wished to evacuate from the school went on to the boat and British officials helped them to embark. The ships had to sail on time. It usually took six hours to load a big ship with refugees and when this was interrupted by air raids the embarkation became very difficult.

Joe and his family went straight from the school to the boat, as there was no time to stop at the house. They had small trunks with a few possessions intended to carry them through for a few days. No fare was paid for this voyage as it was seen as part of an emergency evacuation process. Joe recalls: "It was choc-a-bloc; we slept all crushed together and during the day we had to sit where we were because it was impossible to walk around. We could buy a little vegetarian food from the *khalasees,* (Hi) Indian ratings, on board - (there were ninety-one on the voyage)[16] but we did have a small camping stove on which we cooked rice. In spite of the difficulties we knew we were lucky to be on the very last boat, and the only one which the government had chartered."

Joe's brother-in-law, Elmo Sassoon, was nine years old when he left Rangoon on the last passenger ship. This was the one which sailed before the chartered vessel on which Joe and his family travelled. Conditions were very much the same. But Elmo, being just nine years old, and having a friend and accomplice on board, decided to do something to ease the hunger of their families. They found their way to the officers' mess and from there to the kitchen. They waited for their moment when no one was around and filled their arms with as much bread as they could carry. Then they made a dash for it. Too late! They were caught by the Chinese cook who chased them with a kitchen knife but made sure they got away with their booty.

For boys of nine, there could hardly have been a dull moment with a boat full of people. An Indian lady went into labour during the voyage and when the boys got to know this they managed, in spite of the crowds, to find a place where they would have a good view of the birth of the baby. Having grown up in a town in the days when innocence was prolonged, the boys welcomed the opportunity for first-hand education.

The boats on which Elmo and Joe sailed were both tracked by submarines which meant that it wasn't possible to sail out into the open sea. They hugged the shore and the voyage lasted six days instead of the usual three. They sailed in total darkness at night but there were no complaints. All ocean liners had to wait at the mouth of the Ganges delta until they were piloted up the Hooghly River into Calcutta by a harbour master. This is one of the most difficult rivers in the world to navigate. During the hours they stopped here in the Sunderbunds, the "Chilka" was surrounded by small craft, and the boatmen, who were poor people and had to work very hard to scrape a living, brought the passengers snacks and vegetarian food such as *chappatis, kachowrees, bhaji,* but refused to take any money. They were now familiar with the sight of steamers arriving, filled to the brim with refugees from Rangoon. They had heard that Japanese submarines were tracking the ships on the Burma-India run and that the passages were being delayed. They knew also that food was running out and willingly shared what little they had with boat-load after boat-load of hungry passengers.

When the "Chilka" docked at the Outram Ghat in Calcutta, Joe remembers that they were met by large crowds, many of whom were hoping that their family, their relatives, or their friends might be among the passengers. There were many Jews, including Elmo Sassoon, some of whom had come to welcome other Jews, to offer assistance that might have been needed and to hand over food parcels. "We brought whatever we could. Pastries, cakes, fruit, just whatever we could carry" Elmo said.

Unlike so many Jews from Rangoon, Joe and his family did not have relatives or friends in Calcutta to accommodate them, so they were glad to be told by a representative of the Jewish community that they would be given shelter and food. They stayed in a refuge until a room was found for them temporarily. The accommodation was very basic; an entire family was expected to share a single room, and if that family happened to be a large one, as in the case of Joe Abraham, no alternative housing was provided for them. Aaron Aaron recalls that in the early days the help given to the refugees was purely spontaneous and on an individual basis. "One day my cousin Israel Elias came round and told me that a boat was arriving from Rangoon, and asked me if I would like to go to Outram Ghat with him in case there were people who were in need. I went along, and so did Seemah Menahim (who was to marry him later). She was working for the Tea Marketing Expansion Board and the Chairman was serving hot tea and biscuits himself at the wharf and the Marwaris were giving out food. We went out and bought oranges and hired a few bullock carts to take the baggage. I thought the only place to accommodate so many people at such short notice would be the Jewish Girls' School and as I was the cub master there the *bearers* knew me and

REFUGEES FROM BURMA

I thought they might let us in.

"The school hall was full of refugees that evening. The news spread round the town like wildfire and before I knew it a lady from the school committee came down to tell me in no uncertain terms that we would have to vacate so that the school could function normally. Eventually a compromise was reached and in a day or two a refuge was found to accommodate everybody, for which B.N. Elias & Company paid. Gradually, as people heard about the refugees, there were more and more offers of voluntary help and the poorer people, in particular, came forward to give what practical help they could offer. I don't know what would have happened without them. Some of the people who should be remembered for what they did are Rufoo and Aaron Morris who met the boats and trains, and D.J. Cohen who managed to get rice from the government for the refugees. Gracie Silas was a tower of strength; she tried to find out what people needed and then got help from those she knew. She organised donations of cash, food and clothes, and individual help, not hesitating to take a broom in her own hands to clean the refuge, although she was expecting a baby at the time. B.N. Elias & Company employed many refugees in their expanding industrial enterprises." In the course of time the Calcutta Jews became more organised and coordinated their efforts to assist the refugees. Those who had money refused these offers, but for those who were without, initial gifts of flour, potatoes, rice, and vegetables were very welcome.

A small number of Jews left Burma by air. They were mostly those with business interests who decided to stay on until it no longer made sense for them to do so, or those in essential government posts. One of the businessmen was Abraham Jacob who had a crockery and china store in Mandalay. Therefore, when his wife and their five children registered for the trek to India, and set out from Mandalay on the same train as Albert Judah on the 8th of March, 1942, he stayed on in the hope that he could carry on in business. However, this was not to be. A telegram marked 'most immediate' from the Governor of Burma to the Secretary of State for Burma, dated the 7th of April, 1942, from Maymyo read "I was there (in Mandalay) yesterday. It is the very devil of a mess. The fires were infinitely more devastating than in Rangoon. Railway station, general hospital and Imperial Bank of India are gutted. Although civil police have packed up law and order seem good thanks to military patrols." Three days before, on the 4th of April, 1942, the Governor sent out a plea to the Secretary of State for Burma[17] for American aircraft. "It is clear that unless we can rely on aircraft a very large number of Indians will have to remain in Burma. At present we have some 70,000

REFUGEES FROM BURMA

in the Mandalay district alone ... I feel certain that America will help." His telegram No.758 of the 29th April, 1942 to the Viceroy is desperate "... even at this late hour is it not possible to scrounge a few more planes? Could we not let up on transferring petrol drums even for a short while?"

A resumé of "the problem as we had to face it and the steps taken to solve it" were recorded in a telegram[18] from the Governor General to the Secretary of State for India. "Evacuation by air was started from Magwe (about 150 miles south west of Mandalay) and Shwebo (about 50 miles north west of Mandalay) and at first provided ... (for those) who could not be expected to make the arduous journey by land via Tammu... (the) organisation of convoys from various centres was done by local committees on which all communities were represented... It soon became clear that it would be quite impossible to get away by air all those waiting for passages. Discrimination in one form or another was unavoidable and it was decided to exercise it so as to remove those of whose fate under Japanese occupation there could, in the light of experience, be no doubt. This meant giving preference to Europeans, Anglo Indians and Anglo Burmese, especially women and children, whose fate in Japanese hands would be pitiable whereas our experience showed that Indians were generally left unmolested..."

In this fraught situation, Abraham Jacob was fortunate to have been able to secure air transport out of Burma. It is probable that he flew from Magwe to Asansol; his children cannot be certain. He arrived in Calcutta on the 17th of April, but unfortunately not all his family were safe and well. They had arrived in Calcutta on the 8th of April, 1942 and his wife Sarah had to be hospitalised for treatment for malaria. She was pregnant at the time and this created problems for medication. When Abraham arrived in Calcutta, after his own ordeal in abandoning his business and livelihood in Burma, he had to face the trauma of his wife's death which occurred on April 15th.

The Zaccai family lived in Rangoon at the time of the heavy air raids on the city.[19] They were a family of four. Mr and Mrs Zaccai, their daughter Annie and their son Dick. Bombs fell in front of, and at the back of, the house they occupied. They had a very narrow escape and Nissim Jacob, who lived with them and was about fourteen years old at the time, talked of the carnage. "The outside of the house looked like a battlefield, with human flesh torn apart. I just prayed and prayed that I would not lose my head, and suddenly I became quite brave." After this incident the Zaccai family moved in temporarily with a relative in the suburbs, where they felt safer. However, as the Japanese army was continuing to

REFUGEES FROM BURMA

gain ground they decided to move to Mandalay in January 1942 to live with another relative there. Nissim Jacob accompanied them. Dick was in the ARP, and worked in the Rangoon Town Hall. He decided that as there was useful work to be done in the city, he would remain in Rangoon, confident that the British Army would take whatever care was necessary to protect him if it came to the crunch.

It took seventeen days on the river to Mandalay by boat. Annie remembers that the boat was large, carrying several hundred deck passengers. The water level was low in the river at that time of the year and the large vessel could not, therefore, use its own engines and had to be towed by two tugs. There were villages and small towns all along the banks of the river, and when the boat stopped the passengers disembarked to buy food. Many people had camping stoves on which they cooked simple meals. The Zaccai family needed a clay stove and asked young Nissim Jacob to buy this at one of the stops. The boat left before he returned and he was stranded with very little money and no personal possessions. There was no immediate prospect of getting another boat to Mandalay, and there was nothing for it but for Nissim to return to Rangoon by river craft.

The city was being heavily bombed and young Nissim was terrified. He went to the Town Hall to see what advice he could get there, when quite by chance he met Dick Zaccai who gave him money for the rail fare to Mandalay. Nissim managed to get a train ticket and arrived in Mandalay well in advance of the Zaccai family who were still making their way by boat. They were extremely surprised and relieved to find him waiting for them in Mandalay. Nissim Jacob, his brother and father, who had also evacuated from Rangoon, all lived with relatives of the Zaccai family in Mandalay for about a month, during which time Annie remembers that more and more people joined them there from Rangoon.

In the meantime, Dick recalls being in Rangoon two days before the city fell to the Japanese. Although he and his colleagues were being constantly reassured that they would be looked after, he noticed that "suddenly all the big shots went off. Notices were up all over the city advocating a scorched earth policy. Burn cars, burn gasoline." On February 24th 1942 the Governor reported "a large amount of incendiarism and that the Japanese would find an 'unsatisfying city'.[20] Dick knew that it was time to head north. He managed to get a car and although he had no driving licence, drove to Mandalay together with Benny Jacob and his father Samuel. "The journey took six days as the road was crowded with cars. It was terribly hot, and I found myself dropping off at the wheel." He reached Mandalay safely and joined his parents and sister at the home of his aunt. Not a moment too soon. His uncle by marriage was a Russian Jew, Jack Tass, who owned a small sweet factory. This man "had some influence with the authorities" and the Zaccai family all managed to secure air passages to Chittagong, but not without difficulty. Annie and her brother were considered to be fit enough to trek, but Mr Zaccai said he would not be separated from his children. They had to go to the bottom of the queue, but in the end there was sufficient space to accommodate them all, and the family was not separated. They travelled to Shwebo, where they paid Rupees 280 each, or £21 sterling at the time,[21] and boarded a C47 American Army transport aeroplane.[22] The cost of the fare meant that only the professional and business families got out. The journey from Shwebo to Chittagong took an hour and a half. They transferred immediately to a train which took them directly to Calcutta. There were representatives of many communities at the railway station, including the Jewish community. However, the Zaccai family decided that they would take the offer of a lift by coach to the Loreto House, run by nuns, where they were given food and shelter. The following day was a Saturday and Mr Zaccai and Dick went to the synagogue. They met a friend there who knew of a vacant flat and within a few days the family were able to move into satisfactory accommodation. Mr Zaccai was an employee of B.N. Elias & Company, representing their interests in Rangoon, so it was relatively straightforward to make a transfer to the firm in Calcutta.

The Jacob family were not so lucky. They had to stay on in Mandalay for several weeks in spite of the heavy bombardment of the city which started on February 18th, 1942,[23] as there were no means by which they could leave. They did, however, have refugee status, and as the bombing intensified refugees began to congregate in camps in the hope that their evacuation would be organised. Eventually they were able to travel free of cost by train from Mandalay to Myitkyina in the north east, from where there was limited air transport to Dinjan in Assam. Sir Reginald Dorman Smith, Governor of Burma, reported at the time: "When I arrived in Myitkyina on April 28 the town was hopelessly congested ... the offtake by air rarely if ever caught up with the influx."[24] Priority was given to those who were accompanying women and again the Jacob family were in difficulty as their elderly father, who was suffering from chronic asthma, was travelling with two sons. Eventually the evacuation authorities agreed that the father and one son only could travel by air, free of charge, and the other would have to trek. Nissim, being the younger son was allowed to accompany his father. They parted from the older son, who was no more than sixteen years old at the time, with great sorrow, as they knew the journey was very arduous and many were dying en route. "We had no idea if we would ever see him again and we were all weeping" Nissim remembers. When Nissim and his father arrived in Assam after their flight they transferred to a train and made the journey to Calcutta in five days. Nissim went to the Zaccai family who took him into their home as their own son, and he lived with them for many years. "They did more for me than my own mother and father were able to do." Nissim's father went to live in Cochin, where he was born and brought up. His brother survived the trek, but arrived in Calcutta in a state of severe malnutrition.

In an enclosure to a private letter from the Governor of Bengal to the Viceroy, dated 8th April 1942, the problem of the relief of evacuees from Burma and other Far Eastern theatres of war was discussed.[25] On the question of finance, the Governor said: "When the Evacuee Committee was set up it was understood that each community would provide voluntary relief for its own people and up to date this has been done. The main responsibility for feeding, and in some cases clothing, evacuees has fallen on the voluntary efforts of the non official relief sub-committees. The Marwari Relief Society which has been feeding between 7,500 and 10,000 a day has been spending for that purpose up to 1000 rupees a day (equivalent to approximately seventy five pounds sterling at the time),[26] and the European Association has been spending about 15,000 rupees a month for the maintenance of Loreto House and other forms of relief. Other sub-committees have spent in proportion..."

It is estimated that over 1000 Jews from Rangoon[27] settled in Calcutta in 1942 where the Jewish community did not exceed 2500 people.[28] Many Jews from Burma had relatives in Calcutta who gave them help and hospitality until they had time to settle in, when they became independent and contributors to the community in every sense. There were others who went on to Bombay and Poona, determined not to have to uproot themselves again in the event of further Japanese advances. Initially there were pressures on community resources in Calcutta; for school places, burial space,[29] and funding for those who were in permanent need of assistance,[30] for example. There is no indication, however, that such pressure created problems which could not be resolved, or that the relationship between the two communities was unduly stressed. There was good-natured teasing between the two groups, the Rangoon people were given the nick-name *Tanagath,* (A) tin-heads, since tin was mined in Burma, and the Calcutta Jews were called *Khashbas,*(A) wooden-heads because teak wood grew in the forests of Bengal.

REFUGEES FROM BURMA

After the war, four to five hundred Jews returned to Rangoon. Some went to claim compensation, others hoped to retrieve their property and precious articles which they had hidden. Even more went to rebuild their life in a country which they still loved. Most of them met sadness and disappointment. Albert Judah returned in 1946 in the hope of starting up a business. Conditions were very difficult. "Wiring, railings, and wood had all been ripped out of houses for the Japanese war effort. There was no water, no electricity, no dustmen. Life was very difficult and the prospects for business did not look at all bright. So we decided to leave in 1948 with temporary travel documents (he had married a girl from Calcutta in the meantime) and came to live in England via India." Joe Abraham also returned for a while. "I was amazed to see the city; it seemed to be razed to the ground, like a football field." Joe's visit to Rangoon was also temporary. He found work in India, married a girl from Calcutta, and after the birth of their son, emigrated to the U.K.

A handful of Jews remained in Burma during the Second World War. A few were singled out for "special treatment" because of their pro-British leanings, but never because they were Jews. The large synagogue, *Musmeyah Yeshua*, remained protected as were all buildings of worship. They were simply locked up with a notice stating "enemy property." Both Albert and Joe found that all the silver cases of the *120 sifrae torah*[31] were intact. Today the synagogue is a museum and there are no more than twenty Jews in the city.[32] Like other communities from the East, Rangoon Jewry dispersed to Israel, Australia and countries in the western world. There was no recovery of a Jewish community in Burma after the exodus of 1942.

Albert Judah's diary from 14.2.1942 until 8.4.1942, on his trek from Burma to India.

14.2.42	Left Bassein by boat.
15.2.42	Arrived in Rangoon. Joined sister and family.
19.2.42	Left Rangoon by train. Advised to register for trek in Mandalay.
21.2.42	Arrived in Mandalay. Lived from day to day. Registered for trek. Received evacuation certificate and told to report at railway station on the 8 March, early in the morning.
8.3.42	Left Mandalay by train 11.10 a.m.
8.3.42	Arrived Monywa at 4 p.m. Transferred to launch. Moored overnight on River Chindwin. Slept on deck.
9.3.42	Sailed at 5 a.m. Moored in Kalewa at nightfall. Slept on deck.
10.3.42	Sailed early a.m. but water very shallow. Had to disembark and walked three hours in intense heat. Continued journey on launch, stopping overnight.
15.3.42	Reached Mawlaik 10 a.m. Passed whole day on shore.
16.3.42	Divided into groups. Walkers and non-walkers. 60 men, women and children in each group.
	Non-walkers camped at Mawlaik for a few days until arrangements could be made to proceed to Tammu Pass by country boats.
	Walkers boarded another launch, the "Namtu" and set off at 12 noon.
	Fire broke out on "Namtu" but soon under control. No loss of life or cargo.
	Proceeded to Yuwa - village. Stopped for the night.
17.3.42	Started 9 a.m. Reached Sittaung at 2.30 p.m. Given kit numbers.
	Kit taken by Burmese coolies to camp. Thunder and rain all night.

Diary continued -

18.3.42	Half the party left on walking route. Luggage carried by elephants. Those who could not walk rode on elephants. Very little progress. Held up by heavy rain.
19.3.42	Started on walk 7.30 a.m. Batch of 60. Covered six miles. Arrived first camp 10 a.m. No further progress. Rain holding us up.
20.3.42	Second day of walk. Started 7 a.m. Arrived second camp 10.15. Covered ten miles. Place infested with monkeys.
21.3.42	Started 7 a.m. on third day of walk. Started raining. Took shelter in a bungalow from 8 a.m. until 10 a.m. Walked a total of 8 miles. Soft, muddy tracks. Reached next camp at 1.15 p.m. Scarcity of water.
22.3.42	Started 8 a.m. on fourth day of walk. Arrived next camp at 1.15 p.m. Covered 8 miles.
23.3.42	Started 7.50 a.m. Fifth day of walk. Crossed stream after five miles. Hoped to find lorries to transport us to Tammu. Disappointed. We would have to walk the next 36 miles to Tammu.
24.3.42	Stopped for day. Could not proceed because of shortage of coolies.
25.3.42 - 29.3.42	No movement because coolie shortage persisted and elephants late. Sandstorm.
30.3.42	Other half of Mawlaik group joined us. All left early with elephants. Reached Tammu evening, after 8 miles.
31.3.42	Stopped for day. Attack of jungle fever.
1.4.42	Left Tammu 9.30 a.m. Walked 5 miles to first camp in mountains. Arrived 12.10 p.m.
2.4.42	Left camp soon after dawn. Walked 7 miles to next camp.

Diary continued -

3.4.42	Left camp early a.m. Walked 5 miles to third camp. Arrived afternoon.
	Very steep, narrow paths through jungle.
4.4.42	Left third camp early a.m. Covered 6 miles. Arrived fourth camp afternoon.
5.4.42	Left fourth camp early a.m. Walked six miles to Palel, Assam. Arrived evening.
	Had injection for jungle fever. Given tea and hot baths. Drove to Imphal, 20 miles by bus. Stopped overnight. Thundered and rained at night.
6.4.42	8 a.m. Left Imphal by bus with tiffin. Arrived Dimapur 6 p.m. Tea in canteen.
	11.30 p.m. left by train.
7.4.42	Arrived Lumding Junction 6 a.m. Given tea, sandwiches, biscuits. Went on by rail to Pandu. Arrived same evening. Refreshments at canteen. Took ferry from Pandu to Amingoan. Took train at Amingoan same night. Travelled through the night to Parbatipur.
8.4.42	Arrived Parbatipur. Changed train for direct line to Calcutta. Arrived Calcutta 3.30 p.m.

MEMORANDA

4.4 too left of the camp
early morning arrived 4th
camp. the afternoon 6 mile
5.u.u left 4th camp and
morning arrived Pabal afternoon
had dinner just Laxmi ahir
held tent - wanted for tiffin
after ahiu - 3 hrs 05' to
thakurao and drove to
Inglai 20 miles and arrived
evening. then dined abryleship
b. 4.43 left Inglai by
bus at 8 AM with our tiffin
arrived Dunagpur at 6 P.M.
went to the contractor for tea
etc. then at night made
over to the train & left at
11-30 P.M. and in the
morning 7.4.43 arrived
Lumding junction

MEMORANDA
(Kalewa)

Where we were served with
tea [?] instead
then left [?] till we
reached Patdu in the
evening where we made 6-
the camp for tea & grub
and then made over to the
ferry and crossed by
ferry to Amingon
at Amingon got into
the train at night and
left the same night —
in the morning 8.4.43
arrived Parbatipur
and changed train
then started direct —
for Cal. arrived evening
8-30. P.M. (7th day Passover
21st Nisan)

Permit for Evacuation

Name Mr. A. Judah

Occupation

Signature of officer issuing pass

Date, Mandalay 7th March 1942

Date of Inoculation for Cholera

Signature of Medical Officer

U. B. Adv. Press, Mandalay. 88 42 5000

Albert Judah's permit for evacuation from Burma, March, 1942.

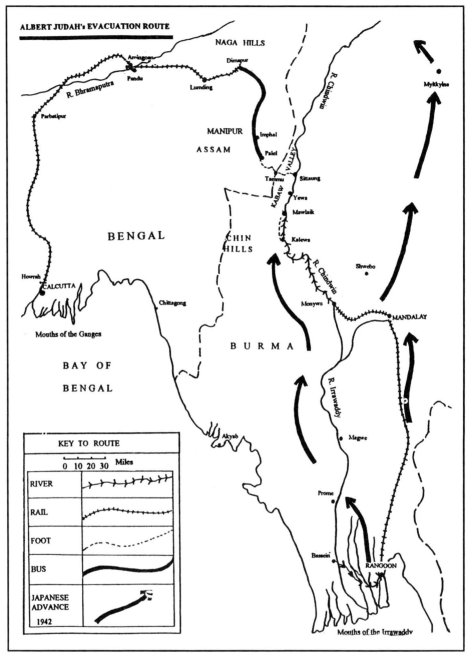

Map showing Albert Judah's evacuation route.

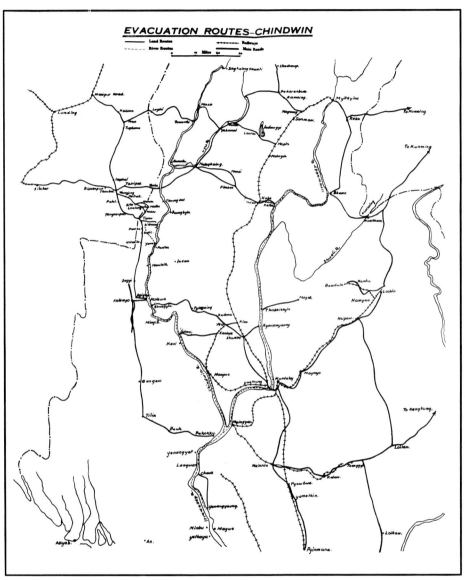

Evacuation Routes – Chindwin, 1942.
Courtesy: The British Library.

Sir Reginald Dorman-Smith, Governor of Burma, 1942, listens to a tale of terror told by a Rangoon refugee. The bombing forced thousands of civilians to leave their homes.
Photo: Hulton Deutsch.

Disembarkation midstream at the Outram Ghat, Calcutta.
Photo: Hulton Deutsch.

Chapter 14

RIOTS

The Jewish settlers who arrived on the Indian scene from Iraq in the early days of the British Raj were mainly merchants, and as such were encouraged by the prospects of stability, security and booming trade.[1] Confidence in the Raj, and loyalty towards the British, grew as the Empire strengthened and all that was British was considered to be worthy of admiration and emulation. For example, the legal system, the administrative system, the railway system were all products of the Raj, which appeared to be awe-inspiring, and were symbols of power and benevolence of the rulers towards their subjects. The attitude of the ruling class was summed up in this statement:[2] "The question of exercising my power (in the police force) never arose in my mind because it seemed so natural that, as an Englishman, I should have power over all my Indian subordinates. The prestige of the Raj enhanced the status of all the British in India. Its advantages in terms of respect and obedience were considerable but it demanded a conscious sense of responsibility towards those under you." Ethnic groups, including Jews, Parsis, Armenians and Chinese, for example, were all free to worship as they wished, and lived together in harmony, respecting their own and each other's faith and way of life. They were all glad and grateful to be British-Indian subjects.

The topmost jobs in commerce and in central administration were the preserve of the British and other Europeans, and although the Baghdadi Jews tried time and again to achieve European classification, they failed to do so.[3] Roland confirms:[4] "... the Baghdadian Jews, particularly those in Calcutta, never wavered in their attempts to be considered European ... for educational purposes, for electoral purposes, and to obtain jobs for which there were quotas in the public services". English was an indispensable entrée to higher paid posts and the Baghdadi Jews, realising this, used it as the medium of instruction in their schools and as their first language at home, by the second quarter of the twentieth century. They were, therefore, equipped to compete for positions which enabled them proportionately, to earn higher salaries than the indigenous population.

There was no doubt in anyone's mind that Indian independence would bring about fundamental economic and social changes and although it was difficult to predict how it would work out economically for any particular group, the slogan

RIOTS

"India for the Indians" would understandably be put into practice. It is not surprising then, that in addition to their strong pro-British leanings, the Baghdadi Jews tended to be wary of Indian nationalism, and like some ethnic groups in India, they took no significant part in the Indian struggle for independence.[5] Traditionalist Muslims supported the nationalist movement and were members of the Indian National Congress, but certain sections of that community, mostly from the upper classes, were uneasy. They believed that their religion and language, Urdu, led them to have political and economic interests which were distinct from Congress, and in 1906 they formed the Muslim League. "Hostility between Muslims, Hindus and Sikhs was generated by the presence of Christian missionaries ... as well as the framework of Government and the competitive style of politics the Raj's changing structures encouraged, and the growing dominance of high and trading Hindu castes in education and provincial administration."[6] Political and social unrest which was beginning to emerge from the mid-nineteenth century was steadily gaining momentum until it started to boil over in the early 1930s.

Gandhi returned to India from South Africa in 1915 and his aim at that time was to achieve Home Rule with Dominion status, i.e. self government within the Empire. He wished for no more than that India be governed on the same basis as the other Dominions in the Empire; South Africa, Australia and Canada. He understood that this would mean a hard struggle and his strategy was a campaign of *satyagraha* (Hi) non-violent civil disobedience. In 1916, at a joint meeting of the Indian National Congress and the Muslim League, it was agreed that the Muslims would support the demand of Congress for representative self government on condition that Congress agreed to separate Muslim constituencies. The Government of India Act of 1919 broadened the base of elected legislatures in the provinces. Race, religion and property were the criteria for the right to vote.

Jawaharlal Nehru returned to India from Britain in 1927 and like his compatriot Subhas Chandra Bose of Bengal, had radical leanings at the time. Together they formed the Indian Independence League which stood for complete independence, which required British withdrawal, and they tried to persuade Congress to adopt this policy. "Bose was in sympathy with the Bengal tradition of the national revolutionaries who preferred violent action to Gandhi's non-violence."[7] The early 1930s was a time of political tension following the doubling of the tax on salt in spite of the fact that the Central Legislative Assembly had rejected it, and the prospect of a peasant revolt against land tax. There were *hartals*, (Hi) literally days of silence or one day strikes, but the political agitation

RIOTS

at the time sometimes led to violence, although this was against Gandhi's policy of *satyagraha*. The economic damage and personal inconvenience was widespread. Political rallies, preceded by mass marches, were noisy and increasingly undisciplined and this contrasted sharply with the days of peace and quiet. It was when mass movements led to mass hysteria that the situation went intolerably out of control. Victims were sought out for attack, and property was burned in what seemed a senseless onslaught of destruction. The Jews, like so many others, sometimes became the unfortunate chance victims of political unrest.

Seemah Jacob Sadka will never forget the day in 1930 when her father bought a car. He and his son could hardly wait to drive it, so father and son, together with a few friends went out together. She said: "A *hartal* had been called at short notice but my family were under the impression it had ended and there would be no problem in going for a drive. While they were out, quite without warning my father and brother found themselves face to face with an angry crowd and under attack with a hail of stones. The car had a soft roof which was lowered at the time and one of the stones struck my father on his head. My brother was afraid that the mob would decide to lie down in the street and force them out of the car but he was fortunate to have been able to drive away from the crowds to the nearby hospital, where my father had an emergency operation lasting four hours. This saved his life but he survived only another seventeen months in very poor health."

The incident reported in The Statesman read: "Mr S Jacob (Seemah's brother) said that about 11 pm on April 15th he was returning along Russa Road. His car contained six people, including his father and two girls. A man gave a shout as a signal, when a large number of men came out from several buildings and by-lanes and started throwing stones. Witness and the two girls received injuries. His father was seriously injured on the head and suffered a fracture of the skull. The car was also damaged." Fifteen Indians were eventually convicted. "Opening the case for the Crown, Mr N N Banerjee (Public Prosecutor) said that as an aftermath of the conviction of Mr Jawaharlal Nehru and Mr J M Sen Gupta, a *hartal* was organised on April 15th last. Some of the *hartalists* were obviously out with the set purpose of creating a disturbance. ... A serious riot took place in the morning in which tramcars were burnt and public servants were seriously injured ... the police quelled the riot and, believing the situation was well in hand, withdrew the police pickets in the evening. This gave an opportunity to the rioters and cowardly assaults were made on European men and women who were passing in their cars."

RIOTS

In the disturbances directed against the British before the war, the prime target on the street was the wearer of the *solar topee*. The British introduced this to India and it was worn by many men but not by the masses of Hindus and Muslims who preferred their own headgear. It was not uncommon for groups of young Indians to board tramcars and order all *solar topee* wearers to get off, toss their hats and even their neckties on to a pile, and set it ablaze in the middle of the street. Seemah Cohen Morris went home one day in considerable distress. She recalls: "I was travelling through the centre of the town in a car with friends. One was wearing a *solar topee*. The car was stopped by a mob and the man was ordered to take off his hat. 'Nothing doing' he protested. 'It's up to you. Get rid of the *solar topee* or we'll get rid of the car'. We knew they meant it and begged our friend to sacrifice his *solar topee*."

An observation of a sign of the times was made by a British resident.[8] "When I first went to Calcutta you could walk down Chowringhee and the Indian walking in the opposite direction would just get out of your way. Time came when they just continued to walk where they were and you got out of the way."

When Britain declared war on Germany in 1939, Lord Linlithgow, Viceroy of India, also declared India to be at war. He did so without consulting Indian politicians, which fuelled their fears that Dominion status would be postponed until the end of the war. Initial support for the cause of the Allies amongst the Indian leadership gradually began to wane as Britain refused immediate agreement to more Indian participation and greater responsibility in central government. A British eye-witness remembers processions in the streets. "They would go along shouting 'no help for the war. Not a man, not a rupee'."[9] Industry was nevertheless speeded up and harnessed to serve the British war effort. "All mill production of wool textiles, all factory production of leather and footwear, nearly three quarters of steel and cement and over two fifths of paper production was directed away from the civilian economy - drawn off for military requirements."[10] When Japan entered the war in 1941 and overran the whole of south east Asia within a year, Congress leaders became alarmed. They believed a Japanese invasion could have been avoided if the British withdrew immediately. Younger, radical nationalists resorted to violence and the Government was getting nervous. Tension in Assam and in Bengal was particularly high as these areas would have been the first obvious targets of any Japanese offensive once Burma was occupied. A complete breakdown between the Government and Congress came at a time when co-operation was imperative in the cause of the Allies. To this end, a Mission led by Sir Stafford Cripps in the spring of 1942, offered "India

RIOTS

full Dominion status at the end of the war, or the chance to secede from the Commonwealth and go for total independence, with the proviso that no part of India could be forced to join the new state. The device failed to weld Congress into the collaborative enterprise and its rejection by the leadership led to open confrontation with Government in 'Quit India'."[11] The violence which followed quietened only after the army was brought in to quell it and by the jailing of prominent Indian political leaders.

In this ferment, the Jews like everyone else, suffered considerable disruption in their everyday lives as *hartal* followed *hartal,* and curfew followed curfew. Inevitably, situations arose when people felt they had to take calculated risks. It was the anniversary of my grandfather's death and as it was the custom, my uncle fasted and wished to pray at the graveside. A *hartal* was not going to stop him if he could help it, so he set off on the six mile round journey on foot. He took the precaution of not wearing a *solar topee* or a necktie and carried only his prayer books. As he expected, he was challenged both on the way to the cemetery and back. "Going about your business as usual, are you?" My uncle explained his purpose and showed his prayer books. He gambled that it would take one sentiment to counter another, and he was lucky. The gamble paid off.

While central government remained under the rule of the Viceroy, gradual self-government was being introduced in the provinces. Originally, Jinnah had anticipated co-operation between Congress and the Muslim League. In the 1937 elections, however, the Muslim League fared only moderately well whilst Congress, with their assured majority in most provinces, declined moves towards coalition with the League. It was then that the League had to re-think policy vis-a-vis Congress. While prominent Congressmen were in prison between 1942 and 1944, Jinnah seized the political initiative and set about working to gain the confidence of the Muslim masses and achieve political strength. In 1940 Pakistan had already been proclaimed as the goal of the Muslim League; this meant they would settle for nothing less than a sovereign Muslim state, which they intended the British should carve out of Indian territory by an act of partition. The boundary lines were to be based on the demographic predominance of Hindus or Muslims by district. Bengal in the east and Punjab in the north-west, were to become the areas of greatest tension and turbulence, as there was no clear majority in all parts of those provinces.

In 1944 the political leaders of Congress were released from jail and the end of the war was imminent. The election of a Labour government in Britain after

RIOTS

the war transferred power to those who believed in Indian Independence, and who wished to work towards a smooth handover at the earliest possible date. In 1946 a "Mission, headed by Lord Pethick-Lawrence, and consisting besides of Sir Stafford Cripps, arrived in Delhi" [12] in the hope of preserving a united India, while trying to allay the fears of the Muslims. Nehru, however, underestimated the strength of the Muslim League and was intransigent about Partition. Gandhi foresaw the human disruption and tragedy which would be involved in Partition and tried to use all his political skill to dissuade Jinnah from pursuing his goal, but he did not succeed. The Mission failed to keep India united, and an interim government was set up in 1946 when Wavell, Viceroy of India, appointed Nehru as prime minister. This infuriated Jinnah, who called for a Direct Action Day on August 16th, 1946. He did not make it clear what action was to be taken, and how it was to be implemented but "in Bengal, Muslim League Chief Minister, H. Shurawardy, engineered a communal holocaust in Calcutta. (Did he wish) to tilt the city's demographic balance in this way in favour of Muslims?" [13] There were large numbers of Hindus working and living in Bengal who originally came from their villages in the neighbouring province of Bihar. Was it intended to drive them back there? Whatever the intention, that is precisely what happened. Factories and mills in Bengal stood idle for months as Hindu workers fled, and as Muslims remained in fear of venturing out of their localities. Until this time Hindus and Muslims had, by and large, worked alongside each other but from 1946 until 1948 Hindu and Muslim wreaked vengeance on each other in an alternating flow and ebb of violence in different parts of the country.

No one who lived in Calcutta at the time of the Great Calcutta Killing in 1946 can forget the complete breakdown of commercial life, the suspension of social life, and the severe food shortage. But all this was as nothing in comparison with the atmosphere, which was dense with fear of murder in all parts of the city. Both day and night, there were constant cries of *Alla u Akbar*, (A) God is great, from Muslims seeking out Hindus, and *Bandey Mathram*, (Bengali) freedom of the motherland, from Hindus seeking out Muslims. In the first wave of violence which lasted nearly a week "Refugees were ... streaming out of the city ... a week after the killings started it was estimated that 110,000 had fled from Calcutta, that another 100,000 had been displaced within the city itself. There were now 45,000 troops in the city and they managed to impose a kind of peace by August 25th."[14] "About 4,000 were killed, and an unknown number, possibly up to 15,000, injured."[15]

Maurice Ezekiel was in the Armed Police in Howrah at the time. He was one of the few Jews in the police force, as the quota system in the public sector gave preference to Anglo-Indians in this service. Maurice said: "I was actually stationed in Midnapur at the time, about a two hour train journey north of Calcutta. I was called in as part of a special reserve force to help quell the riots in the Howrah area, a very troubled district. Our job was to protect life and public property, such as temples and public buildings. Howrah was a Hindu area and there were several little villages along the banks of the river. The Muslims would come in their boats by night, armed with guns, and shoot the Hindus. We kept vigil for at least three or four months and I got very little sleep in those days. We got eight hours off after three days of constant duty. There were many Marwaris living in Howrah at the time and they were quite well off. They would plead with us to escort them to safe areas and offered us money, watches and jewellery, they were so desperate. If one place was being attacked they wanted to move to another area. We saw massacre after massacre in villages along the river, no more than six or seven miles from the centre of the city. It was very traumatic. Those who lived by the river were in the greatest danger because they were easily accessible by boat and bodies could be disposed of without difficulty. Not that this mattered very much to the mob after a time. The police were also protecting Muslims in Hindu areas, it was just chance where one was working, because everyone was caught up in the madness. In the early days of the riots people were being attacked in their own homes. There was little or no activity in the streets and in shops. However, as we were able to get control there were fewer and fewer incidents, as carrying arms was a crime. But it was a joke to attempt to arrest anyone on such a charge in those days as it meant going to court and this would have been too complicated in such a situation. It didn't make sense to charge people while so many were being killed off anyway.

"On one occasion I had a narrow escape. We received information that Muslims had tried to attack a village and had taken refuge in one of the larger houses. When we approached the house they opened fire. Dozens of them appeared to be armed and a bullet just whizzed past my ear. The police never shot to kill but a few boat people were killed in cross-fire.

"The police could not control the situation and the military were eventually called in and the trouble eased off for a while and then it would erupt again." A British army officer at the time said: ".. the high-pitched screaming of the rioting crowd was something you could never forget. You'd hear the screaming coming towards you, they would commit some horrible act and then patter away without a sound ... you'd get the smell of fear, not necessarily from those who were being killed but from the rioting mobs that (were) doing the killing."[16] Maurice

RIOTS

concluded: "It was only when the politicians started talking peace that it became a reality but it took months before they reached decisions and took proper action."

Ray Shellim, desperate to protect both her Hindu and Muslim servants, bought chains with crosses, put them round their necks and told them firmly that they were Christians. They did not demur. No man, woman or child was protected from witnessing disaster and I shall recount an incident to illustrate the fury which was aroused and the passions which were unleashed. All that the ethnic groups could do, in these circumstances, was to provide shelter for either Hindu or Muslim whenever this was possible, and to thank heaven that they worshipped differently.

Diana Isaac told me of the day during the Killing, when a Hindu rushed into the compound of their house. Luckily her mother was around at the time and immediately summed up the situation. Silently, she signalled a hiding place to the beleaguered man. She was astonished, a few moments later, to see that he was being pursued by her brother's cook who lived next door. He was a man she knew from boyhood, who was as decent and honest as anyone could hope for, and she would have been prepared to have vouched for him at any time. Yet here he was, brandishing a knife, almost out of his mind with fury and obviously bent on violence. "I saw that so-and-so Hindu rush in here, and as I've cornered him now I'll cut him down." The lady fell at his feet in the hope that she would thereby humble him into a calmer frame of mind. After all, it was not the place of an employer to plead in this way with a servant.

"I beg of you, don't kill him under my roof. You're right. He is here, and if you are determined to kill him then I know I can't stop you, only don't do it under my roof, in front of my eyes."
"I won't wait a moment!" the cook thundered "now that I have him in the palm of my hand." When Calcutta Jews do a good turn, they don't generally bring it up to demand a favour for themselves or for others. But there was nothing for it, the lady had to use any lever she could clutch.
"Abdul" she pleaded, "were you yourself not at death's door hardly two months ago?"
"So I was, but what of it now? I have to get that beggar."
"Who paid all your medical expenses?"
"You did. Where is he hiding? I'll soon find him."
"And who nursed you back to life as though you were a son of the house?"
"Alright, you did."
"Well surely you owe it to me to respect my wishes when I ask you not to commit

murder under my roof. It is not too much to ask. Go and kill him elsewhere if you must kill, just don't do it where it's going to haunt me for the rest of my life."
She won her point although the servant continued to swear, taking up a position at the gate, his knife at the ready. "I'm telling you, I'll get that so-and-so the moment he steps out of the house. How long can you keep him?"

This wise lady knew that if she could plead for time, rather than for the life of the fugitive, she had a chance of saving him. Hours passed. The cook was forced to leave his post to attend to his own needs and to the demands of his job. Eventually anger gave way to boredom, as he had no personal grudge against the man, he only knew that he was a Hindu. Although the watch at the gate was relaxed, the lady felt that she could not hide the fugitive indefinitely without endangering him and the half dozen other Hindus Abdul knew nothing about, who were already sheltering in the house. They were jewellers who had owned shops in the next street for decades and who had no reason previously to fear for life or property. When trouble flared up they were trapped at work, so they shut shop and did the only thing they could possibly do at that moment, which was to beg for shelter of someone who was not a Muslim. That night the lady's son smuggled all the Hindus into his van and drove them out to a Hindu area.

In the following year the communal killings continued on a smaller scale. A few days would pass without trouble and then flare up again. Ezekiel Musleah recalls: "One day I was having my hair cut by a Muslim barber in a Hindu neighbourhood. Suddenly we heard cries. The barber peered out and discovered general confusion; the blare of sirens, pedestrians on the run, shops closing. He promptly began shutting his own doors and nervously announced that he could not finish cutting my hair. All he could do, in response to my anxious protest was to run his fingers across his throat, signalling that his life was in jeopardy. 'When can I come back to have the job finished?'. '*If* I am alive I'll finish it!' In a few hours, things did get back to normal again, or as normal as one expected things to get in those aberrant times. I plucked up enough courage to return to the barber. I could never have been more relieved than to see him receiving customers. He apologised. He told me he thought of me when he got home safely. As for me, I could not get him out of my thoughts..."

Although the leaders of both sides pleaded for reconciliation, what was actually happening was that civil war was erupting in the Punjab and Jinnah was steadily moving towards success in his demand for Partition. In Bengal, and in Calcutta in particular, the situation was like a running sore. Practically every day

RIOTS

the local newspaper[17] reported ugly incidents in particular areas of the city with figures of the dead and injured as a result of the use of arms, bombs, brickbats and acid. Reinforcements of police and troops were called into the city on August 12th, 1947. The Statesman reported that Gandhi had arrived in Bengal to make "a tour of the most stricken parts of Calcutta to gain a clearer idea of the effects of mob frenzy which has been sweeping the city almost incessantly since August last year." In the meantime the British had set a date for Independence on August 15th, 1947. An Englishman observed at the time: "Independence Day came with such speed and in the midst of such turmoil, that there was little opportunity either for preparation or reflection."[18]

Almost miraculously, the communal riots in Calcutta abated overnight on Independence Day.[19] The streets were crowded with both Hindus and Muslims together, in a remarkable spirit of reconciliation, shouting *"Hindu, Muslim aykh ho"*, Hindu and Muslim are one! Gandhi had been fasting and insisted on continuing it until the killings had stopped. He was on the point of death in one of the Calcutta suburbs on the eve of Independence, and had called prayer meetings in the previous days when he appealed for an end to the riots and murder. It is possible that his personal appeal in the province itself met with a sympathetic response at a time when the excesses had probably spent themselves. The psychology of the masses is never easy to understand. However, the actual transfer of power went through peacefully. Unfortunately, this was a mere respite because the findings of the Boundary Commission, on which Partition was to be based, were not announced until a few days later. These were "ready by 12 August 1947 but Mountbatten, (the last Viceroy of India), decided to make it public after Independence Day so that the responsibility would not fall on the British."[20] On August 19th 1947 the premiers of East and West Bengal issued a joint statement which was reported in The Statesman. "The Boundary Commission has given its final award. We recognise that some portion of the award is open to objection and has caused dissatisfaction. But the leaders of the people of India have given their word of honour that the award will be accepted so that reconstruction may begin in a spirt of peace and goodwill." In spite of the bitter communal unrest before Independence, no practical steps were taken to prepare for Partition, there was no planning for the massive population movements across the boundary lines and no precautions against the riots which accompanied them. It is estimated that "five and a half million travelled *each way* across the ... India-Pakistan border in the Punjab. In addition, about 400,000 Hindus moved from East Pakistan to West Bengal."[21] These movements brought great suffering. "There was general fighting accompanied by every kind of atrocity; convoys were waylaid, refugee trains held up and their passengers slaughtered; men, women and children. The tide of refugees caused an explosion of communal strife in Delhi in early September ... and for a time the stability of the government was threatened."[22] The wealthier and better educated Hindus in East Bengal anticipated pressure to move away, and there was an influx into Calcutta before partition. Any kind of living accommodation was available only at a premium and the word *salami*, (Hi) key money, was heard everywhere by those in the property market. But the peasants could not make provision for themselves and when they arrived in Calcutta they did so with a few pathetic possessions in their hands. At first they squatted on railway platforms and around the railway stations. Then they spilled over into other parts of the city. "Just over four million refugees came into (India) in the first decade (after partition) and three-quarters of them came to West Bengal, perhaps a million to Calcutta itself, which is only thirty-five miles from the border."[23] Most of the refugees came without food or cash, and as the government seemed to be taken completely unawares it meant that the refugees had no shelter or provision. They put up shacks with whatever materials they were able to scavenge, and lived in completely insanitary conditions. "The ones who survived periodic outbreaks of cholera (or) who didn't die of exhaustion and lack of food"[24] begged in the streets and tried to earn what they could, but as this was their first experience of a big city their chances of working their way out of the shanties were very slim. Their wretchedness attracted the attention of the press and at first the refugees hoped that their condition would be publicised and bring relief. But week followed week and month followed month, and there was no sign of any organised help. It took years before the effects of Partition were resolved.

Although the anti-British riots and the communal riots were the worst the city had known, lightning strikes could be provoked for a wide variety of reasons. For example, trade union protests could lead to a *hartal* which would not be observed one hundred percent and this could lead to a riot. Sometimes they were contained within localities but at other times they would spread throughout the city. I had the misfortune to be caught in just such a riot after visiting someone in a nursing home. There was no sign of trouble when I set out after work by car, but when I returned an hour or so later, the driver spotted a car on fire. As we continued to drive we found that the streets were in darkness. There were no pedestrians around, no hawkers, no traffic of any kind and then we heard slogans being shouted from streets nearby. "What shall we do?" I asked the driver in great distress. He didn't show the slightest sign of fear, which was unusual for a Muslim who knew only too well that if we were in a Hindu area he could be victimised if this happened to be a communal riot. "Don't worry" he said, intending to calm my

RIOTS

fears. "First they will burn the car, then they will kill me and only then will they kill you, and as you see, they haven't even burned the car yet." I shivered, he shrugged. He continued to drive in the direction of home, hoping and praying that we would miss the mobs. But we didn't have much of a chance. As we turned into yet another dark street a large gang suddenly surged towards us. The sight of the car was like the scent of blood to a wild beast. I braced myself for disaster as the shouts of abuse came nearer and nearer. When the excited mob surrounded the car I had the inspiration of a lifetime. "Listen to me, brothers" I said. "Here I am, your sister in need of your protection. My honour or my shame lie in your hands. Deal with me as you would deal with your own sister or mother and take the responsibility of protecting me from the danger in the streets tonight. I am relying on you to make sure I return home safely." The appeal worked like magic, and as I look back on the incident I shall never know how I managed to say exactly the right words at the right moment. Both Hindus and Muslims regard the honour of the women in their families as exceedingly precious and they can be expected to be very protective about this. Having identified myself as a sister, the mob instantly substituted calm for hysteria. They encircled the car, as a guard of honour, and we moved slowly through the darkened streets in complete safety as they shouted "let us pass, make way for this car, its alright to let this car go." I kept my nerve until we reached the gates of our house and then, safely in my mother's arms, I decided it was my prerogative to indulge in a little hysteria. "Didn't I tell you" said the driver, completely vindicated "that there was no need to worry?"

Some say the sporadic riots which occasionally still bedevil the Indian scene are a legacy of foreign rule, others say that Independence was premature; the people and their leaders were not ready for it. Still others believe that politicians know only too well that masses can be manipulated and by whipping up emotions they can wield a powerful tool to achieve their own ends. The dynamics of riots cannot be easily understood but what is clear is that the consequences have been, and remain, damaging to the country as a whole, destructive of communal harmony and security and devastating for personal relationships.

The communal riots in Calcutta, 1946. The police using tear gas bombs during an attempt to set fire to a Hindu temple at right. The street is littered with brickbats.
Photo: Hulton Deutsch.

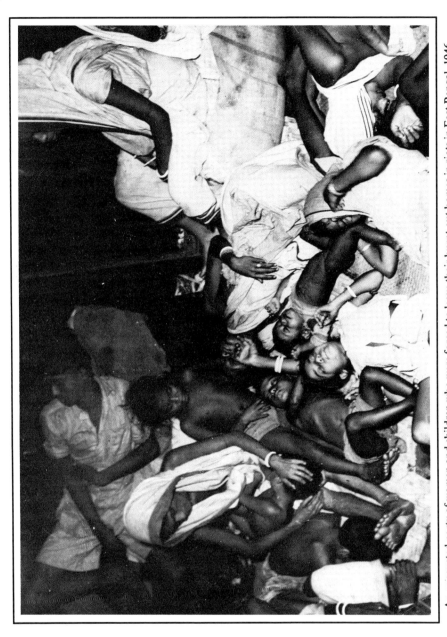

An exhausted party of women and children who were forced to leave their burnt out homes in riots in East Bengal, 1946. Photo: Hulton Deutsch.

Chapter 15

ZIONISM

Until the turn of the nineteenth century, religious Zionism was an integral part of the faith of orthodox Jews in the diaspora, and it was no different for the Jews of the Raj. We referred to Palestine as the Holy Land, to Jerusalem as the Holy City, and to Hebrew as the Holy Language. "The wealthy mentioned some of the Palestinian institutions in their wills as a sign of their religious zeal for the Land of their fathers"[1] and there were a few travellers from the Indian communities who spent short periods on vacation in the Holy Land, spurred by religious fervour. *Shalichim*, (H) emissaries, from religious and charitable institutions in Palestine were usually rewarded with modest success in their fund raising activities. Through our liturgy we constantly kept alive the hope of a return to Zion. Some believed, such as the Bene Israel of Bombay,[2] that this would come about "by some miraculous agency". Few dreamt of political Zionism and the reality of a Jewish state in our own lifetime, and when the first signs began to emerge in the West, the Jews of the Raj were scarcely aware of them. Even if there was some awareness, there was meagre response in terms of community action or initiatives in Calcutta until the latter half of the 1930s. In 1897[3] the Bene Israel community in Bombay were invited to send a delegate to the First Zionist Congress in Basle but refused because they did not support political Zionism at that time. In contrast, the Cochin Zionists founded their first organisation and sent shekels to the Zionist Federation in London in 1903. A Zionist group was also started in Rangoon[4] about the same time.

How then did political Zionism take root among the Jews of Calcutta? I put this question to Meyer Musleah, who was instrumental in founding the Zionist movement for young people in Calcutta in 1941. "Generally speaking, our community was Jewish as far as religion and values were concerned, but quite a backwater as far as any kind of Jewish political consciousness was concerned. When I was about eighteen years old, my memories of a Jewish home surround prayers and religious practices. My own circle of acquaintances was fairly limited, but when I heard the conversation of adults, the subject of Zionism or developments in Palestine hardly ever came up. This area was really a blank, a desert. If life in kibbutzim was referred to at all, it was done deprecatingly

ZIONISM

because of the implications of communal living which were themselves not properly understood. We never worked with our hands, and thought that agriculture was for the lower orders of society. The valiant work being done in the kibbutzim was not appreciated, even if it was known. It was only through the columns of the Jewish Advocate and the Jewish Tribune, both published in Bombay, and through the newspapers, that the problems surrounding the riots in Palestine which began in 1936 reached our community, and even so they didn't seem to stir us very much. In the 1930s there was no Zionist Association and this was symptomatic of the state of mind of the Calcutta community.

"The first breakthrough for me came when there was a talk in the Judean Club by Dr Immanuel Olsvanger[5], an emissary from *Keren Hayesod* (Palestine Restoration Fund set up in 1920 to fund agricultural settlement and small industry). It was in the earlier part of the war, in 1941 before the fighting came closer to Palestine. He was a *shaliah*, (H) emissary sent out to collect funds, and the first one I can remember. He talked about the riots and the Arab attacks and the significance of this for European refugees who wished to settle side by side with the Arabs in Palestine, bringing benefits to both communities. I don't know how much he collected, but he did move me and his other listeners. Yet this is not how I came directly into the picture. It happened through a different route."

The events are picked up by Sally Meyer Lewis. "I went to Bombay on holiday - it was shortly before the war, as I remember it. I met Albert Manasseh and Solomon Ezra there who were both very active in *Habonim* (H) literally, builders. It was like a scout movement, but based on Jewish education and popular with the Bombay Iraqi community. I was very impressed and as we had nothing like it, I was eager to introduce the movement to Calcutta. Albert Manasseh had come to know about *Habonim* through contacts in South Africa. They had strong support from the elders in the community in Bombay who contributed money to the movement. One of the aims was to raise money for Palestine. They had many groups of youngsters between ten and eighteen years old. On my return, I discussed the possibility of bringing *Habonim* to Calcutta with Lady Ezra and she was very supportive of the idea and agreed that we needed enthusiastic young people to be working for the movement. I then thought of Meyer and Ruby Musleah and asked them if they would help. We were working in the dark but we knew that our aim was to do something with our own hands and by our own efforts to remind ourselves of building Palestine. Our venue was the Jewish Girls' School and we met each Sunday, basing our activities on a broad Jewish education and gradually the children became knowledgeable about Zionism

ZIONISM

and enthusiastic about going to Palestine. Their imaginations were fired through our programmes and activities and in time we were able to get hold of more information about the pioneers, the kibbutzim, and the development of the land, and there were books and films which we were able to get from Palestine. Unfortunately the adults were not supportive in Calcutta but the Ezras contributed and we were able to maintain our group. In the late 1930s, Peter and Tehilla Krieger came from Jerusalem to teach Hebrew in our Jewish schools and they introduced political Zionism which was rather different from our cultural zionism."

Meyer Musleah recalls: "One day Sally Meyer came to visit us. It must have been 1938. She had recently returned from a holiday in Bombay where she met Albert Manasseh who had started *Habonim*, a Jewish youth movement, through contacts in South Africa. She brought back some material and was very excited about the activities in Bombay which she hoped to introduce in Calcutta and asked if I would help to start a boys' troop in our neighbourhood. She looked to my sister Ruby to set up a group for girls. Sally wanted me to be a youth leader but I had very little understanding of what was expected of me. I had no guidance apart from the initial meeting and to the best of my recollection there was no training on offer. I had no qualification in education, I had never been part of a youth group - I had never been in the Scouts. My preparation in Jewish matters was restricted to the knowledge I gleaned from home of Bible stories, and of religious practices, which were not an essential part of the *Habonim* programme. Ruby had better preparation; she was a Guide and knew something of Jewish studies since she was in the Jewish Girls' School. There was, at least, a Jewish atmosphere there which I didn't get at St. James's School! I had a good knowledge of the New Testament - having carried off prizes in school and after that at the Scottish Church College." Ruby Musleah Mordecai agrees. "I was in the Guide movement when I switched to *Habonim.* It was a big help having been with the Guides for at least four years, particularly as Iris Moses Ferris was my Group Leader. She was very special. Like everybody else, I adored and admired her and she was my role model."

Meyer continued - "Sally gave me a handbook of the *Habonim* movement in London from which I got an inkling of suitable programmes for a Jewish youth group. I went to the Imperial Library and read Cecil Roth's book on Jewish history and then went on to other works to get an elementary knowledge of Jewish history outside the Bible. Alongside my preparation I set about collecting a troop. Here Ruby had another advantage. She had contacts through the Jewish Girls' School

ZIONISM

and was able to recruit a girls' troop with comparative ease." Ruby confirmed - "I had contacts both from the Jewish Girls' School and the Jewish Girls' Hostel and there was no trouble at all in getting girls between the ages of eleven and sixteen to join. They did so gladly. I was hardly two years older myself! Sally was the *Rosh Gedud,* (H) head of the youth group and I was *S'ganit Rosh Gedud,* (H) her deputy. I got Rae (Levy Musleah) interested and she was in the same position a little later, so there were two separate groups for girls, one under her and one under me. Regina Abraham Meir was my deputy and she took over from me when I went to Palestine. Rae and I would have to go by public transport to the hostel every Sunday to collect the girls - it must have been forty-five minutes each way but we were very enthusiastic. In fact it was because of our obvious dedication as youth leaders that we eventually got entry certificates to Palestine."

Meyer picked up the thread - "It didn't occur to us to have a mixed troop; just as the Scouts and Guides were separate we took it for granted that we too should have separate groups. I had to go from house to house recruiting. The bait was for the recruits to spend a pleasant afternoon in a Jewish movement, something like the Scouts, once a week. We had to find a venue which was easily accessible and I was able to get permission to use the Jewish Girls' School. Miss Luddy, the principal, readily agreed and so did D.J. Cohen, the honorary secretary. I must have got together about ten to fifteen boys between the ages of ten to thirteen, and we had an initiation ceremony - for the officers, including Sally Meyer, for which Albert Manasseh came all the way from Bombay, and for the boys and girls. We had a table with cardboard bricks to symbolise that we were builders, or helping to build the *yeshuv,* (H) settlement, in Palestine. We sang modern Hebrew songs and there was a really good spirit. Our programmes consisted of some scouting activities, Jewish general knowledge, current affairs in Palestine, something of Zionist history and the history of the *yeshuv.* There were special celebrations in memory of Herzl and Bialik. We called ourselves *Gedud Zion*, (H) the Zion Troop and we did have very pleasant meetings. From time to time we would get together with the girls for very enjoyable picnics in the Botanical Gardens, the Eden Gardens, and the *Maidan.* I think the impact on the boys and girls can be judged to have been fruitful, seeing that some of them did end up in Palestine, or Israel later, and some also joined kibbutzim at some stage in their lives.

"These *Habonim* meetings continued after our departure for Palestine in 1945. My direct involvement with this group must have ended about the middle of 1945 before I got married and left India. By this time the boys who first joined

ZIONISM

were in their late teens and they formed an older group - *Shomrim*, (H) guards, who conducted their own meetings and when we left Calcutta they continued until the movement disintegrated as a result of emigration to Israel and other places."

Josh Joshua, one of Meyer Musleah's first recruits to *Habonim* recalls: "I was with Meyer in the very first troop and took an active part in the weekly meetings, which were most enjoyable, and in raising money for Palestine. Meyer was a great leader, and we all looked up to him because he made us feel that we were the nucleus of Zionism in India. When we were older and became *Shomrim*, we had to recruit youngsters ourselves. Meyer trained us very well. A lot was going on in the world at the time and especially in Palestine, and being in the movement awakened our consciousness as Jews and as Zionists. We probably took our Judaism for granted because we felt religious more than anything else but through our activities we felt we were actually taking some part in Zionism in India for which we felt a need. It was because of Meyer's enthusiasm and great leadership that we gained a love for Zionism which we will never forget."

Meyer's account is continued: "So what about the adults? In the late 1930s Florence Joseph was the principal of the Jeshurun Free School, and a small group of people met at her home once a month or once a fortnight. This was not a Zionist group but a get-together of people interested in things Jewish. I remember Florence and Ronnie Jacob speaking in a series of talks, but there must have been many others. This continued fitfully until it gave way to the first Zionist group. The thrust came from Peter Krieger. Peter and Tehilla Krieger came to Calcutta in the late 1930s and stayed for two and a half years. She came on a contract to teach modern Hebrew at the Jewish Girls' School. This was a great achievement for Miss Luddy as Tehilla Krieger brought a different kind of attitude and enthusiasm to Hebrew. For the first time the language began to "live" for her pupils and her sympathetic approach was a great help. Peter got a job in the Elias Meyer Free School and at the same time he set about conducting a group of about fifteen young adults at the Judean Club. For the first time we met with the clear purpose of getting Zionist knowledge. There was only one person in the older generation who attended and took a lively interest and that was Lily Jacob, whose support for every aspect of our work was encouraging."

Ruby said: "The Kriegers had considerable influence on us and gave a tremendous boost to what we were doing. Tehilla was born in Palestine and Peter went there on youth *aliyah*, (H) emigration, from Germany. They were living examples to me of citizens in Palestine and there were so many questions to ask

ZIONISM

and so many answers which we listened to eagerly. In this way we learnt a great deal about Palestine and life there. They lived about an hour's walk from our home, but this didn't stop us from visiting them regularly on *Shabbath.* They were orthodox and so were we, so we couldn't travel by public or private transport."

Meyer continued - "When the Kriegers left Calcutta in 1941 I took on responsibility for the Zionist movement. My aunt, Dinah Musleah Cohen, had a spare room in her house which she very generously put entirely at my disposal and which we used for weekly meetings. We called ourselves the Zionist Organisation of Calcutta. I got people to give talks on Jewish matters, current affairs, Zionist affairs and at some further stage we rented two rooms in a house in Bentinck Street which we called the *Ma'on*, (H), meeting place. The interest among young people started to grow and by this time our membership expanded from those who came regularly to those who came once in a while. Although we met once a week, the senior boys and girls, *Shomrim,* were also able to use the *Ma'on* for their own meetings."

Ruby added: "We had fund raising activities to collect money for Palestine. Lady Ezra let us use her house for our functions, such as dances, plays, bazaars, and so on and we also produced a pageant on Jewish History at the Jewish Girls' School in which Elias Mordecai had a major hand. These activities made the older members of the community conscious of Palestine as a living entity, and in attending our enjoyable functions they too became involved with our work. All this would have had some effect later, I think, after the state of Israel came into being, when more people from our community began to think of making *aliyah.*

"In 1943 large numbers of Servicemen from the British and American Armed Forces came to Calcutta. Among them were Jews who made contact with our community and who had personal experience of adult movements and of youth movements such as *Habonim* and helped us with our seminars, camps and youth groups. They came to our meetings whenever they could and made our discussions better informed and more lively. Some of the Servicemen influenced a few of us to break away from the general Zionist group to become the *Hechalutz*, (H) pioneer group, where the aim was *aliyah*. So instead of simply supporting Palestine with funds we began to set our sights on going there to settle. Eventually, several Servicemen emigrated to Palestine. For instance, Gabby Bick went from London and David Macarov from the United States." David Macarov wrote about Gabby Bick at the time: "I've never heard him spoken ill of and he has free entry into almost any house in Calcutta. His love for Palestine is so deep rooted that although

ZIONISM

rarely expressed, it can almost be felt." Of Solly Marcus he said: "He is an Irishman, and advocates a bi-national state in Palestine, rather than a Jewish commonwealth. However, for purposes of unity before the Jewish community (of Calcutta) we buried all ideological differences." Drew Schwartz was also mentioned. "(He) is a New Yorker (and) chided the Group for having (a servant) to sweep up at the *Ma'on*."[6]

Ruby continued: "Sally Meyer Lewis moved away from the *Hechalutz* movement and also from *Habonim*. She got married and went to Bombay at first and had a baby soon afterwards. Understandably, she felt it was time to go on to other things."

Meyer picked up his story: "By 1942 I had made a fairly firm decision to go to Palestine. I had already obtained a degree in law and served three years of my Articles in a solicitor's office. I gave up a prospective career in law in Calcutta to get a position with a Jewish firm, B.N. Elias & Company, so that I might have some funds of my own when the opportunity for *aliyah* arose. Recognising my enthusiasm, one of the emissaries suggested that if I contributed an entire month's salary to the Zionist cause he could use it as a bargaining point to raise money in the community. He did have some success in raising larger sums from other people. It was not easy to get money in Calcutta from the middle income group and the wealthy were not exactly generous.

"Some time later, Abraham Samet, another emissary from the Jewish Agency came to Calcutta. He had a different mission from the others. He was a member of a kibbutz himself - *Ramat Yohannan* - and was a resident *shaliach* for a while, involved partly in youth work but one of his main purposes, it seems, was to secure a group to go on a kibbutz to Palestine. This was early in 1944. In the meantime the first group of pioneers had gone to Palestine in May 1944. They included Ray Jonah (now Shellim), her husband Alec and their infant daughter, Mercia Rassaby Rembaum and Hannie Joshua Deutsch. Their *aliyah* had quite an impact on us. Once they arrived they wrote us very stirring letters, which were read at the *Ma'on*. This was our first direct link with Palestine and since they were in a group preparatory to joining a kibbutz it was of great interest to us, not necessarily because of the communal way of life but certainly to provide first hand information.

"Abraham Samet suggested we take advantage of the limited final offer by the British Government to make available 75,000 entry certificates for Jews to

ZIONISM

Palestine. There were to be no more certificates - no more Jews entering Palestine to settle, although it was a time when such entry was a matter of life and death for the Jews of Europe. The British had yielded to Arab pressure.

"We rented three rooms off Park Street in 1944 which was known as the *Bayit,* (H) house. It was here that we were meant to get some experience in communal living, on the advice of Samet and some of the Servicemen who helped us to set it up. Seven of us who intended taking advantage of the emigration certificates moved in permanently - four men and three women. One of the seven, originally from Bombay and a recent acquaintance, was unemployed. In typical kibbutz style, the other six brought their entire salaries, which differed considerably in amount, to a common pool. From these funds we paid for rent and food, travel and laundry and any other expenses which arose. Each of us got some spending money - identical amounts and not in any proportion to what we contributed. Individual responsibility of certain members to their parents was not overlooked and their contribution to their families came out of the common fund, including at times, unexpected medical expenses. We did not employ servants and this was most unusual for the way of life to which we had been accustomed. All chores, including 'menial' work was shared betweeen us. Meanwhile, the *Ma'on* continued to function as a place of meetings and talks for members of the wider organisation which, of course, included ourselves.

"The experience was enlightening, for communal living had been an ideal to aspire to; kibbutz living, a goal to achieve. The situation is not dissimilar to a marriage after the courting is over and you come to live with a partner and discover aspects of personality that were not readily apparent previously or that you had been blind to. Individual foibles tend to be less bearable and less forgiveable when you cannot turn your back on them. In equal measure, kindness and generosity and a readiness to compromise are more deeply appreciated because these qualities tend to make communal living more acceptable. The very meaning of communal living was sometimes a problem. I had taken many of my personal possessions, including books of sentimental value, with me to the *Bayit* as had some of the others. Imagine my dismay and annoyance when I discovered one day that all my books, in fact every book in the *Bayit* had been stamped 'Library of the *Bayit*' without permission and without any decision of the 'general meeting'. Our unemployed comrade had used his time at home in an unwelcome fashion.

"Early in 1945 we got a date to leave for Palestine via Bombay. It was to be later that year, in October. It was then that Rae and I fixed a date to get married

ZIONISM

before we left, and Ruby and Elias fixed theirs for a week before ours.

"After we left Calcutta my younger brother Ezekiel and Mervyn Meyer and Jenkins Meyer took over the youth movement and also the Zionist movement. Regina Abraham Meir took the girls' group with the assistance of Esther Moses Solomon, and was also responsible for *Habonim* and the *Hechalutz* group. We were feted before we left Calcutta by our own friends in *Habonim* and the Zionist group and again before we left Bombay by members of a somewhat larger movement, as *halutzim*. We travelled by troop ship to Suez and took a train from Ismalia to Jerusalem where we were the guests of the Jewish Agency for a few days. We met Abe Herman who had been corresponding with me to make all the arrangements. Later he became ambassador of Israel in the United States.

"We travelled to northern Galilee where we were to join Kibbutz *Kfar Blum* with settlers from Britain, the USA and other English speaking countries and a large part also from the Baltic states. It was right in the middle of a valley surrounded by mountains with snow capped Mount Hermon to the north. Beautiful surroundings - but we had to adapt to a new life with very different demands on us. This we set out to do with some zeal and great sincerity. We had to adapt to work in the fields, assisting in the orchards, in the stable and the cowshed and in the fishponds. We took our turn in serving in the dining room and working in the kitchen and laundry and in the kibbutz industry which turned vast logs of wood into clothes pegs.

"We took the work in our stride, some of us probably being more efficient than others in the new environment which was sometimes a little raw so far as creature comforts were concerned. The collective had taken possession of their land barely a year before we arrived. The veteran members of the kibbutz were very helpful to the 'Indians', an appellation we did not, at first, take to easily. The *Bayit* had been a passing phase. This new existence with its restrictions and limitations was for life. We realised at different stages and in varying degrees, and not necessarily to the same extent by partners, that the price of the kind of idealism demanded by this lifestyle was more than we were prepared to pay. Ruby and Elias Mordecai left after about six to seven months; Rae and I lasted close to a year. Hanny Joshua and Dick Zaccai married some time later and remained on the kibbutz for some years. So did our friend from Bombay. For the next thirteen years we were in Israel, making our lives in the cities. Three out of the original seven are still there and some members of *Habonim* are also in Israel.

ZIONISM

"The seven to eight years of Zionist experience in Calcutta was a slow period of growth of Jewish and Zionist consciousness which led me to the decision that I needed to be with Jewish people, building the Jewish state, which did not even exist at the time we reached Palestine. I gave up a career in law and took up a life that was fraught with uncertainty at first. It was a new and difficult life trying to adjust in the kibbutz, and the city was not entirely easy but we did settle down quite well. I regret nothing. I think the greatest thing I did in my life was to have gone to Israel."

Ray Shellim's path to Zionism was highly individualistic and unique. She recalls: "When I was thirteen years old - this was in the early 1930s - I went to a slide lecture with my mother. Every Monday evening a lecture was organised by womens' organisations, and on this particular evening the subject happened to be Palestine. There were slides of beautiful orange groves, there were girls in shorts working in the groves, and everyone was singing and seemed so happy. All I knew about Palestine at the time was that the Jewish Agency collected money for *Karen Kayemeth* (Jewish National Fund, founded in 1901, to purchase and develop land in Palestine by Jews), and we put our coins in the blue and white collection boxes. The slides really stirred my imagination and immediately afterwards I started looking for more information but there was very little I could lay my hands on. I talked to my cousin Ramah Luddy, principal of the Jewish Girls' School, about this and she got in touch with WIZO, through whom I linked up with two pen friends; a boy who lived on a kibbutz, and a girl who lived outside Tel Aviv. I got letters from them every three months or so, and kept up the correspondence all through my teens.

"The next thing of importance was that Ramah Luddy wanted a trained Hebrew teacher from Palestine for the Jewish Girls' School, and Tehilla Krieger came on a contract basis. She and Peter had been married for a year and in the two years or so they lived in our community they got to know us very well. While the war was on they remained an important source of information and stimulation, and it was through them that we got to know a little modern Hebrew and learnt a few songs from Palestine. I kept in touch with them for years and so did many other friends they made in Calcutta. Apart from the Kriegers there were visits from emissaries of the Jewish Agency almost every year, even during the war, but they restricted themselves to large meetings where the main purpose was to collect money. In 1943 - 44 the Jewish Servicemen in Calcutta got to know the community and many of them were in and out of our homes. Some of the men had been active in Zionism in the United States and Britain before the war and they

ZIONISM

knew a great deal about the movement. They brought a breath of fresh air into Zionism in Calcutta and were most helpful in giving us information and in taking part in our regular discussions. They were very supportive of those of us who were eager and ready to go to Palestine.

"By this time the Zionist Organisation had really got off the ground in Calcutta. There were many young, enthusiastic members and we had very lively meetings once a week where we had talks and discussions on Zionism and current affairs in Palestine. More material - books and films - were coming through and it was possible to keep much better informed.

"In 1944 we heard that 75,000 immigration certificates would be available to Jews and I wrote to the Jewish Agency in Jerusalem requesting entry, as there were a few of us who were quite ready to go. In reply they informed me 'you are not living under oppression and therefore we cannot give you entry. Preference has to be given to Europeans'. Hope was running out of going to Palestine under the British Mandate and in the meantime I got married and had a baby. Then permits arrived out of the blue, later on that year. One was for my husband, myself and our infant daughter, plus two for our friends Mercia Rassaby and Hanny Joshua.

"I felt like a bird let out of a cage but my poor husband was very alarmed. Nevertheless, he agreed to emigrate out of love for me and I was ecstatic. He gave up job, family and friends and went along. Everybody we knew was at the station to see us off.[7] We arrived in Bombay with arrangements to stay there with refugees from Poland who were hosted by the community in Calcutta before they moved on to Bombay. We were in Bombay for three to four weeks while waiting for a boat, and our Polish friends were wonderful and welcomed us as their guests.

"We arrived in Palestine on my birthday - 14th June 1944. We travelled by troop ship, stopping in Aden and going through the Suez Canal. We were the only civilians on board and the troops spoiled our daughter completely. We were chased by a submarine en route and had to zigzag which delayed our travel considerably and in the meantime we ran out of baby food. The delay was also harrowing because Rupees 5,000 had to be deposited with the Egyptian authorities in Bombay as surety that we would leave that country by June 14th, and would not be a burden on the Egyptian state when we disembarked. We did not know about this condition until we arrived in Bombay and the money had to be raised by our friends in Calcutta within days. Luckily we just made the deadline and the money

ZIONISM

was refunded on our departure from Egyptian territory. We got off the boat at Suez and there was only one train a day from Ismalia to Jerusalem which we had just missed. The following night we boarded the train for Jerusalem and I didn't sleep a wink from excitement. We arrived early in the morning and were met by Abe Herman from the Jewish Agency. He greeted us with: 'Who is Rachel Luddy?' (my maiden name). I put my hand up, not knowing what to expect. 'Thank goodness you are here! At last I can close my huge file of correspondence with you over years'.

"We were given VIP treatment when we got to Jerusalem. Accommodation was arranged and we were booked for sight-seeing. Abe Herman decided that the best plan would be to put us temporarily with an English speaking group in the village of Binyamina, just south of Haifa. In the meantime the development of a kibbutz in *Kfar Blum* in Galilee was in progress and we went there as soon as they were ready to take settlers. My husband worked in the saw-mill and I did a range of domestic work and also took my turn in making wooden clothes pegs. All the work was back-breaking and sometimes it was monotonous, but the atmosphere was quite wonderful. People were so welcoming and everyone put their hearts into what they were doing, whether this was hard work, like scrubbing thick mud off the dining room floor, or an evening of dancing and singing. I was in my element. My dream over many years had finally come true. Our little daughter took to life in the open air and sunshine like a duck to water. It was not long before she was responding to her house-mother who spoke to her only in Hebrew. The food was fresh and plentiful - mostly vegetables and fruit. From time to time, however, we did yearn for spices and chillies." In letters to the family in Calcutta, her husband Alec wrote: "What I miss most here in the kibbutz is my home food and ... I am longing to get my hands on that parcel of *masalas* as I am just dying to make myself a curry".

The main sustained contact between Palestine and India had been through emissaries; first from religious institutions, and since the early 1920s from various branches of the Jewish Agency. It was very difficult for the Jews of the Raj to make a mental leap between the objectives of those emissaries who either travelled as private citizens or as representatives of seminaries, orphanages and other projects, and those who represented the Jewish Agency. All of them were essentially fund-raisers. It must have come as a shock, therefore, for an audience in Bombay to have been faced with an outraged emissary[8] who felt the need to ask - "Did you think for one moment that I had come to *beg*, either for myself or for the ... Jews of Palestine? I certainly do not need your money; nor do they. It is not

ZIONISM

in *their* name that I come to ask your help and support, but in the name of the whole Jewish people and in the name of generations of Jews as yet unborn." Clearly, his message of supporting the *yeshuv* had missed its mark and so far as his audience was concerned this was a straightforward fund raising appeal; they would be expected, as usual, to dig into their pockets and offer the best they could in hospitality.

Calcutta had a very small number of wealthy Jews in the 1920s and 1930s. As a community we were generally apolitical, absorbed in internal affairs, with a firm belief that charity began at home. We were fairly isolated from other Jewish communities and only regular readers of newspapers, including Jewish newspapers, and a few travellers abroad were fully aware of what was going on elsewhere, particularly in Europe and the Far East. The significance of Zionism for the plight of politically oppressed Jews was not properly understood in a community without any direct experience of anti-Semitism.

Physical work, and work on the land, which was at the heart of the Zionist movement was certainly not appreciated by the Jews of the Raj. In our world, agriculture was the domain of peasant farmers, and the Baghdadi Jews who were essentially merchants and traders, and later white collar workers and professionals, worked and lived in cities. This was the reality of our situation.

It was a reality to which most of the Zionist emissaries to India and the Far East could not relate. Mechner, an emissary in 1944, described the Indian Jews as "orientals, fond of rhetoric, sentimental (and) prone to mystical concepts."[9] There were very limited attempts by the majority of emissaries to harness the energy of local young people, many of whom were well educated and highly intelligent, self-taught in cultural and political Zionism. There is little evidence that the emissaries interested themselves in consolidating local groups to instill the message of Zionism in between their yearly or two yearly fund raising visits. The exception was Dr Olsvanger, who, in 1941, persuaded the Jewish Agency to fund the training in Israel of a local representative from the Bombay Baghdadi community. It was also through his intervention that the Bene Israel community were drawn into the Bombay Zionist Association for "although poor, the community was by far the largest section of Indian Jewry."[10] In Calcutta, the efforts of Peter and Tehilla Krieger, who were not emissaries, and Abraham Samet who was an emissary of a different ilk, stirred young people to action. The fact that most emissaries saw it mainly as their business to target wealthy Jews for funds, meant that their scope in the communities of the Raj was limited. Very little, if anything, was therefore

ZIONISM

done through their efforts to convey the ideology of Zionism across income groups.

The emissaries who visited India travelled to the East as far as Shanghai. Meyer observes:[11] "Shanghai Sephardim remained critical of the Zionist bureaucracy, and the large payments to its emissaries ... the attitude of some (of them) had a negative effect ... particularly those who came with high expectations, assuming that they could collect large sums without much effort. ... Most importantly they had serious misgivings that the Sephardim were not well represented in the leadership of the World Zionist Movement."

India voted against the creation of the Jewish state in the United Nations Assembly in 1948 in spite of the efforts of the political wing of the Jewish Agency and local Zionists to plead their cause. It was not until 1950 that India recognised Israel and that a consulate was set up in Bombay to pave the way for emigration to Israel. Only a limited number of Indian Jews were able to settle there in the early years as priority had to be given to refugees from Europe. In 1950 approximately fifty young boys and girls aged between thirteen and sixteen, went on youth *aliyah* from Calcutta.

Helene Sopher recalls: "I was a member of *Habonim* and from about 1949 until 1951 in particular, there was a tremendous atmosphere of togetherness among the members. We had meetings in the *Ma'on* and our one aim was to settle in Israel. We learnt Hebrew songs, we danced the *hora*, and had discussions. So far as I was concerned our own leaders were more influential than the *shalichim* in making us think about *aliyah,* and I was devastated when my parents refused to allow me to go to Israel with most of my friends."

Danny Daniels was just over thirteen years old at the time. He says: "We influenced each other, child to child, and put pressure on our parents to let us go." Joe Manasseh was fifteen in 1950. He remembers: "We gathered together in groups in the *Maon;* and I remember the *Shaliah* Benny Port was involved in the preparations for the departure of the first group from Calcutta. We were promised we could take up any trade or any profession in Israel and we were ambitious. Our parents saw hope of a new life for us in a country we could call our own. The idea was that the youngsters should go on ahead and our parents would follow after about six months or so, and we were to be their eyes."

Aaron Aaron wrote:[12] "The group were waiting for weeks before they got clearance from Bombay about a flight to Israel. I accompanied them to Bombay

ZIONISM

from where I had to get a boat myself to Australia. Ben Arakie was principal of the Elias Meyer School at the time and he paid for the rail fares to Bombay for all the boys and girls out of school funds. There was a wait of a few days in Bombay before a flight became available. Some of the youngsters stayed with friends or relatives and the others were looked after in the synagogue."

The Jewish Agency paid for the flight from Bombay to Israel and the group were taken to *Sha'ar Aliyah* on their arrival. "It was a massive camp, with the young and old all together. We slept in tents. There appeared to be no leaders and we felt lost" said Joe. Danny added: "We stayed there for a few days before moving on to Ahuza in Carmel which was a youth centre. We were all given a set of clothes and toiletries and it was here that it had to be decided in which kibbutz we would settle. There was a lot of internal politics going on about this and we were influenced to go to kibbutz *Gal Ed.*" Joe continued: "We thought we were going to kibbutz *En Dor* where Benny Port came from and this would have been a good choice for us because there were many American settlers there and it would have helped us to overcome the strangeness of those early days if we could have spoken more English. It was also one of the older kibbutzim and life would have been comparatively more comfortable. *Gal Ed* was not a religious kibbutz, and we were not aware of this when we went to Israel in spite of the fact it was well known that we all came from religious families. It was a surprise for us because we never imagined that Jews in Israel would not be observant. What happened is that most of us became non-observant in time and this was considered to be the norm. We were easily influenced by our surroundings."

Danny and Joe found their paths diverged at Ahuza because Danny had a medical problem and was sent to school in Ben Yaakov. He said "a great deal of care was taken of the children there. I was not at all home-sick and don't know of anyone who was; there was a lot of excitement to start with and the excitement stayed with me. After a few months I moved to Kibbutz *Afek,* outside Haifa. My aunt and cousins had arrived from India and settled there and I joined them so the possibility of home-sickness was avoided for me. There were mostly people from Iraq and Turkey on this kibbutz and we felt quite at home, except for the food. This was the most difficult adjustment to make but children adapt very quickly and all those who were children at that time agree that this was the best time of our lives. We went to school for four hours a day and worked on the land for another four hours. I grew vegetables, which meant planting, watering, weeding, and I really enjoyed it. I liked being independent and making decisions for myself as it gave me a sense of freedom. I lived in this kibbutz for two and a half years."

ZIONISM

Joe Manasseh described Ahuza as a youth group gathering where "we were looked after well, learnt a little Hebrew, songs and dances, and familiarised ourselves with Israeli social attitudes. There were groups from all over the world and we took part in dozens of activities but there we did no work. At that time there was a shortage of food in the country and we filled ourselves with bread and salad cream and some fruit. Meat, eggs and fish were hardly available at the time.

"After a few weeks the group went on to *Gal Ed* which is in *Emek Ha Yarden,* (the Jordan Valley) where most of the members were German, and culturally very different from us, although our *madrikhim* (H) leaders in the kibbutz, an Englishman and a German woman, were very helpful. We studied Hebrew only for half a day and worked the other half of the day. There was no question of finishing our education or getting technical or professional qualifications. The country was very young at the time and what they needed desperately was a work force to defend the borders and develop the land. The work was very hard physically, for example we had to break rocks and level the ground and our hands took real punishment. I was asked if I wanted to be trained as an electrician and jumped at the chance. But I found myself just drilling holes in concrete walls with very basic tools and dropped the idea. Many of us felt that promises of an education were not kept and we were disappointed, disillusioned and home sick. We told our parents not to come and the parents of some of the youngsters migrated to other countries, such as Canada and England.

After a few months, five boys, including myself, decided to leave the kibbutz and try to join the air force. We wanted to train as pilots but we were told that we were too young. When we were just over seventeen we joined the army and again it was work on the land. The other lads thought that because we had come from India we were ignorant and were surprised that we came from a city of cinemas, theatres, schools and universities. They thought we came from the jungle and lived perched up in trees while wild animals roamed below! However, when they came to realise that we knew English, English songs, and could converse at their level they began to appreciate our worth and we felt happier because we were more accepted. This helped us to integrate better with the others while we were in a three month army training camp in Jerusalem.

We then went to Kibbutz *Ha Maccabi* (near Haifa) where we continued our army training for part of the time and worked on a kibbutz for part of the time. In the second year we could opt to work in any kibbutz or continue army service and we opted for the latter. We were posted near the Syrian border in upper

ZIONISM

Galilee, known as the Hula valley, which was marshland and had not yet been drained. It was an area which, at the time, was infested with mosquitos, flies and scorpions. There was danger also from wild boar, field mines and border raids. It was necessary to be alert to every sound and movement, especially at night when we were on watch. On one pitch black night I came close to being shot accidentally by my companion on guard duty and he became hysterical when he discovered how near he had come to shooting me.

"The nearest I came to technical training in the army was being a wireless operator. When I finished my military service I tried to get a job but it was extremely difficult. I did manual work when I could find it; sometimes I ate and sometimes I didn't. A friend let me sleep in his house but I was very embarrassed as I could not pay my way. In the meantime my family had left India and were living in England where jobs were easy to find at the time, so I had no choice but to join them. So far as I know only two out of the original group stayed on in *Gal Ed*. Gradually most of them left; some went to other kibbutzim, some joined a *moshav,* others went to the city, and there were those who eventually left the country.

Musleah wrote:[13] "Other groups followed the first in quick succession and soon a regular stream of immigrants were arriving in Israel from Calcutta, Bombay and Cochin ... In the first year 250 people had emigrated and 700 more were registered. That was the general pattern until 1952 when Aliyah slowed down." It is likely that news of the difficulties people had to face in absorption centres and transit camps reached India and deterred people from emigrating until conditions improved. Moreover, Roland suggests:[14] "Conditions in Israel turned out to be very difficult: Certain professionals who had ... high qualifications and experience in India as physicians, teachers and government officials ... found that in Israel, where Western-educated professionals seemed to be preferred, they were given subordinate posts. Immigration from India peaked in 1950-52. ... By the end of 1952 there were approximately three thousand Indian Jews in Israel, and Calcutta's Jewish population, mainly Baghdadi, dropped from approximately 3,400 to fewer than 2,000, a large proportion having settled in Israel."

There are indications that in the late 1950s immigration to Israel stepped up again. News from the *Shema* in 1956 suggests that emigration to Israel was suspended in January as priority had to be given to Jews from Morocco, although there was a group in Calcutta "packed and ready."[15] A further report in April that same year[16] read - "On March 14th a group of twenty-one adults and children left

ZIONISM

Howrah for Bombay, where they boarded a plane for Israel on the 18th. Their patience has been rewarded."

According to Musleah,[17] "By 1962 the Jewish population (in Calcutta) had dwindled to less than a thousand ... and was decreasing at the rate of a hundred per year." Many had continued to emigrate to Israel, which shows that there was a complete change in the attitude of the community towards Zionism when the State actually came into being and as conditions for immigrants began to improve. In the first decade of the existence of the State, life was very harsh for those who left on flights financed by the Jewish Agency, with no funds of their own to cover the period of transition. These emigrants were living in *ma'abarot*, (H) refugee camps, for long periods before more permanent homes could be found for them. The poor conditions were no secret to those still in India, who had a reasonably good idea of what they would have to endure, particularly in the short term, through letters and from the few who left Israel. The fact that emigration continued from the mid 1950s suggests that for the poorer people in the community, the offer of free fares for themselves and for their children was a chance to escape from the cycle of poverty they had known in India. They were willing rather, to place their faith in a future in Israel.

Rabbi David Seligson, American chaplain, China-Burma-India sector, addressing a *Habonim* meeting in 1943 on Theodore Herzl Day.
Courtesy: Ruby Mordecai.

Gathering at the *Bayit*, Park Lane, Calcutta, 1943. Back row: Standing: Moses Sultoon, Mervyn Meyer, Ezekiel Musleah, Meyer Musleah. Standing: Front row: Sunoo Moses, Solly Marcus, Dov Sinclair, Unknown, Zvi Temple, Abraham Samet, Rae Levi, Stanley Battesby. Seated: Unknown, Ruby Musleah, David Macarov, Saul Moses, Jenkins Meyer.
Courtesy: Ruby Mordecai.

Sha'ar Aliyah 1950. All new arrivals spent their first five days here. Most lived in tents but the elderly and ailing were given more comfortable dwellings.
Photo: Hulton Deutsch.

Chapter 16

EXODUS

No one would have been more surprised than Ramah Luddy Leight had she known that her departure from Calcutta, together with other war brides, would open the floodgates of the exodus by the community. The Jews of the Raj formed small communities in some of the main cities in India and Burma, and until the Second World War they lived fairly isolated lives. They were isolated socially from the communities among whom they lived mainly because of taboos, and isolated from other Jewish communities because of limited communications. There were a few wealthy people who had travelled to England, Europe and Palestine, and some even settled abroad from the last quarter of the nineteenth century. Others returned with tales of their travels which made interesting and exciting listening for a short time. However, as there was very little sustained information from abroad which made an impact on our daily life in Calcutta, little interest was taken in a wider world which seemed remote.

This situation changed dramatically during the war. Our patriotism for Britain and the cause of the Allies made us alert to events in Europe as we had never been before. News of the persecution of the Jews, and the arrival in Calcutta of refugees from Germany, Austria and Poland, sharpened our awareness even further. By the time the British, and later, the American Armed Forces began to converge on Calcutta in the early 1940s, we were ready to take a keen interest in the western world. The massive presence of the troops affected the lives of most civilians. There were significant changes in the economy as manufacturing industry reserved production mainly for the war effort, service industries turned their attention first and foremost to the lucrative patronage of the Armed Forces, and many non-combatant jobs were created as local labour was recruited into the Services.

This brings us to our interest in Ramah Luddy Leight. She was working as a secretary for the British Forces in New Delhi and tells her own story. "I went to New Delhi with my mother and aunt in March or April, 1942 because many women and children were leaving Calcutta at the time, as the war with Japan was becoming increasingly threatening. I enjoyed living in New Delhi and when the tide had turned against the Japanese and my mother returned to Calcutta, I persuaded her to go without me. I lived at the YWCA with other girls I had met so we continued to live a fairly sheltered life. I met my future husband, Lenny, on *Tisha B'Av,* (H) 9th of the month of *Ab*, corresponding to July 22nd, 1942. He showed up at the YW with two other GIs and asked for me by name. I was puzzled about this but he explained that he was walking around, lost in New Delhi, and quite by chance ran into one of my relatives, Jeffery Cohen who told him that I was the only person he knew in the city. I was furious that Jeffery could have given my name to a total stranger. Lenny and his friends invited me to join them for dinner and I explained I wasn't eating that evening as it was a traditional fast for Jews who mourned the destruction of the Temple. I found out, at the end of the evening, that he was Jewish too, and belonged to a Reform congregation. I didn't even know the difference between Reform and Orthodox Jews! Gradually Lenny and his friends began to go out with me and my friends in a group because in those days the idea of couples dating was not so common. Eventually we did go out alone and when my father heard, he was very upset. I remember him saying 'East is East and West is West and they don't talk the same language'. Several months later I was going home for Passover in 1943 and was embarrassed when Lenny asked if he could come too. By this time we were going steady and my parents agreed that he should stay in our home. I was even more embarrassed when the whole family turned up to meet us at Howrah Station! The visit turned out to be a great introduction of Lenny to my family and my family to Lenny. It was instant, mutual affection.

"When we returned to New Delhi I transferred my employment from the British to the American Armed Services. In April 1944 Lenny was transferred to Calcutta and I asked for a transfer too. Shortly after arriving in Calcutta, my family arranged for him to stay in my uncle's house. He spent all his spare time at our home for the nine months he was stationed in Calcutta and got to know me and my family in our own environment. It was a source of comfort to my parents who developed a great affection for him as they came to know the kind of person he was and got the feel of the type of family that I was going into. Lenny and I never had an official engagement; there was just an understanding that we would ultimately marry. My parents were well aware of my impending departure, but they were unselfish and understood that I felt very closed-in within the community which was really a small and narrow world. I wanted to be part of the world outside.

"Like so many other families, our doors were always open to Servicemen who frequently brought us things in short supply from their PX. They were pleasantly surprised to discover they could stay for dinner even though it was not

EXODUS

planned beforehand. They did not really visit for the food but to get a taste of normal life at a very abnormal time.

"When Lenny went home in December 1944 he had no idea where he would get his next posting, and he was not prepared to marry if it happened to be in the Pacific Islands. However, we decided to leave together for the United States although this was by no means easy. The war was still on, there was no civilian traffic and there were still very few war brides. Lenny was in the Judge Advocate's office, had many contacts in the Service and was able to arrange for us to travel together in military transportation. Lenny's parents sponsored me to live in the States. My parents were heavy-hearted at my departure but very supportive. I was excited and frightened at the same time but I must have been very much in love as this carried me through.

"The first leg of the journey was to Bombay where we stayed with our Polish refugee friends for ten days. Every day we would go to the docks to see if we could board a ship; it was understood that if we hadn't returned in the evening we had sailed. The experience of being on a troop ship was quite overwhelming as there were only a handful of women, mostly American nurses. I had never been on an ocean liner and was terrified on this navy ship. But not for long, as we made good friendships on board. There was a blackout every night and we were followed by submarines from time to time. We had no idea of our route, the length of our journey, or what clothes to pack, but we had a little clue when the band played 'California Here I Come' as we left Bombay harbour. We sailed East, via Australia, but were not allowed to leave the ship until we got to Wellington in New Zealand. It took us exactly a month to reach Los Angeles; we left on December 16th 1944 and arrived on January 16th 1945, when the troops were sent to their bases and the civilians were taken over by the Red Cross. Luckily, Lenny managed to get us on a civilian train. He was scheduled to go on a troop train but got permission to escort me as his fiancée on the trip to New York, his home town. I stayed with his parents and when we got news that he was not to be posted overseas, we married on February 19th. I was very lucky, I was happy from Day One! When the war was over Lenny went back to the law office he had previously shared with his father. Before he resumed practice, we took a seven week automobile trip across the United States and back so that I could get a better idea of the country and the people.

"After my mother died I was given all the letters I wrote to her after I left India, as she had kept every single one of them. I've been reading them recently

EXODUS

and can tell you some of the things which fascinated me most when I arrived in the United States. The automat was the first surprise; prepared food actually coming out of a machine at the drop of a coin! Household gadgets blew my mind as I discovered that with a few basic machines one person could do the job of four servants. The department stores were a real joy even though the stock was limited at the time of the war. And the escalators drove me mad with delight; I would run up one and down another, time after time. The best surprise of all was when the train from California stopped in Ogden, Utah. I looked out of the window and couldn't believe my eyes when I saw snow on the ground. I was determined to eat it and it was Lenny's turn to be embarrassed. I was disappointed as I expected it to taste like whipped cream, after all that's how it looked, but it just tasted of ice.

"Several war brides from our community sailed soon after me. Many came to the United States and some went to England. From what I've heard, things worked out well for some, but not for others, yet no one went back to India".

The most significant words in Ramah's story are that she became aware of the world outside family and community when she met people from the Armed Forces and from that time onwards, was not content to remain confined. The war brought the world to us and this was a tremendous breakthrough for those who had no idea what it meant to go out into the world. Letters soon began to arrive from the war brides and those who followed in their wake. Letters full of the promise of opportunity stimulated many young people. Those with relatives overseas knew they could enjoy protection until they felt their feet.

If the world came to Ramah Luddy through Servicemen during the war, it came to Sally Meyer Lewis from another unexpected direction in 1959. She was Vice Principal of Bethune College for ladies when a visiting professor of soil arrived from the University of Missouri in 1957. Sally was professor of biology and was involved in research. "He told me I was wasting my time in Calcutta because of lack of equipment and suggested that he would look for a post for me in the United States if I happened to be interested. There were possibilities of sponsoring me as a teaching assistant at his university but he warned me that the salary would be very small. In fact it was really too small to support myself and my son but my mother encouraged me as she believed that initial difficulties could be overcome and the benefits of working and living in the States would outweigh the initial difficulties. I applied for study leave from India as those who had been in service for a long time, twenty years in my case, were entitled to this privilege. I received a small emolument which helped us to scrape through. My basic education was in India and the schools and colleges there are very different from either the U.S. or the U.K., so much so, I only wish that my grand-children could have got the excellent school education we did in India. I did postgraduate work in botany in London and later became an assistant in Kew Gardens for two years before returning to India.

"When the details of my departure from India to the United States were finalised I became very nervous and left with a heavy heart because of leaving my mother and family. I knew I would be isolated without friends or relatives. However, a friend of the family met us at the airport on our arrival and introduced me to the head of the community in that part of the world. There the Jews were *Aam Ayhad*, (H) one people. Everyone was very kind but it is not easy, even so, to be a stranger in a foreign land. The first night my son tripped over a TV wire, cut his head, and bled profusely. It was awful because I felt quite helpless; as if I had been picked up from one point in the world and put down on another, without any connections and without any knowledge of where to go in a simple emergency. Nor was it easy to manage financially although the university helped me by making me a house-mother for seven or eight foreign students. This means we had a self-contained apartment and the use of utilities without charge. I was also given a big reduction in my son's fees at high school because I worked at the university. We managed in this way for two years when my grant from India was stopped.

"Luckily I was able to get a temporary post doing research part-time and lecturing part-time. Even more luckily, this job was eventually extended for three years, after which I got my Ph.D. At this stage I had become an associate professor and my son was already in university, but I was not sure if I should stay in the United States or go to the U.K. where the rest of my family had settled. We decided to stay, and in 1971 we got American citizenship. I applied for, and got a job, in a new university in Cleveland, Cleveland State University, where there were prospects of leading a settled Jewish life and where I had a chance to become involved in the Jewish community and repay some of the kindness I had enjoyed over the years. My son got his doctorate there and started a career in research in physical chemistry.

"Although life was very hard in the early years in the United States as there was no job or income security, I have no regrets overall. The sound foundation of our education in India enabled me to use my knowledge more flexibly than people in the United States and I was able to establish myself over time. I enjoyed

EXODUS

teaching and had very enthusiastic students but there was something about the students in India which I missed; perhaps it was that they were not worldly, not self-conscious, just more natural, which made them more appealing. However, I left Calcutta in the hope of standing on my own feet, and in many ways my professional life was more fulfilling in the States because of the resources for research and I am sure it has been so for my son also. Equally important is that we made many good friends and enjoyed a full social and Jewish life."

For some people, the decision to emigrate was taken largely as a result of fortuitous circumstances. For others, there was a carefully mapped plan. Even so, elements of chance crept in, sometimes in the form of advice at a particular point in time, or in the form of financial support from family, or because these elements came together when an individual was at a crossroads in life. Charlie Silas is a good example. He says: "After partition in 1947 my school teachers, among whom were Jesuits and Indians, advised me to leave India when I had finished my studies so that I could take Chartered Accountancy exams where they are registered all over the world. The time came to leave in 1953 when I was nineteen years old. It was not common at that time for a person as young as I was to go abroad to become qualified, and to pave the way for my family. By 1953 it occurred to me that as the community was on the move,[1] in another ten to fifteen years it would be either the U.K., Australia, Israel or America for us. I felt closest to England because of the British culture with which we were familiar and in our minds London was the centre of the world. I became an articled clerk and like many others in my situation, my parents were supporting me. When my brothers were ready to come to England they all lived with me initially. Simon, my third brother, was the first to arrive, and he went to a *yeshiva*, (H) seminary in Manchester, and then on to Israel, where he qualified as a rabbi. Eze, my youngest brother, came in 1958 to take a qualification in law. Aaron my second brother, qualified as a doctor in India and he and his wife came after they were married in 1959.

"When I arrived in London I lived with my aunt for about six months, but I realised I had to be independent and went to lodge with a Jewish family from Vienna. I found it very strange that I could not recognise other Jews in London nor was it easy to relate to them. Their food too was entirely different and this seemed odd at the time. However, this was in the early days and I adapted quickly.

"One of my biggest shocks was when I first saw Oxford Circus. How could you have a circus in the middle of a street I wondered? When I discovered

EXODUS

it was no more than a little roundabout I was very disappointed. But the shocks were not all on the side of the newcomers. Our contemporaries in London were extremely surprised to discover that even though we came from India, we spoke better English than they did, that we could present ourselves better and that we were not a bit overawed by the world in which we found ourselves. They were not to know that we were used to living amongst a host of cultures in India which made it easier for us to get to grips with new people and new situations and therefore get ahead faster than many Europeans who only had the edge over us by being more worldly and TV-wise!

"My mother came for my wedding in October, 1961 but stayed just two weeks because she could not leave my father for too long to look after his mother by himself in Calcutta. My grandmother had been living with my parents for several years. My mother was resolved now to be reunited with all her children in London and expressed her ardent wish that she and my father would finally emigrate within a year at the latest. Their great worry was how to convince grandma to go to London as she was their responsibility. However, when she was nearly eighty years old, grandma shocked everyone by announcing that she would live in London. We thought she would travel to Israel first to see her daughter and family but she said 'I will go straight to London'. She came to London with my parents on a sunny Sunday morning in March 1963 and after all she had heard about the weather in England and was prepared for the worst, she couldn't believe the sun was shining when she arrived. She was also very pleasantly surprised to see how efficiently my wife Helen and I, with the help of my brothers, had prepared a comfortable home for all the family to share once more. She was amazed and proud to see how her grandsons were now coping with shopping, cleaning, cooking and general household chores, going to work and studying at the same time. Young men were not domesticated in this way in Calcutta! She was visited by many of her family and friends in the first five days after her arrival and was very excited and happy with her new surroundings and her London family. Unfortunately, and very sadly, she died of a stroke on the Friday night of the same week. Her funeral and the days of *shiva,* (H) seven days of mourning which followed, were very well attended by people from our community, so many of whom now live in Golders Green and Hendon."

The fact that Charlie's grandmother was willing to pull up her roots at the age of eighty shows the strength of family ties and the pain of separation when the younger generation left their home town, one by one. This lady was not prepared to face a desolate old age by remaining in Calcutta, neither did she wish this fate

EXODUS

for her son and daughter-in-law who were tied to her. It was customary to take good care of elderly people in the family who were considered a blessing and their advice and opinion was held in high regard. Yet her courage and fortitude in making the break from all that was familiar cannot be underestimated. There were not many of her generation who were prepared to emigrate, but there were dozens of parents who left their home town for the sole purpose of being with their children who remained abroad after they had qualified in a range of professions. Like Ramah Luddy Leight they enjoyed the world beyond the community in Calcutta, and could not be induced to accept anything less than the opportunities and the quality of life in the West.

Helen Jacob Judah's experience is typical of a parent who decided to emigrate to be with her children, in spite of the fact that she had a good job and enjoyed a comfortable lifestyle in India. In 1964 her two daughters decided to go to Israel. One was eighteeen and the other was twenty-one years old. Helen says: "Their intention was to stay on an *ulpan,* (H) school for an intensive course in modern Hebrew, to look around the country and then go on to England, but it didn't turn out quite that way. The Jewish Agency arranged places for the two girls in *Ulpan Ben Yehuda* in Nathanya and I paid their full fare and fees. After five months both of them got jobs, one as a secretary and the other as a teacher and they rented a flat in Tel Aviv.

" In 1967 they were still living there quite happily and I thought I would pay them a visit. I had three and a half months accumulated leave from Reckitt & Colman where I was working at the time, and it so happened I arrived just before the Six Day War. Apart from the fact that the shops were being cleared of food because of panic buying, there was no disruption of daily life. Everyone pulled their weight. Children were delivering letters, women were collecting the garbage, it was most impressive.

"After the war, the three of us toured Europe and England and then I returned to Calcutta. I was doing two jobs at the time, one with Reckitt & Colman, and the other as a private music teacher. I stayed in India for another two years and my children were writing very persuasive letters to join them as they thought there was no point in my doing well in India if we had to pay the price in separation. In any case I don't think I could have hung on much longer because my brothers and sisters and their children had either left or were planning to leave, so I decided to make a break in 1969 and gave up my jobs. The Jewish Agency arranged for me to go on *ulpan* without charge but I paid my own fare. By this time one daughter was married in Israel and I was living with her, so there were no problems of settling in. I knew what to expect because of my previous visit so there were no surprises and no shocks. I completed my course in Hebrew and got a job in an insurance company where my English stood me in good stead because many clients wanted to have the details of their policies completed in English rather than in Hebrew. I returned to India for a brief period in 1970 to wind up my affairs and when I got back to Tel Aviv in 1971 I bought a flat ."

Jackie and Mordie Cohen left Calcutta for Israel in 1950 with their parents and four sisters. Their experience was very different from that of Helen Jacob Judah who emigrated seventeen years later. At the time they arrived in Israel Jackie was fourteen, and Mordie was six years old. Their older brother Moses left the year before on youth *aliyah,* when he was fourteen and went to live, together with a group of young people from India, on Kibbutz *Gal Ed*. Jackie and Mordie remember: "We heard many things which made it sound very attractive to go to Israel. Our father would say 'who needs money when we are going to get everything free; a house, sheep, and cattle. And as we are to live on a *moshav*, we will not miss being in a small community'. He did not realise that these benefits would come, but only after many years. As children, we were very excited when we heard that people danced round camp fires every night and that you could get soda water out of a tap, which was true if you were anywhere near a kiosk, but the kiosks were in the well established towns. Our father, like so many others of his generation, thought of Israel as a holy place and when we were told that we had the right to return there, it stirred his Zionist emotions. When he lost his job it seemed natural that he should set his sights on Israel, and we sold our furniture, gave up our flat, and used all our money to pay for our fares. The trip to Bombay was the start of the journey and we left with a large group from the community. When we arrived we were told that families would have to be split and the two of us were to go ahead with our father, while our mother and sisters would have to wait in Bombay until transport could be arranged to Israel. We were lucky to have an aunt in Bombay who could take them into her home because when families were split, some people had to live in the synagogue for a long time while the Jewish community there cared for them. As it turned out, we were united after a year!

"On our arrival we were first absorbed in an immigration centre where four families were accommodated in one tent. We had to queue for food twice a day and then for the first time we saw our father cry. He couldn't bring himself to stand in line for his food with a bowl in his hand, so we did this for him. The food was strange, for example we were given olives and could not understand how anyone

EXODUS

could eat them, they tasted so horrid! There were no showers and no toilets and the lack of privacy concerned us greatly. There was no school and time went by very slowly.

"We stayed in these conditions for about six to eight weeks when we went to a so-called *moshav,* because it was not a *moshav*, only a waiting place where the waiting could last ten to twelve years. There were approximately three hundred families from India here; from Bombay, Cochin and Calcutta. This place was Kfar Ofer, between Zichron Yaakov and Haifa, a forty minute walk uphill from the main road. There were no houses, only single roomed aluminium sheds erected straight on the ground, and it was very hot during the day and cold at night as we were on the foothills of the Carmel range. When the wind blew the roof would fly off. We had two shower rooms, one for the men and boys, the other for the women and girls. Fifteen people could shower at one time, without any privacy at all. But there was hot water, as we had a large boiler which was a wood burner. We had metal beds with grass matresses and this was our only furniture but everything issued was documented and had to be paid for later. After we had lived in Israel for several years and father received his pension, social security deducted the cost of the beds from his payments. We queued for water once a day. Our brother Moses joined us here and he was given the job of taking water to the workers in the fields by sitting astride a donkey with jerry cans of water on each side of the animal. There were no roads, so this was the only means of transportation. He also watered the trees which the men planted. There was no work apart from forestry and blasting rocks with dynamite to build roads. However, there was a community school and although the conditions were primitive, from the educational point of view it was as good as any other. The men took it in turns to keep guard duty at night with rifles in their hands. Coming from India, they had scarcely seen a rifle, let alone handled one."

Mordie and Jackie both agreed that the best part of those early years in Israel was in Kfar Ofer. "As children, we did not feel deprived so far as poor housing was concerned. We lived in a flat in Calcutta, surrounded by other flats. In Kfar Ofer there were trees all around us, there was endless open space, there were flowers which we had never seen before, such as wild cyclamen and narcissi. There were animals and the birds were singing; it was an open air life for children and we loved it! There was also plenty of scope for improvising fun. We made a makeshift swimming pool, trapping spring water with stones from the quarry, and we did have camp fires and dancing as we made our own dance floor. The social life of the community was very good.

EXODUS

"We lived here for almost a year when our mother and sisters joined us and mother's first thoughts turned towards moving out. Father was too demoralised and depressed to take any initiatives."

At this point Jackie went to a boarding school for boys near Hedera to learn agriculture. He said "I really enjoyed it, the conditions were fine and I was only aware of the misery of my family when I went to visit them. I was here for four years before being drafted into the army."

Mordie continued: "One of our aunts was living in a *shikkun,* (H) dwelling, which was in a military camp occupied by the British in the days of the Mandate. She vacated it to return to India and we were able to move in. We considered ourselves fortunate because we were in an army barracks, had tapped water which was shared by many families, and even electricity for four hours every night. Here too, there was a school where the educational standard was reasonable. When we left Kfar Ofer we gave up our right to a house on a *moshav,* and the *shikkun* was near Lod airport. Life here was somewhat easier but not without its drawbacks. Two families shared one large room which was separated only by a curtain. The family who enjoyed having the front door had to put up with the other family using their room as a passage-way. Our family was getting smaller. Moses went to work on a kibbutz and my older sisters got jobs as shorthand-typists in Tel Aviv and lived there. Their English stood them in good stead and for two years they saved as much money as they could to make a down payment on a small flat in Kiryat Ono, near Tel Aviv. By this time we had been in Israel for four years. Our experience was not unique as there were many, many others like us who had to go through these stages before they could acquire a normal home.

"Our parents shed many bitter tears until we settled in Kiryat Ono. In later life they said that despite everything they were in the Holy Land and that this privilege was so great they could not regret their decision to have settled there. Of the five children who went to Israel, only two live there, but two grand-children have already returned, so the attraction still remains."

Although there was no political pressure on people from the community to emigrate, in some cases there were clear economic reasons for the move. Mordie and Jackie's father lost his job; there were others who were not so hard pressed, but nevertheless had reason to try and improve their working conditions outside India. In some cases local pressure coincided with pressure from abroad. Many people who had made an early break were homesick, or reaping speedy

EXODUS

benefits from their move, and for one reason or another, were writing persuasive letters to their relatives and friends to join them.

This was the case for Sid and Maisie Jacob who left Calcutta in November 1950. He was twenty-three, she was twenty-one and they had been married for just two months before they set sail on the s.s. "Strathmore" bound for Sydney. Their plan was to stop there and take a short vacation while they waited for a sailing to New Zealand, where they intended to settle. Their friends, another young married couple from Calcutta, who had lived there for two years, wrote glowing letters and helped them to get visas. Sid said: "You can imagine how shocked we were when we found them waiting for us in Sydney when the boat docked. They had decided that New Zealand was too cold and too isolated and relatives in Sydney had helped them to get permission to live in Australia. They suggested we should try and do the same. So it was a spur of the moment decision to stay in Australia. We had British passports but there was a quota system and residence was by no means easy to obtain. However, there was a shortage of engineers at the time, and as I had good engineering qualifications and relevant work experience, this tipped the scales in our favour and we were allowed to stay.

"My older brother is also an engineer and we worked together in Calcutta, but I wasn't making very much out of it. This was one consideration. The recent riots and the fact that the going slogan at the time was 'India for the Indians' made me wonder about the future of the Jews in the country. It was another consideration. We were both young and had a sense of adventure and at that stage in our lives we felt we had nothing to lose by leaving India. Maisie was a graduate in Domestic Science and had secretarial experience and I had good engineering qualifications, so we felt it didn't matter very much that we didn't have money. However, we did not appreciate just how sheltered our lives had been, how much we relied on our parents and family for guidance, and how unprepared we were for household chores! Maisie and I had a hard time adjusting because we missed our families terribly. But we got jobs straight away and the Australians were friendly enough although they can give foreigners a hard time. They couldn't believe that we came from India as we had white skins, spoke English better than they did, and were better qualified than they were. It took a good four years before we felt comfortable in Sydney and all this time we felt both frightened and excited. We had to make decisions ourselves all along the line, we had to rely entirely on our own initiative, we knew we could depend only on ourselves. On the one hand we felt we had made a mistake to leave the easy life we lived in Calcutta, but on the other hand we knew that the lifestyle in Sydney was better for us, and would be for

EXODUS

our children. They were tough days but we got through them.

"At first I had to work with my hands, on the floor of an engineering firm and it was only gradually that I was given more responsibility. All this time Maisie and I were saving money as friends advised us that we should try and become independent and set up our own business. In time we put our money into a grocery shop but nobody told us how hard the job was going to be. Both of us worked from eight in the morning until ten at night, day after day, and gradually the investment began to pay off. It was only then that we were able to feel relaxed about living in Australia and no longer had an empty feeling. Our business prospered and expanded and our children were born and brought up in a world which was completely different to the one we had known. We made good friends and over the years more and more Jews from Calcutta had come to settle in Sydney. The early days were tough but we were young and prepared to work hard and looking back it was certainly the right decision to have left India and stuck it out while the going was not good. However ... who knows how things would have turned out if we had kept to our original plan and settled in New Zealand ......"
Sid and Maisie Jacob were very vulnerable when they left Calcutta. They had no capital, no influential friends, no family to fall back on, and very little worldly experience. But at least they had each other.

Reuben Aaron was more defenceless. He says: "I was fifteen years old and just finishing my matriculation. One day I came home from school and my mother said to me in surprise: 'You've got a letter from Australia. Who do you know there?' It was my visa to go to Australia! I could hardly believe it. There was a great deal of discussion between my friends and myself about emigrating because we felt our job prospects in India would be limited. They had applied for tourist visas to Australia and hoped that they would be able to stay, once they got there.

"So far as I was concerned there was another spark of interest. There had been an old family connection for me in Australia. In 1854 my great-grandfather went to Sydney from Baghdad, and I've checked with the Register of Births and Deaths and know that he died here in 1904 as I have a copy of his death certificate. Although my father was born in Baghdad, he lived in Sydney for twenty-one years but he never discussed his brother or other members of his family with us. I had no idea about what it was like in Australia except for what my father had said, and I knew very little about job prospects. Nevertheless, I decided to take my chance and wrote to the High Commissioner in New Delhi. He was very kind to me and

EXODUS

even helped to arrange for a sea passage. This was soon after the war, in 1947. I was the first from the community to get a visa for Australia. But when I applied I never told my mother because my hopes were not particularly high, and when I told her she said 'you are not going without your brother's permission!' This was my eldest brother, who gave me every encouragement. At that time the Labour government was in office and they were not so strict about enforcing the 'white Australia' policy.

"I was dumbfounded when the boat docked in Freemantle. I saw a white man carrying luggage! It was very difficult to get used to the idea that white people served behind counters in shops and even did menial work. In my mind the white man was still the *burra sahib* (Hi) big boss, and not one to wear open necked shirts and short trousers.

"I had no difficulties in settling down as I spoke English, was used to living under British rule, and the Australians simply accepted me. There was no racism when I arrived. There were not many migrants at the time except for the British. It was later, when waves of Italians, Lebanese, Greeks and Poles started to arrive that racism crept in. Jobs were easy to get. Within a week I just went to the Office of Public Services, was interviewed and employed in the sheriff's office straight away. I took my chance; I didn't respond to an advertisement. I then took the opportunity of going to a technical college in the evenings and took a course in accountancy. This was a great advantage of living in this country; you were able to take any course in higher education on a part-time basis which would not have been possible in India. In this way job prospects improved and it was possible to look forward to a brighter future.

"Some of my friends from India were living in rented accommodation in a house and I shared a room with one of them and paid a dollar a week for my rent. The only adjustment which I had to make was to fend for myself without servants. This wasn't easy in the beginning but we had a small gas ring in the room and I gradually learnt to cook, do my own laundry and iron my clothes.

"I saw my uncle six months after I arrived but there was no bond between us. Later a bond developed with his wife as they had no children and she began to look upon me as her son. However, there was never any question of my uncle helping me to settle down in any way.

"Unfortunately, some of the Jewish leaders here did not make life easy for us; in fact they hindered rather than helped. They knew nothing about the

EXODUS

existence of Sephardi Jews and said we were Indians and not Jews. It is unbelievable that they could have been so backward. We were far better educated and advanced in our ideas than they were, yet one man had the cheek to tell me 'I don't know how you came here because you are black'. It wasn't easy at the time that they were so unwelcoming but in the last twenty years or so they started travelling and have come to understand more.

"I didn't find it particularly hard leaving my family behind because I thought I would be the stepping stone and help them to come here but as it happened they went to London in the first instance. The 'white Australia' policy had become stricter within three years of my arriving here. Most Indian Jews came as tourists but intended to settle and when the authorities found out that this was happening at an increasing rate they put a stop to it after three years. My eldest brother, Aaron, was the only one of my family who came here direct in 1950. He too came as a tourist and eventually got the right to stay himself, and permission to get his wife and children over. But he had a fight on his hands first, with Canberra. He is an engineer and I think that helped. I had to fight hard to bring my mother and sisters here late in 1958, about ten years after I arrived. Sometimes it is easier to help others rather than your own family.

"I left the sheriff's office after three years and joined a jewellery company as an accounts clerk. Gradually I rose to the position of acting manager. Now I am with a property trust company as one of their general managers and this would not have been possible without the additional training I took in the early years of coming to this country.

"In 1962 we built our own purpose-built synagogue; the first Sephardi synagogue in Australia. Somehow the news got around that I would be able to help people to come here from Syria, Iraq, India, Egypt and Singapore. I received many letters asking for help but at this time the authorities had become very strict. Nevertheless, with the assistance of my local Member (of parliament) I was able to get visas for about two hundred and fifty people. The others all got the same letter stating that under present immigration policy their application for permanent residence was refused."

I have heard, on good authority, that Reuben Aaron's life has been dedicated to the Sephardi Synagogue and the New South Wales Association of Sephardim, of which he has been president for more years than anyone else; still working tirelessly to enlarge the synagogue and to extend its educational facilities.

EXODUS

He helped many people who had immigration problems and succeeded in the early years. In 1972 he was awarded the OBE for his services to the Jewish community.

By contrast, other immigrants from India left in far more protected circumstances. For example, Anne Cohen Shaya emigrated to England in late 1960, just before she was eighteen years old, when she found herself in the middle of a process of migration of her extended family. "My relatives were already in the U.K. so the gradual departure of the entire family to England had already been set in motion" she said. "I had been to London for a holiday when I was eleven years old and had a great time so that I had fond memories of the place. When I left school I took secretarial training and had a year's work experience when my parents suggested that I should go to London, stay with my grandparents and an aunt and uncle, and see what I thought about settling there. I was quite happy to try it out as my social life in India was getting increasingly limited. So many young people from the community had left, that there seemed to be no future, and life became quite dull and unexciting. We had very few activities laid on, in fact there was nothing except the cinema, as we used to go out in groups and made our own entertainment. As the groups became smaller there was less opportunity for fun.

"I was staying with my family in London so there were no problems in settling down. I got a job straight away and discovered there were unlimited possibilities for studying in evening classes, the like of which never existed in Calcutta. Immediately I took up interesting and creative courses, and over the years before I married I have done painting, flower arranging, pottery, car maintenance, psychology and philosophy. I was also plunged straight away into a wider social life, and there seemed to be no reason to turn back. When my parents realised I had adjusted, they followed a year later. It was not an easy decision for them because my father had a very good job and there was great inducement to hold on. On the other hand they were drawn to England because my father had two brothers, and my mother had three sisters and her parents who had settled very happily in London. My parents also had good friends in London who were writing persuasive letters, but the test was to see what I thought after a year, as there was no way my parents would have tolerated an indefinite separation from their children.

"After I married and my children started school, I went out to work and continued going to evening classes. Later on, while my children were growing up I was able to study law and this opened up career possibilities which would never

EXODUS

have been possible in India. It is not just that my social life improved in London, there were also infinite opportunities to extend myself intellectually and personally, and for this I can have no regrets at all."

Anne confirms the experience of other young people, like myself, who migrated to England for different personal reasons, but who were looking for, and found fulfilment in a variety of ways, not least to obtain professional qualifications and to study. Ever since I left school I had dreams of continuing my education in England and it took eight years for those dreams to become a reality, a reality which only became possible with a great deal of encouragement and support from family and friends both at home and abroad and also, in my case, from employers who kept my job open for a year. Clearly, family and friendship ties were very strong, and it was largely to maintain a 'togetherness' that the pace of the exodus from India was sharply accelerated.

An important spur to emigration was the prospect of good job opportunities abroad. Those who were dissatisfied with their working conditions, or lost their jobs, looked abroad for the first time. They were no longer forced, as they were in Calcutta, to draw on savings while they looked for alternative employment which was very difficult to find, or become dependent on the community if their financial situation was desperate.

Zionism offered an escape route, through the assistance of the Jewish Agency, for those who wished to leave *en famille*, but did not have the means to achieve this without support. Although there were families who had to endure great hardship in Israel soon after 1948, in time there was succour for the deprivation they endured. The escape was from poverty, from illness, from a quality of life which was marginal in every sense, and from a lack of self-esteem.

As communication opened up, and as the points of contact abroad began to grow, emigration became magnetic. The fact that there was no political pressure to leave India meant that each family could take one cautious step at a time if they were in a personal position to do so. The younger generation, in particular, were able to adjust quite quickly to a change in climate, and to living in very large cities such as London and New York. The older generation adjusted to the multitude of household gadgets and the lack of servants in a remarkably short time. All migrants have their store of funny and sad stories which reflect the strangeness of new surroundings, such as trying to get off an escalator without falling off,

EXODUS

working out why there were curly metal contraptions against the walls in so many rooms which were later discovered to be radiators, or trying to understand why people could never be sure whether or not it was going to rain or shine later that very day. Some puzzled over the difficulty of differentiating between one street of terraced houses from another. Others found it difficult to understand why people were rushing everywhere, on and off transport, in the street, and even in office corridors, when it seemed so much more sensible to amble along with gentle ease, as Orientals do.

No matter how well informed we were before moving abroad, life was full of surprise in the first few days, weeks and months. Those who intended to live in England had been warned that "the sun never shines there" so I was overwhelmed to arrive in the middle of a heat wave, weighed down with coats and every woollen garment I owned, in my arms. It seemed to defy reason that men lived through heatwaves wearing heavy pin-stripe suits in dark colours while carrying tightly folded umbrellas. There was no sign of umbrellas being opened for protection against the sun. Nor was there sign of the fine linen and silk suits in cool, pale colours, to which we had been accustomed in the hot weather. Those who came by sea had not been told that spices could be ground by machine at the press of a button, so they brought their own large grinding stones, to the astonishment of customs officials who said: "You people have actually brought your own tombstones with you!" It was more of a shock than a surprise to hear people make jokes about religion. Very little, if anything, appeared to be sacrosanct and socially it was difficult to appear astonished and hurt when everyone else was amused. We were not accustomed to hiding our emotions, to keeping our opinions to ourselves, or to being adept in the art of diplomacy. An awareness of all this took more than a few weeks to dawn, and for some, re-education may not even be achieved in a lifetime, *if* it is considered to be desirable.

I have heard it said that the Jews left India because they wished to continue to live under British rule and that with the end of the Raj they 'naturally' moved to Britain or to a Commonwealth country. I have also heard it said that the Jews were uneasy about living in India after Independence because they had no confidence in communal harmony after they had witnessed the terror of the riots, and that they felt unsure about their own economic position. It is possible that these elements were taken into consideration in broad terms, but it is difficult to be certain to what extent, and on what scale, they were taken into account when individuals made personal decisions to leave.

EXODUS

Like many people from the community in Calcutta who have now dispersed around the world, I returned there recently for a brief visit with my husband and one of my daughters. We went to *Maghen David* to gaze at the largest and reputedly the most beautiful synagogue in Asia. We stood, together with two synagogue *bearers*, in front of the Ark. I turned round to face the entrance doors and take in the full view of the interior. All the windows were shuttered, and the emptiness of the great and magnificent building was overwhelming. The memories came flooding in; memories of the synagogue filled to capacity during the High Holidays. Memories of Servicemen from the West protesting - "its funny, but you people don't really look like Jews!" Memories of the entire congregation of men, women and children celebrating the festival of *Simhat Torah* with uninhibited fervour. Memories of weddings, when we came together in large numbers in personal celebration. Memories of my grandfather, holding my hand to and from the synagogue and introducing me to the atmosphere of community prayer when I was a small child. Tears welled up for a past which so many of us were privileged to experience, and for days which would not be renewed in this place. Then I thought about the present. The present that people from this place were enjoying in other parts of the world, reaping different rewards in other places. Put in perspective, I realised it is the people who matter most. Nevertheless, in these days of technological skill, the seemingly impossible becomes possible. A synagogue in Cochin was moved from there to Jerusalem in its entirety during the year 1994-5, and will continue to be used for worship as it was originally intended. If this could be achieved for one synagogue, then in time it may also be achieved for others. Shalom Cohen came to live in Calcutta in peace in 1798. In 1995 about seventy people from the community he established are still living there. The rest have all left, just as he came, in peace.

Ramah Luddy and Lenny Leight, New Delhi 1943.

Jackie and Mordie Cohen's Aunt Malca Abraham washing up at the communal standpipe outside one of the aluminium huts in Kfar Ofer, 1950.
Courtesy: Jackie Cohen.

Reuben Aaron at the Sephardi Synagogue, Sydney, where he is President.

Sid Jacob at the entrance to his shop in Sydney, 1965.

Celebration of *Simhat Torah* in the *Maghen David* Synagogue, Calcutta, 1944. The *Hakafoth*, circuits round the *Tebah*, Reader's desk, is led by the *Hazan*, cantor, Rev. Albert Morris, wearing a white peaked cap on the right. The congregants take it in turn to carry the *Sefarim*, scrolls of the Law. Many sevicemen from the Allied Armed Forces, stationed in and around Calcutta are in the congregation. The Jewish community made them very welcome.

SOURCES CITED

Allen, C. (1975) "Plain Tales from the Raj - Images of British India in the Twentieth Century". Warner Books, London.

Allen, L. (1984) "Burma: The Longest War, 1941 - 1945". J.M. Dent, London.

Braudel, F. (1984) "The Perspective of the World: Civilization & Capitalism 15th - 18th Century". Collins, London.

Brown, J. M. (1994) "Modern India: The Origins of an Asian Democracy". OUP. Oxford.

Calvocoressi, P. & Wint, G. (1972) "Total War". Penguin Books Ltd. Harmondsworth, Middlesex.

Cernea, R.F. (1988) "Last Jews of Rangoon". *B'nai B'rith* Int. Jewish Monthly. Washington.

Chandra, B. et al. (1989) "India's Struggle for Independence. 1857 -1947". Penguin, London.

Cohen, M. (1895-96) "Superstition among the Jews of Baghdad" In Annual Report of theAnglo-Jewish Association. In The Scribe, No. 46, 1991, London.

Collis, M. (1966) "Last and First in Burma (1941 - 1948)" Faber & Faber, London.

Cooper, J. (1993) "Eat and be Satisfied - A Social History of Jewish Food". Jason Aronson, Inc. Northvale, New Jersey.

Copeland, M. (1986) "The Varied Kitchens of India". M. Evans & Co. Inc. New York.

Dobrinsky, H.C. (1988) "A Treasury of Sephardic Laws & Customs". Ktav Publishing House Inc, Hoboken, New Jersey.

Elias, F & Elias Cooper, J. (1974) "The Jews of Calcutta". The Jewish Association of Calcutta, Calcutta.

Ezra, E.D. (1986) "Turning Back the Pages: A Chronicle of Calcutta Jewry". Brookside Press, London.

Geary, G. (1878) "Through Asiatic Turkey". Extracts in The Scribe, No.35:7:89 & No.37:10:89.

Ghosh, A. (1992) "In an Antique Land" Granta, London.

Goitein, S.D. (1976) "A Mediterranean Society - Economic Foundations". Volume I. University of California Press. Berkeley & Los Angeles.

Goitein, S.D. (1983) "A Mediterranean Society - Daily Life". Volume IV. University of California Press. Berkeley & Los Angeles.

Goldberg, R.C.B. (1991) "Mourning in Halachah". Mesorah Publications Ltd, Brooklyn.

Hertz, J.H. (1937) "The Pentateuch and Haftorahs". Soncino Press, London.

Hyman, M. (1992) "Indian Jewish Cooking". Hyman Publishers, London.
Jackson, S. (1968) "The Sassoons". Heinemann, London.
Katz, N. & Goldberg, E.S. (1992) "The Last Jews of Cochin" University of South Carolina Press, Columbia.
Keen, M.E. (1991) "Jewish Ritual Art in the Victoria & Albert Museum". HMSO, London.
Krohn, R Paysach J. (1983) "Bris Milah". The Artscroll Series. New York.
Kulke, H. & Rothermund, D. (1990) "A History of India". Routledge, London.
Laxton, W.A. (1994) "B.I." World Ship Society, London.
Lewis, G. (1955) "Turkey". Ernest Benn, London.
Meyer, M.J. (1994) "The Sephardi Jewish Community of Shanghai 1845 - 1939 and the Question of Identity." PhD Thesis. London School of Economics & Political Science, University of London.
Moorhouse, G. (1983) "Calcutta" Penguin Books, London.
Musleah, E.N. (1975) "On the Banks of the Ganga - The Sojourn of Jews in Calcutta". The Christopher Publishing House, North Quincy, Massachusetts.
Musleah, E.N. (1990) "Read After Me - A Manual for Mourners". Town House Press, Pittsboro' N.C.
Nathan, E. (1986) "History of the Jews in Singapore - 1830 - 1945". Herbilu Editorial & Marketing Services, Singapore.
Parfitt, T. (1987) "The Thirteenth Gate". Geo. Weidenfeld & Nicolson Ltd. London.
Rejwan, N. (1985) "The Jews of Iraq: 3000 years of history and culture". Weidenfeld & Nicolson, London.
Roden, C. (1987) "A New Book of Middle Eastern Food". Penguin Books Ltd. Harmondsworth, Middlesex.
Rodrigue, A. (1993) "Images of Sephardi and Eastern Jews in Transition: The Teachers of the Alliance Israelite Universelle, 1860 - 1939". University of Washington Press, Seattle.
Rodrigue, A. (1992) In E. Kedourie (Ed) "Spain & the Jews: The Sephardi Experience 1492 and After". Thames & Hudson, London.
Roland, J.G. (1989) "Jews in British India". University Press of New England, Hanover, New Hampshire.
Sassoon, D.S. (1949) "A History of the Jews in Baghdad". Published by S.D. Sassoon, Smith, Letchworth.
V.A. Smith (Ed) Percival Spear.(1981) "The Oxford History of India" OUP. Oxford.

Newsletters & Newspapers

The Scribe, London.
Shema, Calcutta.
The Statesman, Calcutta.

Oriental & India Office Collections, The British Library, London

POL 361. IOR, File L/P&J/8/436:

Governor General to Secretary of State for India. Deciphered telegrams of 15.1.42, 13.4.42, 14.5.43.
Note, Burma Office on Civilian Evacuation of Rangoon, 5.5.42.
Extracts from Report by the Administrator General on the Evacuation of Refugees from Burma to India (Assam). January - July 1942.
Governor of Burma to the Secretary of State for Burma. Deciphered telegram 14.1.42.

IOR, MSS. Eur.E 215/28.

Report on the Burma Campaign 1941-42. Sir Reginald Dorman Smith, Governor of Burma. Govt of India Press, Simla.

Translations from Hebrew

The Old Testament
Gemmara, (1987) Soncino.
Tikkun Zohar, Lech Lecha.
Midrash Shir Ha Shirim, Yalkhuth Shimoni.
Mishnayoth Kelim.
Joseph Caro. *Schulhan Aruk: Yoreh Deah, Orah Hayyim.*
Hachom Yosef Hayyim: Halacha of Ben Ish Hai. Vol. II. Translated by Shomuel Hiley, Jerusalem, 5751.

Encyclopedias

Encyclo. of Islam
Encyclo. Judaica

NOTES

Chapter 1

[1] Braudel, F. (1984) "The Perspective of the World: Civilization & Capitalism 15th - 18th Century". Collins, London. P 522.

[2] Brown, Judith M. (1944) "Modern India: The Origins of an Asian Democracy". P 44. OUP.

[3] Goitein, S.D. (1967) "A Mediterranean Society - Economic Foundations". Vol. I University of California Press. Pp 6 & 7.

[4] Ghosh, A. (1992) "In an Antique Land". Granta, London. P 157.

[5] Sassoon, D.S. (1949) "A History of the Jews in Baghdad." Published by S.D. Sassoon, Letchworth. P 203.

[6] Katz, N. & Goldberg, E.S. (1992) "The Last Jews of Cochin." University of South Carolina Press. North Vale. Pp 35-43.

[7] Smith, V.A. (Ed.) Percival Spear. (1981) "The Oxford History of India." OUP. P 335.

[8] Braudel, F. Op. cit. Pp 495-6.

[9] Roland, J.G. (1989) "Jews in British India." University Press of New England, Hanover, New Hampshire. P 6.

[10] Moorhouse, G. (1983) "Calcutta." Penguin Books, London. P 35. "The Armenians remain a problem to the student of Calcutta. The standard history of their association with the country asserts that they had come overland, by way of Persia, Afghanistan and Tibet as commercial birds of passage before 'any other Europeans ... and settled at the invitation of the Emperor Akbar' (circa 1562)."

[11] Roland, J.G. Op. cit. P 15.

[12] Quoted in D.S. Sassoon. Op. cit. P 205.

[13] Rejwan, N. (1985) "The Jews of Iraq: 3000 years of history and culture." Weidenfeld & Nicolson, London. P 175.

[14] Parfitt, T. (1987) "The Thirteenth Gate." Geo. Weidenfeld & Nicolson Ltd. London. P 40.

[15] Roland, J.G. Op. cit. P 135.

[16] Moorhouse, G. Op. cit. Pp 30, 36.

[17] Ibid. P 73.

[18] Brown, J.M. Op. cit. P 42.

[19] Musleah, E.N. (1975) "On the Banks of the Ganga - The Sojourn of Jews in Calcutta" The Christopher Publishing House, North Quincy, Massachusetts. P 18.

[20] Ibid. Pp 19, 26.

[21] Sassoon, D.S. Op. cit. P 210.

[22] Jackson, S. (1968) "The Sassoons". Heinemann, London. Pp 26 and 45.

[23] Lewis, G. (1955) "Turkey". Ernest Benn, London. P 34.

[24] Rejwan, N. Op. cit. P 178.

[25] Ibid. P 178.

[26] Sassoon, D.S. Op. cit. P 210.

[27] Ibid. P 174.

[28] Ibid. P 174.

[29] Rodrigue, A. (1993) "Images of Sephardi and Eastern Jews in Transition: The Teachers of the Alliance Israelite Universelle, 1860 - 1939." University of Washington Press, Seattle. P 194.

[30] Rejwan, N. Op. cit. Pp 167, 168, 172.

[31] *The Scribe.* Jnl. of Babylonian Jewry, London. No. 35:7:89. P 6 & No.37:10:89 P 3. Extracts from "Through Asiatic Turkey." G. Geary. Editor, *The Times of India,* 1878.

[32] Rodrigue, A. Op. cit. P 172.

[33] Goitein, S.D. Op. cit. P 275.

[34] Rodrigue, A. (1992) In E. Kedourie (Ed) "Spain & the Jews: The Sephardi Experience 1492 & After." Thames & Hudson, London. P 181.

[35] Ibid. P 182.

[36] Ibid. P 183.

[37] Rodrigue, A. (1993) "Images of Sephardi & Eastern Jews in Transition." Op. cit. Pp 191, 192, 194.

[38] Ibid. P 191.

[39] Musleah, E.N. Op. cit. P 25 & 64.

[40] Ibid. P 442.

[41] Ezra, E.D. (1986) "Turning Back the Pages: A Chronicle of Calcutta Jewry." Brookside Press, London. Pp 438, 439.

[42] Musleah, E.N. Op. cit. P 58.

[43] Allen, C. (1975) "Plain Tales from the Raj - Images of British India in the Twentieth Century." Warner Books, London. P 62.

[44] Sassoon, S.D. Op. cit. P 212, quoting from Eben Sapir II, P 98.

[45] Elias, F and Elias Cooper, J. (1974) "The Jews of Calcutta." The Jewish Association of Calcutta. P 207.

[46] Musleah, E.N. Op. cit. Pp 349 - 51.

[47] See J.G. Roland for a review.

48. Roland, J.G. Op. cit. P 12.
49. Musleah, E.N. Pp 349 - 51.
50. Katz, N. & Goldberg, E.S. (1993) Op. cit. P 51.
51. Ibid. P 147.
52. Ibid. P 147.
53. Ibid. P xxiii.
54. Allen, C. Op. cit. P 79.
55. Ibid. P 105.
56. See, for example, E. Nathan (1986) "History of the Jews in Singapore - 1830-1945", Herbilu Editorial & Marketing Services Singapore. M.J. Meyer (1994) "The Sephardi Jewish Community of Shanghai 1845 - 1939 and the Question of Identity." PhD Thesis. London School of Economics & Political Science, University of London.

Chapter 3

1. Rejwan, N. (1985) "The Jews of Iraq: 3000 years of history and culture". Weidenfeld & Nicolson, London. P 173.
2. Cernea, Ruth Fredman. *B'nai B'rith* International Jewish Monthly. (Washington DC) Vol. 102, No. 10 (June/July 1988) Pp 26 - 30.
3. Nathan, E. (1986) "The History of Jews in Singapore (1930 - 1945)". Herbilu Editorial & Marketing Services, Singapore. Pp 6 - 11.
4. Meyer, M.J. (1994) "The Sephardi Jewish Community of Shanghai 1845 - 1939 and the Question of Identity". PhD Thesis. London School of Economics & Political Science. University of London. P 51.
5. Musleah, E.N. (1975) "On the Banks of the Ganga - The Sojourn of Jews in Calcutta". The Christopher Publishing House, North Quincy, Massachusetts. Chapter II.
6. Encyclopedia Judaica.
7. Hyman, M. (1992) "Indian Jewish Cooking". Hyman Publishers, London. Pp 133 - 147.
8. Ibid. P 73.
9. F 17 - 20; F 47 - 50 in the Sir Stewart Hogg Market.
10. Personal correspondence. 1st November, 1994.

Chapter 4

1. The Statesman. 15.8.47. P 7.
2. Allen, C. (1975) "Plain Tales from the Raj - Images of British India in the Twentieth Century." Warner Books, London. P 261.

[3] The Statesman. 15.8.47. P 7.

[4] Allen, C. Op. cit. P. 259

Chapter 5

[1] Roden, C. (1987) "A New Book of Middle Eastern Food". Penguin. Forthcoming: On the Jews and Their Food.

[2] Goitein, S.D. (1976) "A Mediterranean Society - Economic Foundations". Volume I. University of California Press. Pp 6 & 7 refer to the India trade.

[3] Ibid. Pp 154 refers specifically to pepper, cinnamon and cloves.

[4] Lewis, S. Personal correspondence, 2nd March 1995. *Keora* water is made from the flowers and young leaves of a species of screw pine which are sweetly scented and used for ornament and otherwise in the East. The Latin names are *Pandanus Fascicularis* and *Pandanus Odoratissmus*. Bengali names are *Keiya, Keori*. It grows in all the provinces in India; in village thickets and hedges; also near temples and wild in the Sundabunds.

[5] Cooper, J. (1993) "Eat and be Satisfied - A Social History of Jewish Food". Jason Aronson, Inc. North Vale, New Jersey. P 138.

[6] Exodus, 23:19 "Thou shalt not seethe a kid in its mother's milk." Repeated in Exodus, 34:26 and again in Deut. 14:21.

[7] Marks, Copeland (1986) "The Varied Kitchens of India" M. Evans & Co. Inc. New York.

[8] Allen, C. (1975) "Plain Tales from the Raj" P 93. "You could leave your jewellery, your money, your bungalow wide open and nothing would ever be taken from it ... but as regards their little perquisites in the way of food or making a little bit on the bazaar, all this was taken as part of daily life ..."

[9] Cooper, J. (1993) Op. cit. P 129.

[10] Ibid. P 131.

[11] Ibid. P 131 from which it is clear that this was a common Sephardi ritual, prevalent among those of Baghdadi and Spanish origin.

[12] Psalm 137.

Chapter 6

[1] Personal correspondence with Rabbi E.N. Musleah, November 1994.

[2] Allen, C. (1975) "Plain Tales from the Raj - Images of British India in the Twentieth Century", P. 217 Warner Books, London.

Chapter 7

1. Ezra, E.D. (1986) "Turning Back the Pages." Brookside Press, London. P 334.
2. Ezra. E.D. Op. cit. P 335.
3. Leviticus 24:42,43.
4. Ezra, E.D. (1986). Op. cit. P 337.

Chapter 8

1. Allen, C. (1975) "Plain Tales from the Raj - Images of British India in the Twentieth Century". Warner Books, London. P 133.
2. Ghosh, A. (1992) "In an Antique Land." Definition : "Judeo Arabic (is) a colloquial dialect of medieval Arabic written in Hebrew script."

Chapter 9

1. Goitein, S. (1983) "A Mediterranean Society: Daily Life". Volume IV. University of California Press. Berkley & Los Angeles. P 161.
2. Rejwan, N. (1985) "The Jews of Iraq: 3000 years of history and culture." Weidenfeld & Nicolson, London. P 175.
3. Keen, M.E. (1991) "Jewish Ritual Art in the Victoria & Albert Museum". HMSO, London. P 104.
4. Allen, C. (1975) "Plain Tales from the Raj - Images of British India in the Twentieth Century." Warner Books, London. P 129.
5. The Statesman, 19th November, 1938.
6. Musleah, E.N. (1975) "On the Banks of the Ganga - The Sojourn of Jews in Calcutta." The Christopher Publishing House, North Quincy, Massachusetts. P 225.
7. The Statesman, Calcutta. 3rd December, 1952. Back page.
8. Shema. Vol. X. No.7 of March 1956. P 15.
9. Ibid. Pp 13 & 14.

Chapter 10

1. Exodus 20:1 - 14.
2. Brown, Judith M. (1994) "Modern India: The Origins of an Asian Democracy." Second ed. Oxford University Press. Pp 18 & 19.

3   Ibid. P 18.

4   Sassoon, D.S. (1949) "A History of the Jews in Baghdad". Published by S.D. Sassoon, Letchworth. P 182.

5   Encyc. Judaica. "Lilith, a female demon (was) assigned a central position in Jewish demonology. In the *Torah* there is only one reference to Lilith (Isa.34:14) 'Yea the night monster (Lilith) shall repose there and shall find herself a place of rest'. The image of Lilith was fixed in kabbalistic demonology from many ancient traditions, going back to the Sumerians. Here too she has two primary roles: the strangler of children and the seducer of men.

"Midrashic literature expands the legend that Adam, having parted from his wife after it had been ordained that they should die, begat demons from spirits that had attached themselves to him. He was encountered by Lilith who, taken by his beauty, lay with him and bore male and female demons". (Ha Goren, 1914, pp.66 -68). "A midrash of the Gaonic period identifies Lilith with the 'first Eve' created from the earth at the same time as Adam. She demanded equality of him and when this was refused she is said to have flown off into the air in an act of rebellion. Three angels pursued her and pressed her to return, but she refused to do so, stating that it was her mission to kill infants. Eventually she compromised and agreed to relent whenever she saw the names of the three angels, Snwy, Snsnwy, Smnglf written or spoken". (Alphabet of Ben Sira).

The text of amulets includes the story of Elijah encountering Lilith, and threatening to excommunicate her until she gave an undertaking not to harm women in childbirth whenever she saw or heard the names of the angels. H.C. Dobrinsky (1988) "A Treasury of Sephardic Laws and Customs". Ktav Publishing House Inc. P 12.

6   Meyer, M.J. (1994) "The Sephardi Jewish Community of Shanghai 1845 - 1939 and the Question of Identity." PhD Thesis. London School of Economics & Political Science, University of London. P 91.

7   The number forty is frequently associated with Biblical events which were threatening, eg the flood lasted forty days, the wanderings in the desert after the exodus from Egypt lasted forty years, and Moses was on Mount Sinai for forty days to receive the *Torah* when the Children of Israel were vulnerable to idol worship.

8   *Midrash Shir HaShirim* 4:6, *Yalkhuth Shimoni* relates that when Abraham circumcised the members of his household he piled their foreskins on a heap. In recognition of their faith and sacrifice, the odour rose to heaven and was appreciated by God as the fragrance of incense on the Altar in the Temple. Cited in *"Bris Milah"*, R. Paysach J. Krohn (1983) ArtScroll Mesorah Series. This could be the reason why pungent plant life was included among the items to ward off evil influences at childbirth.

9   "Other means of fighting and subduing the activated evil eye stem from attempts to divert the glance from the intended target by hanging 'interesting' objects, e.g. precious stones." Encyc. Judaica.

10 A strong flavoured spice. The explanation for its use is probably linked to footnote 8.

11 "The use of a specific colour such as blue or red, may blight (the) source of the evil eye by reflecting the glance." Encyc. Judaica.

12 ".. the 'evil eye' in Biblical sources denotes selfishness and jealousy. Furthermore, jealousy was linked with magic and fatal consequences. cf. Samuel I, 18:7 & 9. "Saul hath slain in thousands

and David in his ten thousands ... and Saul eyed David from that day and forward." Prov. 28:22. "He that hath an evil eye hasteneth after riches and knoweth not that want shall come upon him." Encyc. Judaica.

[13] "Once the evil eye has been activated ... only confrontation ... can then save the endangered person ... an outstretched hand may stop its rays." Encyc. Judaica.

In body language, the symbol of the hand facing forward is a signal to stop.

The Muslims also have a protective hand in their culture known as the hand of Fatima. Elias, F and Elias Cooper, J. (1974) "The Jews of Calcutta". The Jewish Association of Calcutta. P 131.

[14] The sixth day may be significant in this context because man and woman were both created on the sixth day.

[15] Sassoon, D.S. Op. cit. P 182.

[16] *Tikun Zohar,* Hebrew Mystical Texts, *Lech Lecha.* Compares the foreskin removed by circumcision to the shell which surrounds the nut and is subsequently discarded. Cited in *"Bris Milah"* R. Paysach J. Krohn (1983). Op. cit. P 73. The same principle would apply to the other items in the *shasha,* ie the skin of chick peas, corn, almonds and dates, the shell of pumpkin seeds, the husk of rice and the wrapping on sweets.

[17] It is possible that the noise of the children was believed to have the power of confusing or overpowering demons.

[18] "In the tradition of most Sephardim, names are given for the living, as was done in the Mishnaic period and right through the Middle Ages." "A Treasury of Sephardic Laws & Customs" H.C. Dobrinsky (1988), Ktav Pub. House, P 3.

[19] Elias,F & Elias Cooper, J. Op. cit. P 36.

[20] *Gemarah: Kiddushin.* P 82b. Soncino (1987) states "It is impossible for the world to renew itself without both the male and female species." The passage nevertheless continues: "happy is he whose children are males and woe to him whose children are females." In a footnote the publishers say "daughters were a greater anxiety - a dowry had to be found for them and they easily got into mischief."

[21] In those communities where the Chair of Elijah is used for the *Brit Meela* it symbolises the presence of Elijah the Prophet on the occasion. See *Zohar* I. *Lech Lecha,* 939. "Said R. Abba. 'When a man takes up his son to initiate him in this covenant, God calls to the ministering angels and says 'see what a creature I have made in the world'. At that moment Elijah traverses the world in four sweeps and presents himself there; and it is for this reason we have been taught that it behoves the father to prepare an extra chair for his honour and to say 'this is the Chair of Elijah'; and if he neglects to do so, Elijah does not visit him nor goes up to testify before the Almighty that the circumcision has taken place. Why has Elijah to testify? For this reason. When God said to him 'What doest thou here Elijah?' (Kings I, 19:9), he answered 'I have been very jealous for the Lord, the God of Hosts, for the children of Israel have foresaken Thy covenant'. Said God to him 'As thou livest, wherever my sons imprint this sign upon their flesh, thou shalt be there and the mouth which charged Israel with foresaking the covenant shall testify that they are observing it'."

[22] Hertz, J.H. (1937). "The Pentateuch and Haftorahs." Soncino Press, Footnote Num. 25:11.

"The Rabbis have a saying 'Pinhas is Elijah'." The zeal of the two men for God and for their religion forms the link between them.

[23] "According to Kabbalistic teachings, the myrtle branches serve to protect the newborn male child, as explained in *Zohar*" (H.C. Dobrinsky, op. cit. P 5). Sassoon (Op. cit. P 183) observes "the use of myrtle in burial, wedding and birth ceremonies goes back to Talmudic times and serves the purpose of protecting from demonic powers."

[24] "Henna, the leaf of the plant Lawsonia Alba, was used, *inter alia*, for its medicinal properties, in particular for burns and swelling. It closes the pores and reduces perspiration and poultices are used on the hands and feet. It was used to protect against the evil eye as prophylactic powers are attributed to the colour red. It is grown throughout the Near East and is abundant in Iran and Western India." Encylc. of Islam.

[25] "Since he (the baby) is not yet a complete Jew until he is circumcised, a *limud*, study session, takes place to protect the lad, as instructed in *Zohar*. Once the *limud* is over, everyone sings *pizmoneem*, songs of joy, and takes delight in the delicacies prepared for the occasion." (H.C. Dobrinsky, op. cit. P 5). A baby girl, born of a Jewish mother, is Jewish from birth and therefore no *limud* is necessary.

[26] Genesis, 17:12.

R. Paysach J. Krohn (1983) *"Bris Milah"* says "circumcision on the eighth day, with regard to blood coagulation, would seem to be the optimum time." P 54.

Midrash (Devarim Rabbah 6:1) - "For God had pity on him (the child) and waited until he had strength." Cited in R. Paysach J. Krohn.

[27] Genesis, 17:5. Following the precedent of God who gave Abraham, previously Abram, a new name at his circumcision.

[28] *Siman Tov* is abbreviated Hebrew for "May the birth of the boy be a propitious sign or omen."

[29] Genesis 17: 9-14

[30] Musleah, E.N. (1975) "On the Banks of the Ganga - The Sojourn of the Jews in Calcutta. The Christopher Publishing House, North Quincy, Massachusetts. P 496.

[31] Musleah, E.N. Personal correspondence, February 1995 explains. "The Cohen and male members of his family were appointed to the service of God. The Levite became part of the ministry in place of the first-born Israelites for a sum - five shekels per head (Numbers 3:44 - 48). These Israelites were redeemed - the Hebrew word *Pidyon* - exempted from doing the Lord's service in the Tabernacle on the way to the Promised Land or in the Temple in Jerusalem. Although the traditional ministry was no longer possible after the destruction of the Temple, the formality of redeeming the first-born Israelite continues his exemption from the priesthood. The Cohen and Levite, however, being born into the ministry, cannot opt out, and so are not required to be redeemed."

[32] Exodus, 13:2.

[33] Exodus, 13:13.

[34] Joseph Caro, *Schulhan Aruk, Yoreh Deah* 305:10. Footnote 16.

[35] Joseph Caro, *Schulhan Aruk, Orah Hayyim*, I:282:3 *"Katan oleh le'minyan shiva"*, a minor can

be called amongst the seven persons for the *Torah* readings.

[36] Musleah, E.N. Op. cit. P 195.

[37] In families among the poor, there was never an opportunity to read *Maftir* on a festival day unless it was presented, and this was rare. When it was known that a boy was of age to be called to read in the synagogue, and his parents could not afford to pay very much for the privilege, no one bid against the father, who could then purchase the privilege for a nominal sum.

[38] In orthodox congregations there is a separation in the seating of men and women. In purpose-built synagogues the womens' seats are in a gallery above those for men.

[39] *Tefellin* is the plural of *Tefillah*, prayer. Four sections of the Torah are encased in the phylacteries worn on the forehead and arm. Exodus, 13: 1 - 10, 11 - 16, Deuteronomy 6: 4 - 9, 11, 13 - 21.

[40] Tractate *Nazir*, Soncino, (1987). P 29b. A boy reaches majority when he understands the significance of a vow. Majority here is the translation for the words "until two hairs appear", ie puberty. See also, *Pirkeh Avoth*, Sayings of the Fathers. Ch.5:13. "Judah ben Tema said 'at five years of age a child should study the scripture; at ten the *mishna*, at thirteen he is bound to observe the precepts...'."

[41] Meyer, M.J. (1994) Op. cit. P 93.

[42] The portion of the Law which is read by men immediately after they lay phylacteries is Exodus, 13:1 - 16.

[43] Boys who attended the Elias Meyer Free School laid *tefillin* in school in the company of their class friends and parents. There was food for only two blessings - almonds and raisins for the produce from trees, and *cacas*, savoury biscuits, for produce from flour. It does not matter which food is selected, as long as there is something to bless.

[44] Nathan, E. (1986) "History of the Jews in Singapore - 1930 - 1945." Herbilu Marketing Services, Singapore. P 52.

[45] Cohen, Morris. (1895-96) Annual Report of the Anglo-Jewish Association. Condensed article in The Scribe. London. Issue No.46, 1991. "Superstition among the Jews in Baghdad" notes that child marriage was common among the Jews in Baghdad. "Married at the age of 12 to 14, and becoming mothers very soon after, a young girl is absorbed at once in all the cares and troubles of infant life..."

[46] There was a much more modest selection of sweets among poor families. Sometimes they only had preserved pumpkin, a popular delicacy of Indian origin and *bailfool*, orange blossom, woven into garlands which could be bought for a very modest price.

[47] Musleah, E.N. Op. cit. P 203.

[48] Hyman, M. (1992). "Indian Jewish Cooking." Hyman Publishers, London. P 74.

[49] Musleah, E.N. Op. cit. P 203.

[50] Meyer, M.J. Op. cit. P 95.

[51] "Henna had several uses, such as a dye, to strengthen the hair, and in the cult for perfume. It is used as a cosmetic on all festive occasions, particularly before marriage, and is applied to the hands and feet. In the Muslim tradition (and in contrast to usage amongst Hindus) it must not conform to a design. It was used in Ancient Egypt by the Hebrews and by the Egyptians them-

selves to dye mummies". Encyclopedia of Islam.

Henna is included among the spices ... to which the beloved maiden is compared in the Song of Songs 4:13. "Thy shoots are a park of pomegranates, with precious fruits; henna with spikenard" while she compares her beloved to "a cluster of henna in the vineyards of Ein Gedi." Encyc. Judaica.

[52] Musleah, E.N. Op. cit. P 204.

[53] Ibid. P 236.

[54] It is interesting to observe small differences between Baghdad and India. David Solomon Sassoon. Op. cit. Ch. XXXI, P. 192, calls this custom *Msahbah*, (A) the appeasement of demons. No bible is mentioned, and no green vegetable, but there is mention of rue. This is a strong scented plant of the orange family with bitter leaves, used in the preparation of medicines at one time. It is a symbol of compassion or repentance. As this is a plant of the Mediterranean, it is possible that it was not easily available in India, and the green vegetable was used as a substitute.

The bible is probably a means of neutralising evil, the mirror is an ornament (Encyc. Judaica), water symbolises a vital sign of life (Musleah, "Read After Me - A Manual for Mourners." The Town House Press, North Quincy, North Carolina). P 17. Candy is a sweetener.

Sassoon comments 'It will not be out of place to make here a passing reference to Manasseh Sittehon's work *Kenesiyyah Leshem Shamayim*, Jerusalem, 1874, where such practices are strongly objected to'.

[55] Deuteronomy, 6: 4 - 9, 11: 13 - 21.

[56] Leviticus, 15:31, 32.

[57] The *Halachot* of Ben Ish Hai, Hachom Yosef Hayyim. Translated by Shmuel Hiley, Jerusalem, 5751. Volume II. P 216. *Shofetim:13*. "It is customary for the bridegroom to fast on the day he gets married as, although one is forgiven one's sins on the day that one marries, one requires also the additional effect of a fast. When one fasts one becomes broken-hearted and is more easily stirred to repentence. In Baghdad many follow this custom, but only the men; brides are not accustomed to fast and it has never happened that a girl should fast before her marriage."

Also, *Arukh HaShulhan, Eben Haezer*, 61:21 quoted in H.C. Dobrinsky (op. cit.) Ch.3, footnote 18, p.415 - "Since some fasted only to prevent the bride and bridegroom from becoming intoxicated prior to the wedding ceremony, even those who do not fast are careful not to drink liquor."

[58] Sassoon, D.S. Op. cit. P 185 observes that this is prescribed by the *Talmud*.

[59] Numbers 5:13 P 30a. Soncino 1987. "A witness shall not rise up." Establishes the principle that "whenever it says 'a witness' it implies two unless one is specified in the verse."

[60] The *Halacha* of Ben Ish Hai. Vol. II. *Shofetim:* 3, P 211.

[61] Ibid. P 213. "Some people have the custom to use three coins, one of gold, one of silver and one of copper. However, it is best to use a silver ring, symbolising certain kabbalistic concepts ... based on the writings of our teacher Ari z'l, *Ta'ame Hamizwoth, parashath Ki Theze*."

[62] Ben Ish Hai. Op. cit. Vol. II, *Shofetim:* 5.

[63] Ben Ish Hai. Op. cit. Vol. II, *Shofetim:* 2. "If she was coerced ... and the money or ring forced upon her, the marriage is not *halachically*, legally, valid and she should immediately throw the

[64] money or the ring to the ground."

[64] Psalms 137:5, 6.

[65] "This isolation of bride and groom in complete privacy, after the *chupa* is known as *yihud*. It is not considered necessary if the *Shiva Bra'chot* is said while the couple are covered by a *sissith*." *Mekor Hayyim,* V:237,2b (P 37). See H.C. Dobrinsky Op. cit. P 415.
Zoor is the masculine, singular imperative of the Arabic word 'visit' and was associated with visits to the tombs of the Prophets Ezekiel and Ezra at the time of the festival of Pentecost.

[66] Ch.3:1,2,4.

[67] Genesis, 46:4 ".. and Joseph shall put his hand upon thy eyes." Ibn Ezra's commentary on *Torah* (5729). This is "an idiomatic expression referring to closing of eyes of one who dies."

Mishna Shabbath 23:5. One may not close the eyes of a corpse on the Sabbath. Nor on weekdays when he is about to die, and he who closes the eyes of a dying person at the point of death is a murderer (because he hastens death). The *Mishna* is dated at 200 C.E.

[68] Tractate Shabbath, Soncino, (1987), P 151b "so that air should not enter and swell the body."

[69] Genesis, 3:19.

[70] Goldberg, R. Chaim B. (1991) "Mourning in Halachah" Mesorah Publications, Brooklyn. P 53:75, footnote. "Through this and other things done for the deceased it arouses mercy for him ...". The number and placing of candles varies between communities.

[71] Musleah, E.N. (1990) "Read After Me: A Manual for Mourners." P 17.

[72] Joseph Caro. *Schulhan Aruk, Yoreh Deah 339:5* There are two main reasons: 1. Mystical. The Angel of Death whets his knife on water and a drop of the blood of death falls in. 2. A way of informing people that someone has died so that neighbours can come and perform acts of kindness, e.g. accompany the deceased to burial.

See also, Psalm 22:15 "I am poured out like water" i.e. that life is being drained to an end.

[73] Exodus, 20:4. Moreover, mirrors are traditionally regarded as ornamentation and this is inappropriate at a time of bereavement.

[74] Deuteronomy, 21:23. This is an obligation, even for a criminal.

[75] The use of earthenware vessels means they may be disposed of immediately after use on particular parts of the body. This ensures that the fresh, unadulterated water necessary for ritual purification remains uncontaminated, for it is seen as spiritual purification. *Mishnayoth Kelim.* Ch.2, para 1.

[76] Leviticus 18:7. Sons are not permitted to assist or see the ritual washing of their parents' bodies. The words 'nakedness' and 'shame' in Hebrew are interchangeable. Immorality exposes something that should be covered. *The Humash,* (1993), ArtScroll, Footnote to verse 7.

[77] *Takhrikhim,* shrouds are traditionally sewn by women because it was Eve, the first woman, who caused death to come to the world through her enactment of the "original sin" in the Garden of Eden. (H.C. Dobrinsky, op. cit. P 70).

[78] Tractate *Moed Kattan.* P 27b. Soncino, (1987). Linen rather than wool because it was cheaper, and avoided an undue cost to families of the poor.

[79] Meyer, M.J. Op. cit. P 97 footnote 93. "Talmudic evidence suggests that scented herbs and myrtle were used." *Bezah* 2, Chronicle 16, 14; *Baba Kama,* 16b.

[80] Sassoon, D.S. Op. cit. P 187.

[81] Musleah, E.N. Op. cit. P. 19.

[82] Joseph Caro, *Schulhan Arukh, Yoreh Deah,* 340:1. Reason, *Zohar Noah* 6:6. The body is like a garment for the soul and death is like tearing the garment.

See also, Genesis 37:34. "Jacob rent his garments." Samuel II. 1:11 - "Then David took hold on his clothes, and rent them; and likewise all the men that were with him."

[83] Leviticus, 10:6.

[84] Tractate Sanhedrin. Soncino, (1987). P 20a. "When it is customary for women to follow the bier they may do so. To precede it, they may do so." *Minhag,* custom is the guideline.

[85] Proverbs, XXXI

[86] Musleah, E.N. Op. cit. P 451.

[87] Genesis, 25:6.

[88] Dobrinsky, H.C. Op. cit. P 80.

[89] Genesis, 3:19.

[90] Tractate *Moed Katan,* Soncino, (1987). P 27b "A mourner (during) the first three days should look upon himself as if a sword is resting between his shoulders, from the third to the seventh as if it stands in the corner facing him, thereafter as if it is moving alongside him in the market place." This imagery suggests a gradual decrease in the intensity of suffering over time.

[91] Joseph Caro, *Schulhan Arukh, Orach Hayyim,* Ch.4 Section 18. The fact that we do not dry our hands symbolises not removing attention from the mourning and not casting off the thought of the day of death.

"It also bears the superstition of avoiding carrying symbols of death in our handkerchiefs." Musleah, E.N. Personal correspondence. February 1995.

[92] Meyer, M.J. Op. cit. P 97.

[93] Tractate *Moed Katan.* P 27b, Soncino, (1987). "Since bitter feelings are most pronounced at the time of the first meal after a funeral, friends and neighbours should provide at least that meal."

[94] Sassoon, D.S. Op. cit. P 189.

[95] Musleah, E.N. Op. cit. P 485.

[96] Meyer, M.J. Op. cit. P 98.

Chapter 11

[1] This has been confirmed by both his sons in personal correspondence dated August and November 1994.

[2] Moses, R. (1992) "From Mandalay to Calcutta - 8th March - 7th April, 1942. Recollections

of my Family's Trek from Burma". Limited private circulation.

³ Shema. Vol. IX. No.3.

⁴ Musleah, E.N. (1975) "On the Banks of the Ganga - The Sojourn of Jews in Calcutta". The Christopher Publishing House, North Quincy, Massachusetts. P 276.

⁵ Musleah, E.N. Op. cit. P 444.

⁶ This contrasts with the situation in Singapore and in Shanghai. See, Nathan, E. (1986) "The History of Jews in Singapore, 1830 - 1945" Herbilu Editorial & Marketing Services. P 33. Also, Meyer, M.J. (1994) "The Sephardi Jewish Community of Shanghai 1845 - 1939 and the Question of Identity". PhD Thesis. London School of Economics & Political Science, University of London. P 101.

Chapter 12

¹ Ezra, E.D. (1986) "Turning Back the Pages." Jewish Occupations in Calcutta in 1901. Brookside Press, London. Pp 452 & 453.

² Musleah, E.N. (1975) "On the Banks of the Ganga - The Sojourn of Jews in Calcutta." The Christopher Publishing House, North Quincy, Massachusetts. P 53.

³ Ezra, E.D. Op. cit. Pp 330 and 331.

⁴ Musleah, E.N. Op. cit. P 49.

⁵ Meyer, M.J. (1994) "The Sephardi Jewish Community of Shanghai 1845-1939 and the Question of Identity." PhD Thesis. University of London. P 19.

⁶ Musleah, E.N. Op. cit. P 311.

Chapter 13

¹ Collis, M. (1966) "Last and First in Burma (1941 - 1948)". Faber & Faber, London. P 292.

² Governor General to Secretary of State for India. Deciphered telegram 15.1.42. POL 361. IOR, File L/P&J/8/436. Oriental & India Office Collections (OIOC). The British Library, London.

³ Note by Burma Office on Civilian Evacuation of Rangoon dated 5.5.42. File cit. above.

⁴ Collis, M. (1966). Op. cit. P 56.

⁵ Ibid. P 57.

⁶ Extracts from Report by the Administrator General on the Evacuation of Refugees from Burma to India (Assam). January - July 1942. Section I. IOR, File L/P&J/8/436. (OIOC). The British Library, London.

⁷ Governor General to Secretary of State for India. Telegram New Delhi 14.5.43. IOR, File L/P&J/8/436. (OIOC), The British Library, London.

⁸ See note 6.

[9] Calvocoressi, P. & Wint, G. (1972) "Total War" Allen Lane The Penguin Press, London. P 730.

[10] See note 6.

[11] Govt. of India Press, Simla. IOR, MSS. Eur.E 215/28. (OIOC). The British Library, London.

[12] Mole. R.F. (1942) " The Temple Bells are Calling" MSS Eur C520. IOR, (OIOC), The British Library, London.

[13] Deciphered telegram dated 14.5.42, New Delhi from the Governor General to Secretary of State for India. Burma 12351. The British Library, London.

[14] Deciphered telegram dated 14.1.42, Rangoon, from the Governor of Burma to the Secretary of State for Burma. Burma 10382. The British Library, London.

[15] Laxton, W.A. (1994) "B.I." World Ship Society, London. P 156.

[16] Ibid. P 156.

[17] IOR, File L/P&J/8/436. Burma 11928 (OIOC), The British Library, London.

[18] IOR, File L/P&J/8/436. Burma 12351 (OIOC) The British Library, London.

[19] "The air battle for Burma lasted from December 23rd 1941 until February, 1942. (There were) 31 day and night attacks made." Report on the Burma Campaign 1941-42. Sir Reginald Dorman Smith, Governor of Burma. Govt. of India Press, Simla 1943. Mss. Eur. E 215/28. (OIOC). The British Library, London.

[20] "Civilian Evacuation of Rangoon. Note by Burma Office. Received 5.5.42. IOR, File L/P&J/8/436. (OIOC), The British Library, London.

[21] Thacker's Directory 1941-42. General Section. P 18. 1 rupee = Sh.1/6.

Details of air fare in Louis Allen (1984) "Burma: The Longest War, 1941 - 45" J.M. Dent, London. P 80.

[22] Deciphered telegram from Governor General to Secretary of State for India. New Delhi, 13 April 1942. Pol. 3105. "These (aircraft) will be C47s with a dead load of about 3 tons, ie, able to take approximately 25 men each. Starting about April 16th there will be some surplus space on these aircraft. Suggested Burma army allot priorities ... filling up surplus space with refugees who must not take precedence over wounded." IOR, File L/P&J/8/436. (OIOC), The British Library, London.

[23] Report on the Burma Campaign. 1941-42. Sir Reginald Dorman Smith. cit. above.

[24] Ibid.

[25] Burma file. The British Library, London.

[26] Thacker's Directory 1941 - 42. Cit. above.

[27] Musleah, E.N. (1975) "On the Banks of the Ganga - The Sojourn of Jews in Calcutta". The Christopher Publishing House, North Quincy, Massachusetts. P 432.

[28] Ibid. P 442.

[29] Ibid. P 432.

[30] Ibid. P 324

[31] Cernea, Ruth Fredman. "End of the Road: The Last Burmese Jews." *B'nai B'rith Hillel Foundations*. June-July 1988. Pp 26 - 30.

[32] Ibid.

Chapter 14

[1] Moorhouse, G. (1983) "Calcutta". Penguin, London. Pp 74, 80.

[2] Allen, C. (1975) "Plain Tales from the Raj - Images of British India in the Twentieth Century". Warner Books, London. P 219.

[3] Musleah, E.N. (1975) "On the Banks of the Ganga - The Sojourn of Jews in Calcutta". The Christopher Publishing House, North Quincy, Massachusetts. Pp 345 - 351. "... in 1885 the Jewish community of Calcutta were disturbed when they were declared non-European ... the reason is not clear".

[4] Roland, J.G. (1989) "Jews in British India". University Press of New England, Hanover, New Hampshire. P 125.

[5] Gourgey, P. (1972). Letter to the Jewish Chronicle, London. Quoted in Elias, F and Elias Cooper, J (1974) "The Jews of Calcutta." P 100. "It was Mahatma Gandhi himself who ... advised the small Jewish community to stand aside lest they become crushed by the giant conflicting forces of British imperialism, Congress nationalism and Muslim League separatism."

[6] Brown, Judith M. (1994). "Modern India: the origins of an Asian democracy. OUP. P 179.

[7] Kulke, H & Rothermund, D. (1986). "A History of India." Croom Helm, Australia Pty Ltd. P 285.

[8] Allen, C. Op. cit. P 245.

[9] Ibid. P 250.

[10] Brown, Judith M. Op. cit. P 351.

[11] Ibid. P 327.

[12] Spear, P. (1965) "A History of India" Part 2. Penguin, London. P 233.

[13] Kulke, H. & Rothermund, D (1986). Op. cit. P 308.

[14] Moorhouse, G. Op. cit. P 219.

[15] Brown, Judith M. Op. cit. P 337.

[16] Allen, C. Op. cit. P 253.

[17] The Statesman. Calcutta. Until mid-August, 1947.

[18] Allen, C. Op. cit. P 255.

[19] The Statesman. Calcutta. 15 August 1947. "Remarkable signs of a return to communal amity after a year of bloodshed were seen in Calcutta last night and early this morning. Almost unbelievable scenes of fraternity and rejoicing were witnessed in some of the hitherto worst-affected areas...."

20. Chandra, B. et al. (1989) "India's Struggle for Independence. 1857 - 1947." Penguin, India and London. P 499.

21. Spear, P. (1986). "A History of India" 2. Penguin, U.K. P 238.

22. Ibid. P 238.

23. Moorhouse, G. Op. cit. P 282.

24. Ibid. P 282.

Chapter 15

1. Musleah, E.N. (1975) "On the Banks of the Ganga - The Sojourn of Jews in Calcutta". The Christopher Publishing House, North Quincy, Massachusetts. P 414.

2. Roland, J.G. (1989) "Jews in British India - Identity in a Colonial Era". University Press of New England, Hanover, New Hampshire. P 81.

3. Ibid. P 81.

4. Ibid. P 82.

5. Ibid. (Notes) "Immanuel Olsvanger, Polish born folklorist and Hebrew translator, emigrated to Palestine in 1933. He was among the pioneers in the translation of Sanskrit and Japanese literary texts to Hebrew. In July 1936 the Jewish Agency decided to send (him) as a special emissary to India. This mission was not to be a political campaign conducted by public meetings or interviews in the press but a very cautious and discreet method of procedure. (The Jewish Agency) believed that Olsvanger could not only present the Zionist case on a high cultural level to leaders of Congress who were unsympathetic to Zionism, but could gain the respect, affection and confidence of people and even endear himself to persons with an oriental mentality." P 318.

"In 1941 Immanuel Olsvanger returned to India, five years after his earlier visit. The Jewish Advocate commented that Olsvanger had 'forged a link between Indian Jewry and Palestine as no delegate before him had done ... his campaign had yielded the highest total yet collected by any Zionist delegate in Bombay'. Wealthy Parsis contributed more than one fifth of the total collected." P 232.

6. Copy of letter, courtesy of Ruby Musleah Mordecai.

7. Ray Shellim's account is confirmed in letters she and Alec Jonah wrote to their families at the time, to which she very kindly gave me access.

8. Adolph Myers. Bombay, November 1932. J.G. Roland. Op. cit. P 164.

9. Ibid. P 235.

10. Ibid. P 196.

11. Meyer, M.J. (1994) "The Sephardi Jewish Community of Shanghai 1845 - 1939 and the Question of Identity. PhD Thesis. London School of Economics & Political Science, University of London. Pp 245, 246, 248.

12. Personal correspondence with the author dated February 1955.

[13] Musleah, E.N. Op. cit. P 450.

[14] Roland, J.G. Op. cit. P 248.

[15] Shema, Vol. X No.5, 1:56.

[16] Ibid, Vol. X No.8, 4:56.

[17] Musleah, E.N. Op. cit. P 451.

Chapter 16

[1] This is confirmed by J. Roland: "Between 1945 and 1952 (Calcutta's) Jewish population, mainly Baghdadi, dropped from approximately 3,400 to fewer than 2,000, a large proportion ... having settled in Israel. ... " "India Census 1951, Paper No.1, P.8 lists 1935 Jews in Calcutta." In "Jews in British India". University Press of New England, Hanover, New Hampshire. P 328.

INDEX

Aaron, Aaron 65,66, 125-128 151,168,204,223.
Aaron, Reuben 221-224.
Abraham, Joe 166-168, 174.
Abraham, Lillian 38,117-119
Adjustment to living abroad, 18,98,212,213,215,217.
Accommodation,29,31,57,58,70,71,96, 145,166,168,172,213,214,217-220,222,224-226.
Agarpara Ch.7 passim. 67,93,103.
Agarpara Jute Mill, 67,70,71,76,78,79.
Agriculture,1,27,192,199,200,218.
Ahuza, 205ff.
Air raids, 156,166,167,170-172.
Aleppo, 5,6,8,9,145.
Aliyah, 195,196,197,199,200ff,204, 207,208,216,217ff. 219.
Allen, C. n 234-237, 247,248.
Alliance Israelite Universelle 7,8,9.
Anglicize,4,10.
Anglo-Burmese,170.
Anglo-Indians,13,23,25,44,57,58,64,94, 98,160,170.
Anti-Semitism,13,201.*See* Refugees, Europe.
Arakie, Aaron 97.
Arakie, Marianne Sadka 97,98,101,102.
Arakie, Sammy 97.
Ark, 113,121,122,227.
Armed Forces,24,74,139,156,209,212.
Armenians,3,23,98,179,233.
Army, Allied,166,171,182,183,209,210.
    British,159,184,185,210.
    Israeli,206,207.
    Japanese,156,159,160,209.
Assam, 156,164,182.
Australia, 26,174,205,211,214,220-223.
Australians,220-222.

Background,16,107,134,149.
Baghdad,6,9,13,15,17,25,28,37,41, 42, 52, 53, 99, 108, 126, 128, 131, 141, 145, 221.
Baghdadi,Baghdadian,3,4,10,11,13,17, 18,25,43,49,55,90,108,117,126,129, 203.
Basra,6,145.
Bassein,159,145.
Bayit, Ch.15 passim. 198.
Beliefs 98, 107,108,129,131,134,98, 107,108,129,131,134.*See*Backgroud.
Benaiah, Marina 38,61,62,66.
Benaiah, Rahel 49.
Benaiah, Ruby 108.
Bene Israel,10,11,191,203.
Bengal,1,57,58,62,77,135,156,166 182-184,188,189.
Bick, Gabby 196,197.
Bihar,55,56,184.
Bombay,1,3,4,5,11,41,43,90,124,192, 193,199,202,203,211,217,218.
Bose, Subhas Chandra 180.
Boundary Commission,188.
Boy Scouts, *See* Scouts.
Braudel, F. n.233.
British,1,2,4,10,13,44,120,156,162, 167,179,180,182,188,189,219,220,222
British Indian,13,179.
British influence,18,44,47,73,90,138,139
British Mandate,201,219.
Brown, J.M.107, n.233,238,247.
Burial ground, cemetery, 127,128,173.
Burma trek,133,159,162,165,175-77.

INDEX

Calcutta,1,3,4,5,7,8,10,17,19,25,26,27, 29,41,43,60,69,76,107,159,173, 188,189,209,212,213,214,216, 221,227.
Calvocoressi, P. n.246.
Caro, Joseph n.241,243,244.
Casual work,52,117,153-57.
Casualties,160,162,164,181,184.
Cernea, R.F.n.235,247.
Chandra, B.n.248.
Charity,Ch.12 passsim. 110,203,143-157
Child naming,109,110.
Childbirth,107,108.
Children,18,19,22,28,29,32,35,58,46,64 69-71,74,80,109,113,114,147,149, 151,161,208,209,216,217,220.
Chindwin River,161.
Christian, 6,7,8,25,107,139,180,186.
Cochin,2,11,12,37,41,43,90,173,191, 227.
Cochini Jews,5,11,12,191.
Cohen, Azeeza 133,134.
Cohen, D.J. 168,194.
Cohen, Ellis 92,121.
Cohen, Jackie 217-219.
Cohen, Joe 119-124.
Cohen, Mordecai 64-66.
Cohen, Mordie 217,218.
Cohen, priests 17,41.
Cohen, Ruby 119-124.
Cohen, Sassoon 111,112.
Cohen, Seemah Musleah 62,115.
Cohen, Shalom 5,59,227.
Collis, M. n.245.
Communal living,Ch.5 passim.
Communal relief, 147-151,173.
Coolies, 18,19,57,162.
Cooper, J. 43,47,
Craganore,12.
Cripps, Sir Stafford 183,184.
Culture,*See* Background.

Customs, Traditions,107-128.

Daily life, 107,108.
Daniels, Danny 204.
Daud Pasha 7.
David, Noreen Ezra 71 passim. 95, 102.
Death, 107,108,125.
Demons,108,119,127, n.238,240.
Deuteronomy,51,n..241-243.
Deutsch, Hanny Joshua 197,199,201.
Dhoolie, 162.
Direct Action Day, 184.
Discrimination,13,170.
Dobrinsky, H.C. 127, n.239,240,242-244.
Dominion status, 180,182,183.
Dress, 29,30,59,81,89,90.

Educational opportunities,8,9,13,143, 146,212,213,218,222,226.
Education in India,13,18,64,90,144, 146,151,179,213,223.
Eighteenth century,143.
Einy, Arleen 55,61,62,96.
Einy, David 60,90,101,110-112.
Elias, B.N. & Company Ch.7 passim. 67, 138, 169,172.
Elias, David 110-112.
Elias, Ellis 111.
Elias, Flower 10,25,34,,109,131, 135,137,140,180, n.234,239,247.
Elias Cooper, J. 10,109,180.
Elias, Nissim 103,121.
Elias, Sophie 110,111,112.
Elijah, chair of 110,111.
Elijah, the prophet 110.
Emigration,9,216,219,224,225.
Emissary,191,203,204
Empire,179,180.
Employment,27,28,29,36,38,52,67,70, 75,143,144,166,179,212.

INDEX

Encyclopedia of Islam n.240.
Encyclopedia Judaica n238,239,242.
Engagement,60,115,117,119,225,226.
Engineer,220,223.
England,26,80,116,139,144,174,209, 212,214,216,224.
English,13,47,58,118,145,166,179, 217,219,220.
Estad,112,114,138.
Europe,2,9,19,25,80,116,156,209,216.
European Association,173.
European classification,11,179.
European(s),1,6,10,13,23,30,107,143, 179,201.
Evacuation,160,162,166,167,172.
Evil eye,108.
Exodus,Ch.16 passim. 80,120,152, 165,241.
Exodus, Book of 238,241,243.
Ezekiel, Aisey 162.
Ezekiel, Maurice 185,186.
Ezekiel, Norman 64.
Ezra, David Sir, 121.
Ezra, E.D. 9,78,n.234,237,245.
Ezra, Moses 65.
Ezra, Lady Rachel 100,120,124,192ff. 193.

Factory,68,69,71. Ch.7 passim.
Faith, Ch.11 passim. 131-41.
Far East,2,4,5,6,8,18,20,30,131.
Fatah Wooch,124.
Fatalities, 160,162,164,184,189.
Ferris, Dan 135.
Ferris, Iris Moses 131,135,136,193.
Festivals,24,75,140,141.
Festival foods, 50,140.
First Zionist Congress, Basle,191.
Food,Ch.5 passim. 16,32,35,36,62,66, 68,75,151,161,166,202,205,206
Foreign trade,3,4.

Gandhi, M.K. 180,181,188.
Ganges River,4. Also *See* Hooghly.
Gedud Zion,194-197.
Genesis, Book of n.240,243,244.
Ghosh, A. 2.n.233,n.237.
Giridih,60.
Girl Guides, 134,135,136.
Goitein, S.D.2,89,n.233,234,236,237.
Goldberg, E.S. *See*Katz,N.
Goldberg, R.C.B.n.243.
Governor of Burma, 159,161,163,169, 170.
Great Calcutta Killing,80,184,186.
Great Indies Companies,1,2.
Gubbay, Adrian 75,79.

Habonim, Ch.15 passim.
Hai, Ben Ish, n.242,243.
Hannukah,,53,99,117.
Hartal,80,180,183,189.
Hawkers,30,57,66,143,189.
Hebrew teaching,35,123,193.
    language,138,191,206,217.
    script,113.
Henna,110,117,118.
Herbs,Ch.5 passim.
Herman, Abe 199,202.
Hertz, J.H.n.240.
Hertzl, Theodore 194.
High Holidays,*See*Festivals.
Himmelschein, Helen Jacob 19,22,216, 217.
Hindus,5,11,23,25,28,43,44,53,54,72 76,77,80,107,118,180,183, 185-190.
Holy Land,127,191,219.
Home Rule, 180.
Hooghly River,4,67,76,168.
See Ganges.
Horse racing, Ch.8 passim.
Hyman, M. n.235,241.

INDEX

Immigration,217,223,224.
Income,132,143,152,154.
Income groups,144,149,150.
Independence, Indian 78,179,184,188.
India,3,9,15-18,20,37-39,41,42,52,
57,93,102,120,133,134,152,162,
163,174,179,180,182,184,209,
211-213,215-217,219,220,222,
223,225,226.
Indians,10,39,54,61,79,93,98,133,143,
159,160,166,179,180,182,183,
190,199,214,220,223.
India Tea Association,165.
Indian Independence League,180.
Indian National Congress,180-184.
Indigenous population,5,11,179.
Industry,1,19,23,136,143,166,182,184,
202,209.
Iraq,1,7,9,54,143,179,205,223.
Isaac, Benny 74.
Isaac, Diana 69,passim. 186,187.
Isaac, Joe 67 passim.
Israel,26,100,174,199,200,205,208,214,
217-219,225.

Jackson, S. 234.
Jacob, Abraham 169,170.
Jacob, Benny 172.
Jacob, J.R.75,77,104.
Jacob, Maisie Ezra 220,221.
Jacob, Nissim 170,171,173.
Jacob, Ronnie 137, 195.
Jacob, Sid 220,221.
Jewish Advocate, The 191,192.
Japan, 155,156,159,182,209,210.
Jewish Agency,199-202,205,21,217,225.
Jewish heritage,39,41,42,134,141,149.
Jewish Law,11,17,53,136,143.
Jewish National Fund,200.
Jewish Tribune, The 191,192.
Jews,5-9,11,12,19,44,47,50,55,56,67,
77,107,117,129,179,183,185,
209,210,213,220,221,223,226.
Jews of the Raj,10,13,43,47,48,54,107,
129,139,141,155,191,202,203,209,
214,220.
Jinnah, M.A.183,184,188.
Jobs,131,135,138,166,179,185,209,213,
217,218,219,220,222,225. *See*
Employment.
Jonah, Alec 201,202,203,248.
Joseph, Florence 195.
Joshua, Josh 195.
Judah, Albert 159-166,169,174,175-
177.
Judean club,21,100,192.

K'far Ofer 218,219.
Kaddish,56,114,127,128.
Kasher,20,28,33,43,76,138,156.
Katz, N.233,235. *See* Goldberg,E.S.
Keen, M.E.n.237.
Khadba,117.
Kibbutz,Ch.15 passim.
Kibbutz Afek,205ff.
Kibbutz En Dor,205.
Kibbutz Gal Ed,205ff. 217.
Kibbutz Kfar Blum,199,202.
Kiryat Ono,219.
Kraft,Michelle 131.
Krieger, Peter 195,196,200,203.
Krieger, Tehilla 195,196,200,203.
Krohn Paysach J. n.238,240.
Kulke, H.n.247.

Lanyado, Moshe 91,92.
Lanyado, Seemah 34,91,92.
Laxton, W.A. 246.
Leight, Lenny 210,211.
Leight, Ramah Luddy 209,210,211,216.
Leviticus, Book of n.242,243,244.
Lewis, G.n.234.

INDEX

Lewis, Sally Meyer 192-194,197,212, n.236.
Lillith, n.238.
Linlithgow, Lord 182.
London,26,135,152,214,215,224-226.
Luddy, Rahma, principal Jewish Girls' School,95,100,194,200.
Luddy, Sam 100.

Macarov, David 196.
Maccabi Association of Calcutta,99-104.
Maccabiah Games,96,100.
Madhupur,Ch.6 passim. 115,151.
Maftir,112,113,n.241.
Maghen David Synagogue, Calcutta, 121,227.
Manasseh, Albert 192-194.
Manasseh, Joe 204 ff.
Mansfield, Mercia 131,135.
Ma'on. Ch.15 passim.
Marcus, Solly 197.
Margulies, Rina Einy 95,96.
Markets, bazaars,17,19,21,26,41,59,61, 64,92,160,155.
Marks, Copeland, n.236.
Marriage,6,115,118,122.
Marwari Relief Society,173.
Marwaris,10,121,124,185.
Matza,52.
Meir, Regina Abraham 103,194.
Merchants,2,3,12,41,143,179.
Meshuchrarim,12.
Meyer, Benny 25.
Meyer, Bertie 103.
Meyer, Ellis 112-115.
Meyer, Florence 150.
Meyer, Jenkins 199.
Meyer, Maisie J. 22,102,108,117,128, 129 n.235,238,241,242,244,245, 249.

Meyer, Mervyn 199.
Meyuhasim, 11.
Middle East,2,11,18,20,41-43,48,50,54, 90,145.
Missionary, 152,180.
Mofussil,20.
Mole, R.F. n.246.
Moorhouse, G. 4ff.n.233,247,248.
Mordecai, E. 196,199.
Mordecai, Ruby Musleah, 35,192,193, 199.n.248.
Morris, Aaron 168.
Morris, Rev. Albert, 121,122.
Morris, Rufoo 168.
Morris, Sally 69
Morris, Sammy 59,66.
Morris, Seemah 182.
Morris, Sunoo 68 passim.
Moses, Rahma 134.
Moses, Renee Cohen 26,133.
Moses, Sydney 78.
Moshav,217-219.
Mountbatten, Lord Louis,116-119,125-126,187,188.
Musleah, Rabbi Ezekiel, 5,99,187,199, 207,208,n.233-235,237,240-249.
Musleah, Isaac 131.
Musleah, Meyer 191 passim.
Musleah, Rae Levi 194,199.
Musleah, Ramah 25.
Muslim League,180,183.
Muslims,9,11,23,25,28,29,43,44,54,72, 80,98,107,118,180,183-190.
Musmeyah Yeshua,174.
Myers, Adolph n.249.

Nahoum, David 103,
Nahoum, Hannah 21
Nahoum, Nahoum Ch.3 passim.

INDEX

Nahoum, Ramah 20,21.
Nahoum, Sollo 24,25.
Nahoums 17, Ch.3 passim. 104,116,121, 140,151.
Nathan, E. 115,n.235,241,245.
National Tobacco Co. of India, Ch.7 passim.
Nehru, J. 180,181,184.
New Delhi, 165,166,184,189,209, 210,222.
New South Wales Association of Sephardim, 224.
New York,19,211,226.
New Zealand,211,220,221.
Nicknames,154,155,173.174.
Nineteenth century,2,8,9,90,108, 131,143,145,180,209.
Nissim, Ruby 45.
Numbers, Book of 242.

Olsvanger, Immanuel 192,203,248.

Pakistan 79,98,183,189.
Palestine 35,191,192,194,196,199, 200,201,209.
Parfitt, T. n.233.
Parokheth,126,141.
Parsis,5,44,98,108,179,248.
Partition,184,187-189.
Passover,23,50,52,53,66,98,99,109, 117,133,146,149,165.
Patriotism,10,66,155,157,180,209.
Pethic-Lawrence, Lord 184.
Pidyon ha-ben, redemption of firstborn son,111,112.
Population,9,10,207,208.
Poverty,131-133,144-147,149-152, 154,225.

Prayers,services
52,92,120,128,140,150.

Professions, professional training,172, 214,216,223,225.
Proverbs, Book of,n.244.
Pujas,76,77.
Punjab,107,188,189.
Purim,36,52,53,99,146.

Quota system,111,220,223.

Race,36,81,223.
Rahabi, David 11.
Rahim 32,33,34.
Railways/trains,55,57,59,60,65,67, 70,160,165,179,211,212.
Raj,3,5,20,32,63,79,81,115,123,141, 143,144,151,179,180,226.
Rangoon,2,159,166,169,173,174.
Raymond, Jack 143.
Refugees, Burma 78,160,162,166,169.
    Calcutta 184,188,189.
    East Bengal 188,189.
    Europe 78.
Rejwan, N. 6,17ff,89,n.233-235,237.
Rembaum, Bolek 101.
Riots,Ch.14 passim. 77,226.
Rites of passage,Ch.10 passim.
Roden, C. 41,n.236.
Rodrigue, A. 9,n.234.
Roland, J.G. 3ff,179,206,n.233,234, 247-249.
Rosh Hashana,50-53,137,140,146,148, 149.
Rothermund, D.n.247.

Sabbath,24,26,34,47,48,49.87,98,107, 120,124,126,132,138,140, 150-152,196.
Sabt el Niswan,124.
Sadka, Seemah 181.
Salary,131,132,149,179,212.
Samet, A. 197,198.

INDEX

Sassoon, D.S. 5,7,108,126, n.233,234, 238,239,240,242,244.
Sassoon, David & Company 4,138.
Sassoon, E.D. & Company 4.
Sassoon, Elmo 159,167,168.
School, 132,139,173.
 Elias Meyer Free, 65,139,145,195,205.
Jeshurun Free, Calcutta 72,195.
Jewish Girls,46,71,99,136,101,136, 139,192-196.
Jewish, Rangoon,166,167.
Jewish schools, general,139,146,151, 179,218.
Schwartz, Drew 197.
Scouts, 64,65,136,151.
Second World War,23,24,67,124,139, 155,174,209,212.
Secretary of State for Burma,169,170.
Secretary of State for India,159,161.
Seder, 52,113,165.
Seligson, Rabbi David 139.
Servants,Ch.4 passim,38,53,64,70,72-74,154,222.
Servicemen,24,196ff. 200,210,212,227.
Sha'ar Aliyah,205.
Sha'aray Rason Synagogue,22.
Shanghai,2,19,20,112,144,151,204.
Shasha,108,109.
Shavuoth,53,98,99.
Shaya, Anne 224,225.
Shellim, Ray Luddy 35,39,135,136,186, 195,200,n.248.
Shema, The 104,208,n.237,245,249.
Shohet,5,6,66,72,143.
Shomre Miswa,7.
Sikhs,107,108.
Silas, Abraham, Rev.97,98,104.
Silas, Charlie 22,214,215.
Silas, Eze 97,98,99.
Silas, Gracie 168.
Silas, Simon, Rabbi 22.
Simhat Torah,52,112,113,141,227.

Singapore,2,18,115,144,159,223.
Smith, V.A. n.233.
Skills,132,143.
Social isolation,209,210,212.,
Socialising within the community, 55,72,74,83,97,98,104,218.
Solar topee,132,182,183.
Solomon, Elmo 159,167,168.
Solomon, Esther Moses 102.
Solomon, Jochebed 137.
Solomon, Joe 93,94.
Solomon, Samuel 136,137.
Sopher, Eric 100.
Sopher, Helene 98,101,103,204.
Spear, P. n.247,248.
Spices,Ch.5 passim. 2,41,42.
Sports,63,68,74,82.
Statesman, The 94,181,188,236,237,248.
Status,11,143.
Submarines,168,211.
Succoth,51,52,75.
Superstitions,28,83,107,108,123,127.
Synagogue,12,34,47,56,112,113,118 , 120-122,124,126,139,140,146, 154,174,217,223,224,227.
Sydney,220,221.
Syria,1,18,41,207,223.

Taboos,58,75,135,209.
Tea Marketing Expansion Board,168.
Tefellin,114,241.
Torah,52,56,112,113,114,120,124,129 52,56,174.
Trade,2,5,3,8,17,31,46,143-145,179.
Traders,12,145.
Traditions,15,16,54.
Turf Club, Calcutta. Ch.8 passim. 91.
Turf Club, Tollygunj 90,101.
Twena, Mozelle 69-71.
Twentieth century,107,131,138,143,179.

INDEX

UK,19,21,25,35,79,96,136,174,213,214, 224.
Unemployed,144,151,198,217,219.
USA,26,80,120,199,201,211,214.

Values,Standards,16,28,107,108,131,133 134,137,138,143,151,153.
Viceroy,170,173,182-184,188.

Wages,144.
War brides,211,212.
Wedding,120,123,227.
White Australia policy,222,223.
Wint, G.n246..
Women,15,33,45,74,89,96,115,117, 161,162,209,218,227.
World Zionist Movement,204

Yemen,5,8,9,12,18.
Yom Kippur,22,23,51.

Zaccai, Annie 170.
Zaccai, Dick 170,171.
Zachariah, N. 94,100,101.
Zionism, Ch.15 passim. 16,141,217,225 n.248.
Zionist Association, Calcutta,196.
Zionist Congress, First 191.
Zohar,n.239,240.
Zoor,122.